O9-ABF-607

praise for
turn left at the trojan horse

"Thank you Brad Herzog for taking me on a great cross-country journey. To quote another storyteller, his words winged like arrows to the mark."
—**AJ Jacobs**, author of *The Guinea Pig Diaries*
and *The Year of Living Biblically*

"*Turn Left at the Trojan Horse* had me howling with laughter and nodding pensively at the razor-sharp observation. His epic road trip, tinged with local culture and flavored with the Greek myths, is the stuff of legend itself and puts Herzog at the forefront of the genre."
—**Tabir Shah**, author of *The Caliph's House*
and *In Search of King Solomon's Mines*

"Brad Herzog is the perfect travel companion: funny, wise, and as good a storyteller as you'll find on the open road. You can't help but want to spend a month in his passenger seat after reading this book."
—**Chad Millman**, author of *The Detonators* and *The Odds*

"A midlife quest that while grounded in mythology, transports the reader along a redemptive, poetic journey through small-town America."
—**Doreen Orion**, author of *Queen of the Road*

"Herzog cleverly reinvents the original 'road trip' in his new book, one that is more than just a timeless journey of self-discovery. He is at his best when taking the reader to little-known towns born of Homer's itinerary and introducing us to the endearing people who make these places so uniquely American. As we sit in Herzog's passenger seat, we cannot help but stare out the window and even see our own reflection in the glass.
—**Liz Robbins**, author of *A Race Like No Other*

"Herzog is that rare person blessed with an innovative spirit and creative mind, persistence in pinpointing the heart of the issue . . . and skill in applying his reflections to paper."
—*Houston Chronicle*

Also by Brad Herzog

States of Mind
Small World

turn left at the trojan horse

A WOULD-BE HERO'S AMERICAN ODYSSEY

─────────

brad herzog

Citadel Press
Kensington Publishing Corp.
www.kensingtonbooks.com

CITADEL PRESS BOOKS are published by

Kensington Publishing Corp.
119 West 40th Street
New York, NY 10018

Copyright © 2010 Brad Herzog

Grateful acknowledgment is made to the following for permission to reprint previously published material: Quotations from *The Hero with a Thousand Faces* by Joseph Campbell, copyright © 1949, 1968, 2008; reprinted by permission of Joseph Campbell Foundation (jcf.org). Excerpt from "Ithaka" by C. P. Cavafy (Aliki Barnstone, translation), copyright © 2006; reprinted by permission of W. W. Norton & Company.

All rights reserved. No part of this book may be reproduced in any form or by any means without the prior written consent of the publisher, excepting brief quotes used in reviews.

All Kensington titles, imprints, and distributed lines are available at special quantity discounts for bulk purchases for sales promotions, premiums, fund-raising, educational, or institutional use. Special book excerpts or customized printings can also be created to fit specific needs. For details, write or phone the office of the Kensington special sales manager: Kensington Publishing Corp., 119 West 40th Street, New York, NY 10018, attn: Special Sales Department; phone 1-800-221-2647.

CITADEL PRESS and the Citadel logo are Reg. U.S. Pat. & TM Off.

First printing: June 2010

10 9 8 7 6 5 4 3 2

Printed in the United States of America

Library of Congress Control Number: 2008054495

ISBN-13: 978-0-8065-3202-8
ISBN-10: 0-8065-3202-5

To Mom and Dad

There is in every constitution a certain solstice when the stars stand still in our inward firmament, and when there is required some foreign force, some diversion or alternative to prevent stagnation. And, as a medical remedy, travel seems one of the best.

—Ralph Waldo Emerson

Tell me, O muse, of that ingenious hero who traveled far and wide . . .

—Homer, the *Odyssey*

contents

turn left at the
trojan horse

I

high noon

Mount Olympus has vanished, so I order another beer.

Around me, the patrons in this lofty bubble stab at pan-seared mahi mahi and sip chardonnays as the restaurant rotates, revealing the wonders of Puget Sound in a slow-motion panorama. One floor up, tourists ooh and aah their way around the Space Needle's observation deck. Some five hundred feet below, the Emerald City continues with its daily bustle.

A silent procession hums along Interstate 5. Hulking vessels inch across the sound. A seaplane lands and glides to a stop on Lake Union. A cruise ship — the *Sapphire Princess* — sits patiently dockside in Elliott Bay. To the east is the Seattle skyline backed by distant vistas of the Cascades. To the west is the Olympic Peninsula, where Mount Olympus rises regally from its center. But the sky is brimming with low stratus clouds, like ceiling tiles, and the mountain is hidden.

So this is where it begins — with my view obscured, but with the world revolving around me, one degree of perspective at a time.

I reach into my backpack, thumbing past tattered translations of the *Iliad* and the *Odyssey* and a few back issues of *Sports Illustrated* until I find an envelope containing a breathless invitation: "Calling all classmates around the world to join us in Ithaca!"

This is what brought me here. I have been invited — along with three thousand or so Cornell University classmates — to a fifteenth reunion at the gleaming school on the hill in Ithaca, New York. *Come enjoy the guest lecturers and the glee club concert! Hear the president's State of the*

University address! Take in an alumni baseball game! It might have added: *Consider the stratospheric success of your classmates, and wallow in a sense of underachievement!*

When asked to revisit where you have been, you tend to assess where you are. You realize that the gradual march of days has accumulated into years and that the years are forming decades. When midlife approaches like a mugger in an alleyway, you don't merely take stock of your life; you recall your original goals — and perhaps you notice the gulf between the former and the latter.

I seem to arrive at such an existential crisis every decade or so. I assume we all do, in one way or another. My first one happened when I was thirteen and about to celebrate my bar mitzvah, the Jewish rite of passage that was supposed to mean I was entering into some form of adulthood. I felt the weight of the world on my still-narrow shoulders, mostly because the world seemed suddenly complex and chaotic. I was overwhelmed by the onslaught of junior high school — the Darwinian game of social standing, the increasing imbalance of work and play, the shock of adolescence.

I recall the pressure of trying to memorize Hebrew text that — to my blurry and unconvinced eyes — looked like hieroglyphs and squiggles. I heard somewhere that girls preferred boys with dimples, so for my seventh-grade class photo I tried to surreptitiously suck in my cheeks while smiling. When the yearbook came out, I looked creepy and constipated. I remember silently sitting on my girlfriend's basement couch with my arm draped around her shoulder for what seemed like hours as I tried to summon the courage to make any sort of move. I thought: If I am becoming a man, this is a hell of an unimpressive start.

So I confronted this crisis of confidence by traveling inward, by delving further into my imagination. I escaped the chaos by creating worlds in which I was in command. I became a writer.

A few years later, in high school, I met Amy — as a result of my writing, in fact. An English teacher had decided to read one of my papers to her class. I stopped in to chat for a moment. Amy says she liked my smile. I think she was smitten by my metaphors. We attended a couple of proms together, weathered college in Ithaca, and saved our pennies to pay for a walk-up apartment on a leafy street in Chicago's Lincoln Park neighborhood. Following the thrill of our wedding day, we found ourselves falling into a routine and a future laid out before us like a straight track to the horizon. True adulthood had arrived, and responsibilities along with it. But we yearned for options. We wanted to sample life's possibilities before settling down. So this time I responded by traveling outward. We collected our meager savings, bought a thirty-four-foot RV, and hit the highway.

Through forty-eight states and nearly eleven months, we allowed our thoughts to expand and fill the open spaces, crystallizing our criteria of what we wanted out of a place to live. In the end, we opted for small-town serenity on California's central coast, a place where John Steinbeck, Doc Ricketts, and Joseph Campbell used to clink beers, stare into tide pools, and ponder the human condition. I was self-satisfied at my ability to control my destiny and certain that the sky was the limit as long as I didn't settle for anything less than the ideal. But that was when I was a young phenom, newly married, already published at age twenty-six, still clinging to the idea that I could somehow change the world, one word at a time. That was before I had kids and a minivan and an unfathomable mortgage and the notion that my achievements were not meeting my expectations.

Before I found myself humbled by the vagaries of my profession, I would joke to friends that my sole objective was to someday gain entry into the encyclopedia. I figured the folks who make it into those glossy pages had been rewarded for being universally impressive or constructive or, at the very least, memorable. They discovered chemical elements or trekked into lands unknown or churned out literary classics. They earned their immortality. So I aspired to join them. Was that too much to ask?

Be careful what you wish for.

Several years ago, at the peak of the *Who Wants to Be a Millionaire* phenomenon, I tried out for the show. By that I mean I phoned the I-800 number they flashed on the screen and attempted to answer three trivia questions. I did it once a day for a couple of weeks. Why not? I am self-employed. There are worse ways to take a work break. It was a diversion, a lark — until I passed the initial round and received a fortunate random phone call telling me I had moved on to the next tryout hurdle.

So in rapid succession I answered five more questions, tougher ones, on subjects ranging from Mary Lou Retton to the Teapot Dome scandal. Finally, there was this synapse-snapper: "Put the following ancient civilizations in the order in which they were established — Assyrian, Mayan, Sumerian, Classical Greek." Wise Athena must have been smiling down on me. More likely, it was Tyche, goddess of luck. Soon enough, I found myself in Manhattan, along with nine other contestants, hoping for an opportunity to sit across from diminutive Regis Philbin and his shiny teeth, each of us craving a chance to conquer trivia questions for gobs of money in front of an audience of millions.

Then I won the "fastest-finger" round — by thirteen-hundredths of a second. This meant I was headed for something called the "hot seat," which at the time was the epicenter of pop culture in America, a piece of furniture as iconic as Archie Bunker's chair. Surreal doesn't even begin to describe it, and because I tend to be rather cynical and inhibited, it was as out of character as if I had joined the cast of *A Chorus Line.*

For the next forty minutes, I did my best not to humiliate myself in front of twenty-five million people. I am sure I didn't impress the ten million or so folks who were screaming at the boob on the tube who wasn't quite sure about the name of Dilbert's pet dog or the logo of Hallmark cards. But, using my lifelines early and often, I clawed my way through the murk of ignorance until suddenly this little television host was showing me a fake check for $64,000.

Then came a question for $125,000: Which of these American

westerns was not a remake of a Japanese film? Possible answers: *The Magnificent Seven, The Outrage, High Noon, A Fistful of Dollars.*

I knew that the first one was a remake of *The Seven Samurai*. I had no clue about the rest. If I wanted to hazard a guess, I had a one-in-three chance. However, if I guessed incorrectly, I would lose half my money. I kept focusing on *High Noon*, mumbling it over and over, whispering my suspicion that it was the answer.

Before jetting off to New York I had considered possible scenarios with my friends, and I actually had declared that if I were in that exact situation — with an inkling of an idea at that particular level of the game — I would go for it. You only live once, I announced. The name of the show isn't *Who Wants to Be Slightly Better Off.*

But when the real moment arrived, I hemmed and hawed and squirmed. Then, rather suddenly, I decided to stop. I took the money and walked away.

The next question would have been for a quarter of a million dollars. I would give anything to know what the subject would have been. In my daydreams, it is a bit of trivia about baseball or U.S. geography, something very much in my cerebral wheelhouse. All I had to do was answer three more questions correctly, and I would have been an instant millionaire.

The answer, of course, was *High Noon*. The irony — that I didn't have the guts to choose a film about one man's gallantry in the face of long odds — is not lost on me. While I was overjoyed at my windfall, I reflect on that moment of decision and feel pangs of weakness. I know that it took a certain daring to get there in the first place. And I very much believe that we make our own breaks in life. But that decision nags at me. How many people are handed such a black-and-white litmus test of their nerve? Isn't boldness the one trait shared by most every encyclopedia-worthy historical figure? Did my fears win the day?

It was my Scylla-and-Charybdis moment. In Homer's mythological epics, this is brave Odysseus's most heart-wrenching dilemma, as he pilots his ships through what may have been the Straits of Messina, off the coast of Sicily. On one side is Charybdis, an unpredictable whirlpool that may — or may not — swallow entire ships. On the other side, in a gloomy cliffside cave, dwells Scylla, a monster with "twelve flapping feet, and six necks enormously long, and at the end of each neck a horrible head with three rows of teeth set thick and close, full of black death." She is guaranteed to snatch a half-dozen crew members in her deadly jaws. So this is Odysseus's choice — if he steers clear of one, he falls prey to the other. It is the genesis of the rock-and-hard-place metaphor. Do you risk everything for success, or do you sacrifice for safety?

Like Odysseus, I chose conservatively — security over audacity. And I regret it, both fiscally and spiritually. But that isn't the end of the story.

After every commercial break, Regis would ask contestants a personal question or two, his note cards stocked with information gleaned from a producer's pre-interview. We chatted about how I met Amy and what magazines I write for. We discussed the one-in-a-billion coincidence that the person in the hot seat right before me was a good friend of mine whose husband I have known since the age of nine. We even touched on the fact that I suffer from cremnophobia, the fear of precipices (which — let's face it — is really the fear of death). Finally, after I had won the $64,000, Regis said, "So you've written a few books. What's the latest one?"

So for about thirty seconds I described a book I had written, an account of my life-altering year on the road with my wife. *States of Mind* had been published to little fanfare by a small press in North Carolina. It had been sporadically, if kindly, reviewed, and only a few thousand copies had been sold. Before my moment of *Millionaire* glory aired, I had logged on to Amazon.com and discovered that it was the online bookseller's 122,040th best-selling book. That's humbling. But there were twenty-five million people watching — and paying attention. Within twenty-four hours, *States of Mind* was ranked No. 7.

USA Today ran a blurb revealing the book's meteoric rise. *Enter-*

tainment Weekly called, followed by a parade of newspapers and national magazines. After I flew back to New York and chatted with Matt Lauer on NBC's *Today* show for five minutes, *States of Mind* rose to No. 2, behind only an unpublished Harry Potter novel.

Damn wizard.

By the time *People* magazine and the *Oprah* show contacted me, my excitement had evolved into bemused fascination. It was thrilling, of course, but I also struggled with ambivalence. My book chronicled a search for virtue in America — a literal and figurative trip through places like Inspiration (Arizona), Honor (Michigan), and Wisdom (Montana)—yet I had promoted it on a mind-numbing television show predicated on greed. It was a bit like Harper Lee using *Let's Make a Deal* as a platform, if you will pardon the comparison. And while the ensuing publicity was a hoot, it focused almost entirely on the book's sales, not necessarily the merits of the book itself. I feared that I had sold out and peaked at the same time. Other than quarterbacks and porn stars, who wants to max out at age thirty-one?

I am not a believer in predestination. But the ancient Greeks, the folks whose myths are driving my current excursion, were consumed by it. They believed their fortunes were at the mercy of the Morae — the three sisters known collectively as the Fates. Clotho, the youngest, spun the thread of life. Lachesis, the middle sister, measured it with a rod. Atropos, the oldest, snipped it with shears when Death arrived. It was said that even Zeus was powerless against them.

However, the mythic Morae determined not only the time and manner of one's death but also one's lifelong destiny. A thousand years after Homer's day, an Athenian sophist named Flavius Philostratus mused that the threads that the Fates spin are so unalterable that "a man who the Fates have decreed that he shall be an eminent archer will not miss the mark, even though he lost his eyesight." But I have begun to wonder if I was fated to slightly miss the mark.

"Brad Herzog. Remember the name," began a *USA Today* story in the midst of my fleeting media maelstrom. "He just might be the next Stephen King or John Grisham." Surely I am the only reader who

recalls the words, but they now strike me as having a DEWEY DEFEATS
TRUMAN quality to them. Acquaintances will refer to my *Millionaire*
moment and joke that I somehow managed to double my fifteen minutes of fame. But I didn't seek fleeting tabloid renown, and I have no
desire that my obituary someday begin with a reference to a TV quiz
show. In the long run, I became neither rich nor famous — just a bit
more professionally established and briefly celebrated for being mo-
mentarily well-known.

Now I am pushing forty. I seem to have aches where I didn't know
I had muscles, rogue hairs where I didn't realize I had follicles, and
frustration where I wasn't aware I had ambition. I have reached that
psychochronological tipping point at which my life is no longer entirely a forward-looking phenomenon, and sporadic regrets have
begun to creep in like cockroaches. And I am being beckoned to the
place where my grandiose dreams took root.

It has been nearly two decades since I first arrived in Ithaca, unpacking my bags and my potential. What kind of existence have I
crafted for myself? Can I claim to have lived a good life? Are my con-
tributions in any way heroic? And in contemporary America, what
constitutes a heroic life anyhow?

Funny thing is, I am wholly satisfied with my surroundings. How
many people can say that? I lucked into an adorable and compassionate wife, two precious sons, loyal friends, and a fine house in a
charming town. What I can't figure out is why, amid so much exter-
nal contentment, I can harbor so much disillusionment. Lately, my
angst has coalesced into a bit of a black cloud over my head, and it
has begun to permeate the small world that means everything to me.

I used to write from the heart — experimentally, enthusiastically.
But in recent years my grand literary dreams have softened into moderate ambitions revolving around paying the mortgage. Whereas once
I was inspired by a shifting view of the big picture, now I constantly
find myself sweating the small stuff, micromanaging my family like a
retired guy who hangs around the house and annoys everybody —
only I may never be able to afford retirement. I have bouts of irri-

tability, periods in which I have difficulty living in the moment, times where I notice my innate cynicism evolving into a sort of nihilistic grunt.

I don't want to be *that guy*. My wife doesn't want it either.

Amy is always the optimist, impossibly sunny — a Pooh to my Eeyore — and she has taken on the tiring responsibility of bolstering my sense of self-worth. But when I begin to cross the line — when my unreasonable expectations are thrust on my life partner and two little boys, who, after all, will be boys — her exhaustion turns to exasperation. The last thing I want is to unravel my near-perfect universe because I can't come to grips with my own imperfections.

"Go take a drive," Amy insisted. "I'll meet you in Ithaca."

I might have taken this to mean simply that I should light out after the kind of self-knowledge that only a journey can provide, that I should clear the existential cobwebs by crafting a unique itinerary through a nation's nooks and crannies, figuring it would take me to places I had not yet explored. But when she said it, she held my gaze for just a half-second longer than usual, a moment dripping with subtext.

Go away. Figure it out, she was saying. *Don't come back until you do.*

She looked at the calendar. "You have thirty-one days."

It was a Greek philosopher, Socrates, who believed, "The unexamined life is not worth living." And it was the son of French Canadian immigrants, Jack Kerouac, who opined, "The road is life." Some combustible combination of the two notions is the spark of my mission.

I have decided to let Homer ride shotgun. It was he, a supposedly blind minstrel nearly three millennia ago, who crafted the original hero's journey. Odysseus's was a practical quest — return home to his beloved isle of Ithaka after twenty years of war and wayward travel. But at its heart, the voyage of Odysseus represents an intellectual adventure. For all the gods and monsters he encounters, his is a pilgrimage toward an understanding of humanity.

In fact, much the same could be said about all ancient myths. "Society's dream" is how they were characterized by Joseph Campbell, the famed mythologist, who described myths as stories of man's constant search for meaning. The heroes are archetypes, replicated in many cultures over various ages. Their tests and ordeals are the wrappings of truth, a sort of collective unconscious, a vehicle for the communication of universal insight—all in the guise of a good yarn. In other words, we were not made in the image of gods; gods were made in our image—our fears, our foibles, our fantasies. In my journey, I am not aspiring to the deeds of ancient heroes; rather those ancient heroes are manifestations of the symbolic expression of my psyche.

I don't claim to be Odysseus. It is simply the other way around.

So Campbell will be a key companion of mine too, sitting in the back, occasionally looking over Homer's shoulder. Our ride is a cushy little house on wheels—a twenty-six-foot Winnebago Aspect, which is the perfect name, given my quest. It suggests a facet, a part of a whole—a component of the big picture. Campbell, an atheist's icon, will have to share space back there with a pastor-turned-philosopher because I brought a collection of Ralph Waldo Emerson's essays along—treatises on concepts like Power, Truth, and Experience, just in case I need a dose of nineteenth-century self-reliance. So this is my traveling band—Homer navigating blindly, while a mythologist and a transcendentalist try to help me determine exactly where his tales should lead me.

My goal: Visit with other lives. Explore other places. Find coherence in the diversity I am sure to encounter. Accumulate the knowledge of journeys past and present as I rumble toward an understanding of the heroic ideal. Locate exemplars of that elusive concept. Court adventure and epiphany and insight. Then come home in one piece, and possibly at peace with myself.

I descend the Space Needle and spend an hour wandering around Seattle's trendy Belltown neighborhood, past assorted sushi bars and billiard halls and jazz clubs. Nothing much catches my eye until I reach . . . the single eye. Here it is, on the corner of First Avenue and

Wall Street—blue-irised, red-lidded, rimmed in neon orange. It hangs over the sidewalk, three-dimensional and hypnotic, protruding from a red brick building. I have stumbled upon the Cyclops Café.

Seattle's Cyclops Café

The menu sounds appealing, in an ocular sort of way—a Greek-tinged Cyclops Omelette, a two-egg meal called the Bi-clops, drinks with names like Eye Caramba and Pink Eye—but it is midafternoon, too early for dinner. The door is locked, the lights dim, the chairs stacked on tables. This is one Cyclops lair that will have to remain unexplored.

I consider this a good omen. Odysseus would have been wise to skip it himself. Early in his journey, when he and his twelve ships catch sight of the Island of the Cyclops—a race of precommunal cave dwellers—Odysseus's prudence loses out to his curiosity. He takes a handful of men to the island, enters a cave, and starts feasting on the food there, only to be somehow surprised when the resident one-eyed giant, Polyphemus, returns. The Cyclops places a massive boulder in front of the cave entrance to trap his uninvited visitors and proceeds to cannibalize a few of them.

Odysseus utilizes his famed cunning to extract himself from the situation—first getting the Cyclops drunk and then, when he falls asleep, using a fire-sharpened pole to destroy the creature's single eye.

In the morning, when blinded Polyphemus moves the boulder so that his sheep may graze outside, Odysseus and his men, who have tied themselves to the animals' undersides, are able to escape.

But this scene is really a tale of Odysseus's flaws. Hubris bookends the story. First, he deems his personal curiosity more important than the safety of his crew. Then, after their escape, his excessive pride puts them at even greater risk. When Polyphemus first asks his visitor's name, Odysseus calls himself Noman. After being blinded, Polyphemus cries out to his fellow Cyclops that Noman has hurt him. So they don't intervene. Clever move. But as Odysseus sails away, he stoops to perhaps history's first account of trash-talking, shouting, "If ever anyone asks you who put out your ugly eye, tell them your blinder was Odysseus, the conqueror of Troy, the son of Laertes, whose address is in Ithaka." Bad move. Turns out Polyphemus is one of the sons of Poseidon, who will take vengeance on Odysseus by constantly driving him away from his home and happiness, precipitating some ten years of wandering.

This is why I can identify with this ancient king of Ithaka. Although he claims to be Noman, he is essentially Everyman, in the sense that he is far from perfect. In the course of his adventures, Odysseus lies, steals, and schemes. He can be clear-minded and determined and remarkably courageous, but at times he is also distrustful and devious and hypocritical and merciless. He is not a particularly successful leader: His men often ignore his warnings and pay dearly for doing so, and he loses every single one of his ships and crew. His wife, Penelope, a daughter of Spartan royalty, is the very paragon of fidelity, yet he certainly isn't faithful to her during his long journey home. And when he finally reaches Ithaka, he murders the dozens of unarmed men who have been courting her, thinking her husband long dead.

Even physically, Homer describes Odysseus as unimposing. In the *Iliad*, an older man points to him and asks who the fellow is "who is shorter by a head than Agamemnon." Later, another admits, "No other man alive could come near Odysseus. But then we did not think him so very much to look at." By the time of the *Odyssey*, he is probably well into his forties, maybe with bags under his eyes from his constant travails, possibly out of shape. Even one-eyed Polyphemus calls him a "short worthless-looking runt." You know you are no physical marvel when you are dissed by a Cyclops.

So Odysseus is the prototype of not only the hero but also all *flawed* fictional heroes who followed. He is why Superman falls prey to kryptonite and Sherlock Holmes prefers his 7 percent solution and Indiana Jones hates snakes. And for a guy like me — somewhat vertically challenged, battling a paunch, not always taking the high road — his is a template to which I can relate.

Come to think of it, my imperfection has been immortalized. You see, there is one final addendum to my *Who Wants to Be a Millionaire* tale. A few weeks after the silliness subsided, the phone rang. It was a fellow from Grolier, the folks who publish *The Encyclopedia Americana.* They were putting together *The Americana Annual,* a six-hundred-page recap of the events of the year 2000. Could I write 800 words about the history of quiz shows and the current craze? Sure, I said, only a tad reluctantly. At least it's one way to get into the encyclopedia. The lesson: When revealing aspirations, be specific.

Several months later, the volume arrived, a handsomely bound yearbook with Al Gore and George Bush awkwardly shaking hands on the cover. Squeezed in between an account of "Monkeys in Peril" and a spread about tall ships was my summary of quiz show history. To my surprise, the article began with a half-page color photo of my final moments on the *Millionaire* set. So in perpetuity, anyone can turn to page 90 of the 2001 *Americana Annual* and catch the forever frozen image of me sitting in the hot seat, smiling wanly at my old pal Regis, having just failed a test of courage.

II
family plots

The original *Encyclopedia Britannica*, published nearly a century ago, described suicide as "an act of cowardice disguised as heroism." It is a fascinating perspective, and it may have its origins in the ancient Greek myths, which are rife with dozens of tales of men and women who find death preferable to a troubled life. They hang themselves, stab themselves, drink poison, self-castrate, leap into the sea, and hurl themselves into the mouths of dragons. Usually, the gods are to blame.

At about the time of the inaugural *Britannica*, my great-great-great uncle took an easier route than most of the ancients. He simply shot himself—after shooting someone else. I am on a mission to find him and perhaps figure out why.

I have made this my first task because I have decided that I cannot examine the parameters of a heroic life without first considering the phenomenon of personal expectations. How does one's course compare to one's potential and, more important, to one's aspirations? If the decision to end it all may be oversimplified and described as an extreme reaction to an existence unfulfilled, doesn't it boil down to expectations? What society expects of us. What we expect of our world. What we expect of ourselves. And if the expectations are so unreasonable that they are all but impossible to meet, what is the source of such high standards?

So I am making my way toward a cemetery in eastern Washington, but first I am lunching in Paradise, a thin-aired hamlet at the foot of massive Mount Rainier that receives nearly seven hundred inches of snowfall annually. It is midday in mid-May, and the sun has turned the blanket of snow around me into a billion crystalline wonders. As my companion Emerson once put it, on "one of those celestial days when heaven and earth meet and adorn each other, it seems a poverty that we can only spend it once."

The mountain as holy place is a notion present in nearly every culture, of course, and in every era — whether it be Mount Fuji to the Japanese or the Smoky Mountains to the Cherokee or Ararat and Sinai in Judeo-Christian teachings. We celebrate them as an opportunity to rise above humanity, literally and figuratively. Really, they are metaphors for aspirations.

Alpinists seem to find the climb itself — the challenge — to be a sort of stairway to the realm and the revelations of the gods. In 1950, when Maurice Herzog (no relation to my decidedly earthbound family) reached the peak of Annapurna, at the time the highest mountain ever summited, he returned with the conviction that "in touching the extreme boundaries of man's world, we have come to know something of its true splendor." Those concerned with the big picture — the philosophers and photographers among us — tend to find a glimpse of immortality in the view. If one accepts the contention, articulated even in ancient times, that gods are heroes glorified over time, then these two perspectives of the mount might represent the dichotomy of the Hero, of what constitutes heroic attempt — ascent versus awareness, effort versus insight, the challenge of overcoming man's limitations versus the possibility of actually understanding them.

The story of Odysseus embodies both. His is a search for both Ithaka and illumination. Joseph Campbell's blueprint for all myths, which he called the nuclear unit of the monomyth, is simply the following: "A hero ventures forth from the world of common day into a region of supernatural wonder: fabulous forces are there encountered and a decisive victory is won: the hero comes back from this mysterious adventure with the power to bestow boons on his fellow man." The last part, while it may be least exciting, is actually most important. It implies that one falls short of the heroic ideal if there is achievement without understanding, forces overcome without lessons learned and dispersed — that is, if you climb the mountain without absorbing the view.

But while this might be paradise after all, someday it will be annihilated. Mount Rainier is an active volcano, one of more than a dozen in the Cascade Range. Volcanologists keep an especially wary eye on it because a large lava eruption would melt the white sheet covering its massive dome — more snow and ice than all the other Cascade volcanoes combined — and send a flood of mud and rock rushing toward the river valleys that radiate from the mountain.

Less than fifty miles south of here and almost exactly twenty-five years earlier, a tremendous blast blew the top off Mount St. Helens. An ash column rose more than fifteen miles and dumped volcanic dust across the Northwest. A hundred-mile-per-hour landslide covered twenty-three square miles and left debris and ash as much as six hundred feet deep. Fifty-seven people died. By contrast, Rainier's environs are far more populated than those surrounding Mount St. Helens; more than three million people live within one hundred miles of the mountain.

The ancient Greeks knew nothing of magma reservoirs, of course. To them, the rumble and steam from volcanoes were the hammer and forge of Hephaestus, the blacksmith of Olympus, god of fire and metallurgy. Unlike the other gods, who were usually portrayed as having exceptional beauty, he was short, fat, and, most remarkably, disabled — the result of being tossed from Olympus by either his mother, Hera, or his father, Zeus, depending on which version of parental rejection one prefers.

His is a mythos of great contradiction. He was a god, but he actually worked tirelessly, sweating over his fiery forge, wearing a smudged face and a sleeveless tunic. He was lame and ugly, yet he hammered out great power (Zeus's thunderbolts, Apollo's arrows) and unmatched beauty (the thrones of Olympus, Dionysus's golden cup). He was married to lovely Aphrodite, but her unfaithfulness led him to act on his vengeful desires, and so he tried to rape virginal Athena.

It was the three women in Hephaestus's life — Athena, Aphrodite, and Hera — whose I'm-prettier-than-you contest was judged by the Trojan prince Paris. Athena and Hera tried to bribe Paris with power and victory in battle, but Aphrodite promised him the love of the most beautiful woman in the world. She was Helen, wife to the king of Sparta and daughter of the king of the gods, conceived during one of Zeus's frequent adulterous endeavors. But it was her own adulterous elopement with this Trojan prince that led to a god-squabble played out on an epic human scale, launching a thousand ships, one of them captained by the reluctant Odysseus, amid the ten-year Trojan War.

Both mythographies — Hephaestus the unwanted god and Helen the wanted woman, he the repulsive creator of beauty and she the beautiful seed of ruination — share similar, almost paradoxical motifs: ugly attractiveness, blighted purity. The existence of a Mount St. Helens, bearing the forge of the god and the name of the woman — or a Rainier, even grander and deadlier — would seem to be a lesson in moderating expectations. The ability to both inspire and obliterate is a reminder that, however heroic we may deem ourselves, we are earthbound and at the mercy of something greater. They are monuments to the impossibility of perfection.

A few hours later, I have come upon a high desert mirage for the atomic age. In the distance, out past the sagebrush, beneath an armada of cumulus clouds, a cluster of smokestacks and boxy buildings rise from the flatlands of Benton County like rows of Montecristos and packs of Marlboros. It is what John Steinbeck used to call the "yellow smoke of progress." The forested mounds of western Washington have flattened into the dry grasslands of eastern Washington, and I am driving along the fringe of a 560-square-mile region overseen by the Department of Energy — the Hanford site, an anti-oasis if ever there was one.

Two centuries earlier, when Lewis and Clark arrived at this curve

in the Columbia River, they found the remains of Indian villages dating from prehistoric times. Today, more than 120,000 people reside
in the Tri-Cities of Richland, Pasco, and Kennewick. Most of them
are here because a few scientists discovered the devastating potential
of nuclear fission.

With the launch of the Manhattan Project in January 1943,
Hanford, a tiny farming community here in Benton County, was chosen as the nation's first large-scale plutonium production site. The area
was selected for its distance from major population centers, its acces-
sibility to railroad transportation, its semi-arid climate, and the fact
that the Columbia River offered plenty of cold water to cool reactors,
while nearby dams made abundant and inexpensive electricity available. As for the folks who lived there, the War Powers Act allowed the
government to buy the land and force all the residents to move within
a month. By March, more than fifty thousand construction workers
were living in makeshift housing (Hanford immediately became Washington's fourth most populous city), and only a few dozen people
knew what the hell they were building.

Just thirteen months later, Hanford's first nuclear reactor went
online. Plutonium manufactured at Hanford was used in the first
atomic bomb tested at New Mexico's Trinity Site and the second
atomic bomb ever used in warfare — the "Fat Man" bomb dropped
on Nagasaki. Afterward, the newspaper in Richland shouted, "IT'S
ATOMIC BOMBS," reporting that the reaction in the Hanford area was
"disbelief . . . followed by enthusiasm." Richland High School
adopted "Bombers" as its nickname. The school's coat of arms
featured an adorable mushroom cloud. You can buy bumper stickers
there — still, to this day — that declare, PROUD OF THE CLOUD.

These days, Hanford's reactors lie dormant, but the Tri-Cities
continue to thrive, based not on what is produced here but rather on
what has accumulated. The Hanford Nuclear Reservation is the largest
nuclear waste dump in the Western Hemisphere. It is one of the most
toxic places on earth. Nearly 10,000 workers are involved in what has
been called the world's largest environmental cleanup. Their task:

Guard 25 tons of plutonium (which has a half-life of some 24,000 years), dig up 10 million tons of contaminated soil, mitigate 2,300 tons of corroded nuclear fuel rods sitting in two huge indoor pools that might at any time crack open during an earthquake and spill into the Columbia, and clean up more than 50 million gallons of radioactive and chemical waste stored in 177 underground tanks, each the size of a three-story building, many of which are leaking. It is a task worthy of Hercules, and the cleanup will last for decades.

So here is the man-made version of the volcanic metaphor. Native American writer Sherman Alexie, who grew up on the Spokane Indian Reservation, about one hundred miles north of the Hanford site, has observed how myth and science are "first cousins who strongly resemble each other and passionately hate the resemblance." It could be argued that at some point, when we began messing with the atom and developing enough destructive power to obliterate the planet, we started poaching the divine powers. Our aspirations outpaced our aptitude.

Indeed, a great many mythological tales warn of the dangers of hubris. Arachne challenges Athena to a weaving contest and is forever transformed into a spider. Phaethon learns that his father is Helios, god of the sun, and tries to drive his chariot across the sky, only to be struck dead by a thunderbolt from Zeus. Sisphyus, believing his cleverness surpasses that of Zeus, is left to constantly roll a huge rock up a hill in the underworld, only to have it roll back down just as he reaches the top. The Greeks and their gods didn't much care for overweening pride.

And what is that middle ground between earthbound man and divinity? The hero. The paragon of humankind. But given that even the gods seem to have their flaws — a constant narrative of jealousy, rage, arrogance, infidelity — I have to remind myself again as I stumble forward that although the heroic may be the ideal, there is room for imperfection.

Perhaps the best indication that the hero has long been viewed as a sort of God Lite is the fact that most of antiquity's most celebrated heroes were born of a union between the human and the divine. Hercules and Perseus, for instance, were direct offspring of ever-philandering Zeus. However, Odysseus was a man of comparatively low birth. For one thing, his parents — Laertes and Anticleia — were human. Yes, Laertes was king of Ithaka, but Ithaka was just a rocky, barren island on the fringes of what was then the Mycenaean civilization. Odysseus's maternal grandfather, Autolycus, was a thief — a notorious, brilliant expert at trickery but a thief nonetheless. It is from him that Odysseus received his oft-mentioned wiles, not to mention the helmet he wore during the Trojan War. His gramps had stolen it.

Of course, Autolycus was said to be the son of Hermes, the god of thieves, and he inherited some impressive skills. And since Hermes was the son of Zeus, that would make Odyseus the great-great-grandson of the king of the gods. But by Hellenistic hero standards, that ain't much. This I admire about Odysseus, not least because I am on a mission to find the murderer in my ancestry.

I had always thought my paternal roots were firmly entrenched in Chicago, where I and my father and his parents were born and raised. I figured a handful of folks came over from the Old World sometime in the late nineteenth century and made straight for the Windy City — until my paternal grandmother began to tell me foggy tales of how *her* family came to Chicago via eastern Washington, somewhere near Walla Walla. She claimed, though there was conviction missing from her voice, that a family patriarch was awarded plots of land in eastern Washington in gratitude for his gallantry in battle. One of Teddy Roosevelt's Rough Riders, she seemed to recall. Or something like that.

But then I talked with a cousin of mine one day, and he shrugged his shoulders at the Rough Rider reference. Instead, he mentioned rumors of a sordid event in the family history — a disgruntled uncle, a mystery, a murder-suicide. Rumor has it that this uncle is buried, he said, in a small town called Dayton, about an hour west of Washington's Tri-Cities along a road touted as the Lewis and Clark Forgotten Trail.

These days, it is a trek through farmland, much of it nearly vertical. The layered hills — dark green wheat fields, light green pea fields, brown fallow soil — look like striped gumdrops. Just west of Dayton, on the north side of Highway 12, one of the foothills comes alive in the shape of a giant — a green giant, actually, over three hundred feet tall and made of colored eight-by-twelve-inch patio blocks set into the hillside.

My Homer-saturated mind conjures up images of gigantic cannibals — the Laestrygonians, who welcome three envoys sent by Odysseus by grabbing one of them and preparing him for dinner. When the other two men race back to the harbor, the Laestrygonians rush in from every direction and toss massive boulders at Odysseus's ships, smashing them to pieces. Then they spear the men like fish, carrying them home for supper. The confrontation amounts to all of a dozen lines in Homer's epic, but in an instant Odysseus loses eleven of his twelve ships — all but his own.

This is typical of Homer, by the way. He spends only a few lines describing horrific scenes: sinking ships, terrifying maelstroms, ghastly deaths. But he uses dozens of lines to explain how Odysseus's old wet nurse recognizes him upon his return to Ithaka by a scar he received while hunting a wild boar as a young man. It is a strange imbalance of event and exposition, but it isn't necessarily inconsistent with Homer's intent. The *Odyssey* is a story about a man's journey home, rather than simply a man's journey.

Regardless, the all-too-brief encounter with the cannibals begins with an encounter with a sturdy girl who is drawing water from a spring. She points the men toward her home, where they expect to be welcomed as traveling strangers. *Beware your friends*, the scene seems to suggest — which, it turns out, well describes the tale of the green giant.

The hillside giant is the logo of the Green Giant label, which was long represented here in Columbia County by the Seneca Foods asparagus cannery. For seven decades, the cannery reigned as one of the major employers in the region — until 2004, when Seneca announced it would shift its operations to Peru, where workers earn in a day what Americans make in an hour. The Dayton facility, touted as the largest in the world, had been the last remaining asparagus cannery in the state, and the move left a huge void in Columbia County's economy, eliminating thousands of full-time and seasonal jobs in a region with a total population of only 4,100 people. But the green giant is still there, decorating the hillside, only now it must seem like a massive chalk body outline at a crime scene.

For the time being, Dayton remains a charming little community, the kind of nineteenth-century hamlet — with the oldest continuously operating courthouse in the state and the oldest train depot — that clings to the significance of its past amid a modern world that has rendered the place largely insignificant. It has been the Columbia County seat since 1875. I head for the public library, where a woman named Liz assists me in my exploration; we go through old newspapers, census records, deed records, history books. And a story begins to emerge.

There were no Rough Riders in my family. I come from a long line of Dry Cleaners and Insurance Brokers. If old Teddy Roosevelt wanted his shirts pressed or his claims paid, we were of heroic stock. Adolph Roth made it to America first, emigrating from Austria-Hungary to New York City in 1873 at the age of eighteen. How and why he found his way to the southeastern corner of Washington remains a mystery, but he did so less than a decade later, well before the Spanish-American War. He was the first of three Roth brothers to arrive.

By 1883, the Adolph Roth Mercantile Company was advertising in the *Columbia Chronicle*. Adolph married a woman from New York a few years later, and they raised three daughters and a son in Dayton. The son died suddenly at the age of five in February 1906 and was buried in Dayton Cemetery. Almost immediately thereafter, Adolph must have moved his family to San Francisco, just in time for the city's infamous earthquake. Records show that Adolph wrote to his brother to tell him about the unfortunate timing.

Henry Roth, the oldest Roth brother, was the second to come over, following his brother to Dayton in 1895 and lasting about fifteen years there, before moving to Chicago, where he and his sons ran a dry cleaning business. Henry was my great-great-grandfather. The story I always heard about his second son, my great-grandfather, was that he was originally called Otto. However, for some reason he despised the fact that his name could be spelled the same forward as backward. So he renamed himself after his uncle — Adolph. History will record that as lousy timing, too.

Of the original immigrants, there was also a third son. His name was Joseph. My grandmother, Celia Roth, is in her nineties now but still as sharp as the spear of Achilles. She lived across the street from her grandfather in Chicago and heard tales of his brother, the elder Adolph. But she had never heard of the other brother, Joseph. Apparently, the family was keen on keeping him a secret.

This I know: Joe Roth was born in Hungary in 1862. He lived in Dayton for a dozen years, and he is buried in Dayton. In between, he lived in Hermiston, Oregon, for four years, and he died there, violently. After a good deal of digging, I discover the family secret on the front page of the *Columbia Chronicle*, dated June 3, 1916, which reprinted a report of a few days earlier from the *Hermiston Herald*:

> Goaded on by a crazed brain crying for a righting of fancied wrongs, Joe Roth Thursday lay in wait for James Ralph, shooting him twice, and a moment later turned the gun to his own head and fired. The shooting took place just a few minutes past 9 Thursday evening. There was no warning and both apparently died instantly.
>
> James Ralph had been out riding during the evening and on his return ran his car up to the front door of the Sapper Bros. garage. This large door has

no lock on it nor a means of opening it from the outside. The garage was closed and Mr. Ralph did not have a key to the side door. He knew, however, that by taking a screwdriver he could lift the door sufficiently to get his fingers under and then raise it. He did this and just as he succeeded in raising the door as high as his shoulders there were two shots in quick succession and Mr. Ralph fell backward to the walk. A moment later a third shot was fired . . .

It seems that both Joe Roth and James Ralph had worked at the Dayton Electric and Power Company, which brought the first electric lights to the town. In 1912, both sold out and moved about one hundred miles southwest to Hermiston, where they purchased interests in the Hermiston Power and Light Company. At the time of the shooting, Joe was the company's president; James was the vice president and general manager. Again, *beware your friends.*

Apparently, that night Joe came home from work and sat for a while with the evening paper. Then he left, telling his wife and two daughters that he was going to the office. That is the last they saw him alive. Joe seems to have gained entry to the garage through a side door. He left through a rear door and was found behind the building with a bullet in his head. A revolver with the spent bullets was found next to his body; another revolver with one exploded shell was found in his coat pocket.

Records indicate that in 1909, at least, Joe Roth lived at 703 South Third Street in Dayton. But there is no 703 South Third Street; it is an absent address, although it would have been located across the street from what is now the high school gymnasium. So instead, I trudge to Dayton Cemetery, where Adolph Roth bought a dozen plots 115 years earlier. The city clerk informs me that, had I arrived only a few years earlier — before the city changed its policy on such things — I could have sold nine plots back to the city for $800 each. Again, bad timing.

In section A, I find a trio of gravestones in a neat row. Two belong to Adolph Roth's children — ten-week-old May and five-year-
old Sammie. The third, a square slab of granite, smaller and less
adorned, is Joseph Roth's. He was fifty-four.

The final resting place of Joe Roth in Dayton, Washington

I stand there, listening to the birds chirp blissfully, and I think
back to the last words of the *Hermiston Herald*'s account of the tragedy:
"Mr. Roth was a kind, loving husband and father." So what caused Joe
Roth's descent into madness? Did he discover that Ralph had em-
bezzled money? Was he trying to cover up his own thievery? Had he
found Ralph in bed with his wife? Had the stress of business led him
to snap? Or was he a man destroyed by miscommunication? Did he
simply think Ralph was a burglar trying to enter the garage? Then
again, why was Joe in the garage in the first place?

There are no real answers, only clues, as gleaned from the newspapers: "Mr. Roth was in Dayton several weeks ago, and it was noted

at that time that he was worried about something, but no one knew what it was. . . . It is also learned that for the past two years Mr. Roth has wanted to buy the electric plant and own it all to himself, but Mr. Ralph did not want to sell. . . . Mr. Roth had a bruise on the back of his head which cannot be accounted for unless it was caused from falling."

Most intriguing to me is the third bullet. Why did he kill himself? Was he distraught over his place in life? Or was he remorseful over his involvement in death?

Among the myriad tales of suicide in the ancient Greek myths, several are directly tied to Odysseus himself, including the death of his mother, whom Odysseus had thought very much alive. But when he encounters her spirit during his trip to the underworld, she tells him, "It was no disease that made me pine away, but I missed you so much, and your clever wit and your gay merry ways, and life was sweet no longer, so I died."

Still if I were to guess at what might have driven Joe Roth to murder-suicide, I might point to Odysseus's experiences in Troy. The legendary Ajax, tallest and strongest of all the Achaeans and second only to Achilles as a warrior, is the only main character in the *Iliad* whose prowess on the battlefield is absent any help from the gods. With the death of Achilles at Troy, Ajax and Odysseus both claim his armor for themselves. Both men deliver speeches, and Odysseus, far more eloquent, takes the prize. Ajax then goes into a narcissistic rage, vowing to kill the Greek leaders who deprived him of what he considers his rightful inheritance. It is a tale of unmet expectations.

To stop Ajax, Athena makes him temporarily insane, and so he slaughters a flock of sheep instead, mistaking them for his former comrades-in-arms. It has been described as vengeance against the social order, a rebellion against the notion of honoring a negotiator over a true warrior. When his madness leaves him, blood on his hands, his honor diminished, he sees death as the only way to reestablish his heroic stature. He fastens a sword to the ground and falls on it.

So maybe Joe Roth was equally enraged by the order of things. Perhaps he, too, considered himself worthy of sole ownership and went mad when his ambitions were thwarted. It could be that he came to his senses in time to see the blood on his hands and did what he considered to be the only honorable thing.

I can only hope that my great-great-great uncle was humbled by his grave error in judgment, perhaps understanding — as I am beginning to — that obsessing about unrealized life goals might only serve to undermine a life entirely. Ajax? He never learned. When Odysseus visits the underworld, all his fallen comrades-in-arms are there. He speaks with Achilles and Agamemnon and Patroclus . . . but Ajax simply walks away in silence.

III

athena

"Should I call you Mr. President?"

The man loosens his grip on the lawn mower and offers a smile and a handshake. "Bill would be fine."

I am in Oregon now, some fifty miles southwest of Dayton, having enjoyed a gorgeous drive that took me through quintessential rolling hills to a hamlet called Athena, home to about 1,200 God-fearing souls. It wasn't always Athena. When a New Yorker named Darwin Richards settled the area in 1866, the stagecoach operators who stopped there called it Richards' Station. Later, the town that sprang up was known as Centerville, as it was halfway between Pendleton and Walla Walla, which must have seemed like metropolises back in the day. But, predictably, there were already a few Centervilles in the region. So a local school superintendent, a classical scholar, suggested a name change. He claimed the hills of what is now called Umatilla County were similar to those around Athens, Greece. So Athena it became.

And why not? There is no harm in aiming high when christening a settlement. You can harbor big-city dreams, and since a community far outlasts its original settlers, you don't have to deal with the angst of unrealized expectations. So it seems sensible enough to name a burgeoning hamlet after an immortal, especially one who ranked among the most feared and revered of the Olympians. Particularly in Athena, though, birth seems to have been accompanied by lofty aspirations. Among the town's early settlers was a fellow named Isaac

Newton Richardson, a minister and dentist. His relatives included George Washington Richardson, Thomas Jefferson Richardson, Benjamin Franklin Richardson, Andrew Jackson Richardson, and Lewis Clark Richardson. To be sure, living up to such names seems an unenviable challenge, but it is significant that more than a few Americans choose to saddle their offspring with such historical burdens. The Leader of Men is a hero for all time.

I suppose I am here in Athena to explore exactly what that makes the rest of us.

"I'm a fifth-generation Athenian," Bill Hansell begins. He is sixty years old, with a head of white hair that is thinning but hanging on gamely and glasses set in rectangular frames that rest slightly askew on his face. He leads me into his living room and hands me a soda, and for the next twenty minutes I hear a family history like something out of a James Michener novel.

The paternal side of Bill's family reached the West Coast via the Oregon Trail, settling in the Willamette Valley. Two sets of families made the trek together, each with teenaged children. Two of these teenagers fell in love and, as many pioneers did, returned to land that they passed through along the way — back to Umatilla County. They raised a daughter, who married a carpenter named George Hansell, a fellow who had come out from the Midwest on the train.

One of George's children, M. W. Hansell, used his eighth-grade education to become a horse trader—literally, rounding up strays and selling them in the Athena area. He had a business partner whose family boarded a schoolteacher assigned to a one-room schoolhouse out in the country. She and M. W. fell in love, but she told him, "I don't want to be the gypsy wife of an itinerant horse trader. If you're serious about marriage, then I want roots." So they bought a 640-acre farm just north of Athena, raising wheat and peas. The family eventually got into ranching, too, primarily a cattle and hog operation. But M. W. never quite lost his horse trader's instincts, which paid off considerably during the Great Depression when he purchased another 640 acres, much of it covered by forest, for $640. When he died nearly a half-century later, the family sold the timber from that section of land to Boise Cascade for nearly three quarters of a million dollars.

"That money paid the inheritance tax and saved the ranch," Bill says with a grin.

Bill's mother, Joyce, was a pharmacist. His father, also named Bill, was a veterinarian who was shipped over to China during World War II, where he doctored animals as they came over the Himalayas. When he came back home, he decided to return to farming, which is all he ever desired in the first place.

"So my dad is one of the few people who, for his entire adult life, did exactly what he wanted to do more than anything else in the world," says Bill, and he says it with great pride in his voice, as if it represents the pinnacle of existence. Which, come to think of it, it damn well might.

The younger Bill, on the other hand, didn't much care for farming. He had been born when his father was overseas, and it may be impossible to have a more enviable birth date than his: He arrived on 01/23/45. Bill lived in Athena until the third grade, then moved to the family ranch and was raised on the farm. At the University of Oregon, he met his wife, Margaret. They were married during their senior year.

"When I enrolled, John Kennedy was in the White House. Everybody had a crew cut. I remember an article about what a unique thing it was on campus that one of the professors had a beard. As far as I know, the only drug on campus was alcohol. And I couldn't have found Vietnam on a world map if my life depended on it," says Bill. "By the time I graduated four years later, we had Vietnam, Berkeley, the Summer of Love, the riots, just a cauldron of turmoil."

Bill was the furthest thing from a radical. In fact, after he graduated with a degree in political science, he and Margaret joined the staff of Campus Crusade for Christ, an interdenominational ministry dedicated to spreading the gospel of Jesus.

"I knew a lot about God, but I never recall feeling that I had a personal relationship with Him. I remember hearing how many of my peers made decisions. They were telling me they heard God's call, and I was envious because I wasn't hearing any voices or seeing any direction. I remember praying and saying, 'God, I'm willing to do anything you want me to do, but I need to know it's Your call on my life. I don't want to just respond to something emotionally. And unless You lead, I'm going to law school.'"

Instead, Bill was assigned to minister in Berkeley, of all places, in the summer of 1967 — quite a revelation, if you will, to a straitlaced Oregon farm boy. Apparently, God has a sense of humor.

There is a touch of Odysseus in Bill's account. Early in the *Odyssey*, Aeolus, king of the winds, takes measure of our protagonist's run of misfortune and suspects that he must be hated by the gods. Odysseus himself is tempted to agree. But over the course of his adventure, he learns to trust in the gods, specifically Athena, who becomes to him the voice of the Olympians. In Joseph Campbell's monomyth, Athena is the model of supernatural aid—"a protective figure . . . who provides the adventurer with amulets against the dragon forces he is about to pass." So Odysseus's spiritual journey is much the same one Bill has made (and I have not)—passage from uncertainty to faith.

"I was born again," Bill announces. "I know at times that has a negative connotation, but that was the experience I had."

After Berkeley, Bill and Margaret ministered for six years in Sacramento and for another five in Sydney, Australia, before returning to Athena to raise their children in the kind of rural environment they preferred. For a few years, Bill worked on the family farm. But, he says, "Farming's pretty isolated. I'm more of a people person."

So he ran for public office instead, becoming Umatilla County commissioner in 1983. His is the kind of family history — intrepid pioneers, soldiers shipped to war, generations of farmers, and a country teacher and horse trader thrown in for good measure — that makes for a solid politician's backstory. But don't call him a politician.

"The word I've used is servant leader. You serve the people you lead, if you will. That's sort of the philosophy," says Bill. "My time in the ministry prepared me in a whole lot of ways for public office. I've never been a Christian candidate. I happen to be a Christian who's running for office. But I'm not part of the Religious Right or this or that. I am who I am. I pray for guidance. I pray for understanding of

Umatilla County commissioner Bill Hansell in Athena, Oregon

the issues. But that's not all I do. I study. I do the research. I get the background."

Here again, Athena is a suitable reference. She is a remarkable figure in Greek mythology, because she seems to represent two opposing concepts. On the one hand, Athena is boldness personified — from the very beginning. Her birth consists of splitting open the head of Zeus and climbing out fully formed and clad in armor with shield and spear at the ready (which is something I will have to remember the next time I hear one of my wife's friends claim that males could never endure the pain of childbirth). She is the goddess of war, who descends from Olympus and strides between the two armies at the battle of Troy.

But Athena is also unlike the other Olympians in that she has found a harmonious equilibrium between extremes. She is said to be the immortal who walks most often with the mortals, frequently taking human form, as if approximating humanity herself. While the other gods are rather one-dimensional in their behavior — Aphrodite the lustful, Ares the wrathful, Hermes the rogue — Athena seems more complex. She is belligerent in battle but benevolent in peace. Although she is the archetype of the invincible warrior and is credited with inventing the war chariot, she is also the goddess of intellect, a model of measured judgment, inventor of the flute and the potter's wheel.

Sometimes bold, sometimes conciliatory, appealing to various interests — of the twelve Olympians, Athena would seem to have made the best politician. She values cleverness above all, and what is Mount Olympus if not a jumble of faith and politics and concealed trickery?

Over two decades, Bill has been reelected county commissioner five times, usually going unopposed. He has served as president of the Association of Oregon Counties. About ten months before my arrival in Athena, he discovered that his most recent campaign had been fruitful and had multiplied his influence exponentially. He had been elected president of the National Association of Counties, an organization giving voice to the nation's 3,066 counties, nearly two-thirds of which are members, including most of the nation's largest.

Bill offers the usual motives for pursuing a career in public service — the joy of helping people, whether that means creating dozens of jobs by relocating a big business to the area or assisting an elderly lady on Cabbage Hill whose chickens won't come down from the rafters of her barn.

"In the county, I can help seventy-two thousand people," he explains. "When I was president of the state association, I could help several million people, most of whom had no idea who I was. All running for the national association did was expand my base."

But it seems to me that with this last campaign he also has entered the maelstrom of politics. He has testified before Congress and has visited the White House, shaking hands with the man who lives there. Bill's schedule in the weeks after my visit includes trips to Washington, Montana, Mississippi, Florida, New Mexico, even Germany. He is the face of a national organization, a sort of mega lobbyist.

More than that, he is a man in charge. And that is why I wanted to meet Bill Hansell. Because I most certainly am not.

Leadership is not a prerequisite for a heroic legacy, and it certainly doesn't guarantee one. But it is a fine start. The minions may do the dirty work, but the managers get the credit. History has never recorded the names of the frostbitten fellows who paddled Washington across the icy Delaware, imploring him to please sit down; or the brave Carthaginians who followed Hannibal over the Alps, dodging mountains of elephant crap — just as Homer never bothered with the names of Odysseus's men who were snatched by the jaws of the monstrous Scylla or turned into swine by Circe. General, commander, emperor, king . . . those are the titles that allow access to immortality.

My driving buddy Emerson defined heroism as "a self-trust which slights the restraints of prudence." I don't seem to possess the fearlessness, the ambition, or the self-belief to strive for a position of leadership — and by that I mean management of any sort. I have pals from my days in Ithaca, old buddies whose juvenile antics are seared into my collegiate memory, and now they have titles like vice president for acquisitions and development. My close friend and neighbor since the age of four, a guy who was so terrified of junior high that he puked on the first day of school, is now president and CEO of a real estate development corporation. They have accepted the notion that much of professional life is predicated on hierarchy, and they have impressed their way toward the top. They have underlings and personal assistants — people who actually answer the phone on their behalf.

In contrast, I have crafted a career in which I am my own boss but also my only employee. I am instinctively antiauthoritarian, so I have never been much of a follower. But I am also uncomfortable with the idea of giving instructions, evaluating performance, handing down grand decisions that actually affect the lives of other professionals. Not that I wouldn't mind a minion or two, but it is enough of a challenge for me to take responsibility for myself. And I am not sure I would ever feel entitled to such a position.

"This is not an endowment. It's not something that people owe to me. I've been hired by them through the voting mechanism to perform a service. I never take it for granted," says Bill.

"And what about politics, in general?" I wonder. "What kinds of motivations have you seen?"

"I have found people who have run for office because they really focused on a single issue. I think that's the wrong reason. I've seen people for whom it's just an ego trip. I've seen people who have done it, believe it or not, for the benefits package. And I've seen people who are retired and bored and they think, 'Hey, I'll run for office.' And sometimes, the people who go in maybe for the wrong reasons turn out pretty good."

But it is the purpose-meets-poise aspect of leadership that dominates my thoughts — the self-assurance. There is the story of ancient Chaerephon, who traveled to Delphi and boldly asked Apollo to tell him if anyone had greater intellectual powers than his friend Socrates.

The oracle replied that no man was wiser. But when Socrates heard of this, he was dismayed. He did not believe he was the wisest, nor did he believe the oracle would tell an untruth. He concluded that it was a riddle of words — that no man was truly wise, only the gods, and that the only true wisdom is in knowing that you know nothing.

"As much as you may want to help people," I tell Bill, sounding a bit more cynical than I intend, "it seems to me that it requires a healthy ego — some sort of gene that leads you to say, 'I can do this. I'm worthy of this. I'm qualified and skilled and intelligent enough to be able to handle it and to be able to lead.' "

"If you're talking about confidence"—Bill smiles—"that often comes with experience."

During his brief college days, Bill was president of his dorm, fraternity representative on the student senate, and president of his junior class. On the other hand, I can think of only two times in my entire life when I accepted any sort of mantle of leadership. Just two.

When I was nearly fifteen years old and nearing the end of my six-summer stint as a camper at a boys' camp in northern Wisconsin, I was tapped to lead one of the teams during an all-camp competition. Back then, before political correctness reached the North Woods, the event was known as Pow Wow Day. The camp would divide into four tribes — Cherokee, Chippewa, Navajo, and Sioux — and compete in activities ranging from basketball to archery to canoeing relays. I was a Big Chief, which is about as close as I will ever come to CEO. Essentially, my role was to dress in faux Indian garb and convince a collection of several dozen campers that, no, they weren't just a bunch of scrawny suburbanites. They were the mighty Cherokee.

I well recall my first few Pow Wow Days, when I was nine or ten. I would stand openmouthed, marveling at the muscle and command of the big chiefs. They were *teenagers*, for goodness' sake, confident and vaguely heroic and ten feet tall and fully deserving of their lofty titles. Now that I was one of them — a nearsighted, shallow-chested, self-doubting big chief — it was like discovering that the great and terrible wizard was a bumbling oaf behind a curtain.

We mighty Cherokees lost each and every one of our first thirteen preliminary events — nearly a statistical impossibility. Ours was a comedic montage of errant jump shots, missed targets, and tipped canoes. Heading into Pow Wow Day itself, we were already so far behind that victory was virtually unattainable. So I borrowed a notion from the Bill Murray movie *Meatballs*, which had been released a few years earlier, and led a procession of Cherokees through the dining hall at lunchtime: "It just doesn't matter! It just doesn't matter! It just doesn't matter!" And significantly, it didn't.

I wish I had recalled that sentiment four years later when I was a freshman in college and a fraternity pledge. For some reason, I decided it would be a sensible idea to run for pledge president. It was a "What was I thinking?" moment, not unlike the time when brave Odysseus arrived at the land of the Cyclops and said to his men, "My good fellows, the rest of you stay here, while I take my ship and crew and see who these people are; whether they are wild savages who know no law, or hospitable men who know right from wrong."

I suppose I wanted instant credibility in my new collective, having been previously acquainted with only a handful of my pledge brothers. So in this, the one leadership position I ever chose to pursue, I was motivated primarily by social panic. And what did I get out of it? I became a target for the slings and arrows of a bunch of upperclassmen drunk on power and Mad Dog grape wine. That semester, I lost ten pounds and earned the only C-minus of my life (in a philosophy class, no less), not to mention the enmity of a few of my pledge brothers, who fancied themselves Fletcher Christian to my Captain Bligh.

Of course, given their series of hardships, it is a wonder that Odysseus's men didn't plan a mutiny themselves. But I suspect that some men simply have the makeup of a leader, while the rest of us are easily revealed as mere imposters.

Bill, the rancher's son, likes to refer to his history working with the animals that populated the family farm. His constituents are smart, he says, more like hogs than sheep. From a farmer, that is a high compliment indeed, and it may well describe life's universal managerial system. But even wily Odysseus puts his trust in Athena, just as Bill often refers to the Twenty-third Psalm: *The Lord is my shepherd; I shall not want.*

We all need guidance, one way or the other. Heroic leadership, of course, is another animal entirely.

"Often, we view our heroes in response to a crisis situation and how they react to that — 9/11 or Pearl Harbor. You save somebody from drowning. You fight back a grizzly bear. You crash-land a plane to safety," says Bill. "Most of the time, in the average occupation, you don't have that type of crisis situation. I think politics probably fits into that as well. Even if you make a courageous vote, often the consequences of that aren't evident until years later."

The phone rings, and Bill answers it. He talks for a while in another room, pacing a bit while I sip my soda. Then he returns and adds a caboose to his previous train of thought.

"And anyway, the people whom I would most want to call me a hero are my children."

Bill's father was one of five children. His grandfather was one of five children. His great-grandfather was one of five children. Not counting the two foster children they took in and the four exchange students they housed, Bill and Margaret have raised five daughters, as well. They all graduated from college and pursued advanced degrees. They were Dean's List students and multisport letter winners, and one was even an NAIA college basketball All-American. Successful shepherding, no doubt.

But he also has a son, and for a while his son strayed. Bill has never touched a drink in his life. Dry Bill is what they called him in college. He has never allowed beer, wine, or any sort of alcohol in his house. But his son — who, yes, is also named Bill — became an alcoholic and drug addict.

For the better part of a decade, the family dealt with the struggle. The father turned again to the Twenty-third Psalm for explanation and comfort. *Even though I walk through the valley of the shadow of death, I fear no evil, for Thou are with me.* The verse, he explains, refers to a practice in Palestine in which sheep were moved from winter quarters to spring and summer pastures, moving through valleys that were both life-giving and treacherous. The father focused on the "through" part of the verse, the suggestion that greener pastures await.

And then one day, the son woke up in a motel room in Idaho, full of self-loathing. He pulled out a Gideon Bible from the bedside stand and randomly opened it, his finger landing on Exodus 30. He interpreted the words according to his state of mind. *Thou shall not offer strange incense . . . nor shall you pour a drink offering on it. . . .* He stood up, flushed his drugs down the toilet, poured out his booze, and called his dad.

"He just celebrated his first complete year of being clean and sober," says the father, and I can only guess at the sense of relief that must provide. He smiles. "Do you have kids?"

I smile back.

My oldest son, Luke, was born nine months after my *Who Wants to Be a Millionaire* adventure. In fact, he was conceived in a Manhattan hotel room the morning after the show was taped. What can I say? It was a good twenty-four hours. Given the circumstances, we considered naming our newborn Regis.

That is, we considered it a really bad idea.

His brother, Jesse, arrived only eighteen months later. The first child was the result of a carefully orchestrated bit of coupling and timing, following a few months of frustration and worry. His brother's conception, on the other hand, was totally unexpected (although we are now grateful for the accidental miracle). We might have named them Luke and Fluke.

My sons are tiny, all innocence and devotion, energy and wonder. They are best pals who enjoy many shared enthusiasms, but I have grown to appreciate how their personalities have diverged. One is insightful, physical, and somewhat self-conscious. The other is inventive, artistic, and rather blissfully lacking in self-awareness. Two thousand years ago, Aristotle compared a child's mind to "a tablet which bears no actual writing." But he sorely underestimated human nature. My children are no more blank slates than was Odysseus when he first sailed from Troy.

But at this point in our lives, I am their journey-guide, and I revel in the role. For a few more years at least, they will view me as the ancients viewed Athena — a paragon of strength and wisdom, able to lift chairs over my head and open pickle jars and explain what happens when the toilet flushes.

"It's a heck of a lot easier for a four-year-old to see me as a hero than for a thirty-four-year-old to see you as one," I tell Bill.

"That's exactly right," he nods. "But you lay the foundation from which they launch. One of the primary goals of any parent is to prepare our lambs to be independent."

My sons will experience great lows and great highs. The valleys beckon, as do the tops of mountains. Will their failings and successes be a reflection on me? In spite of me? Will their estimation of their father diminish as their innocence fades and their wonder weakens? On their own hero's journey, will they heed the call for separation? Will they answer the call to return? And will they reach out to me when they need me?

So I have procreated myself into a position of leadership. My sons look up to me, if only because I am much taller than they. Back when I wore a faux Indian costume and led a parade of preteens around a summer camp, I could pretend on some absurd level that I was a molder of men. But now it is the real thing. And if I want them to love and respect me, I think I have to regain a love and respect for myself.

I can't say it just doesn't matter.

IV
troy

I am near Troy, and a fall appears to be imminent.

I have reached the far corner of Oregon — unspoiled and virtually unoccupied Wallowa County. High into the Wallowa Mountains, past snow-capped Sacajawea Peak, along the Hells Canyon Scenic Byway (those are the kinds of names this region seems to engender — Leap Lane, Starvation Creek, Seven Devils). North on Highway 3, past Joseph Canyon, where the Nez Perce Indians used to spend their winters — a breathtaking vista of great green folds of earth with the late-afternoon sun deepening every crevasse. Tradition has it that Chief Joseph was born and died here, despite his forced travels in between, and I can see why he fought so valiantly to stay. A left turn toward the setting sun, and all of the collected debris on my windshield is suddenly backlit and blinding me, so that the handful of turn-of-the-century buildings that constitute the tiny hamlet of Flora passes by me as if in a dream.

And then the peril begins.

I start down. And down. The road tightens; the pavement becomes gravel; the gravel becomes loose, and then looser. I can hear stones pelting the Aspect's wheel rims and an incessant crunching as if I am driving on broken glass. A sign warns, somewhat paradoxically, PRIMITIVE ROAD: NO WARNING SIGNS. Here and there, I spot a lonely black Angus chewing absentmindedly by the roadside. Or a tiny, decrepit shack leaning half-hidden in the trees, remnants of a land rush amid land better suited to black bears and bighorn sheep.

For a few miles, I hug a hillside, enjoying a glorious view of a fertile valley below — wide grassy meadows rippling in the wind. Then comes the real descent. The road turns to dirt and the switch-backs curl tightly, so much so that I soon lose count of the twists and turns. The rains have made the dirt soft in spots. I can feel the Aspect pleading for traction. I can smell the brakes. There is no shoulder, and the drop-off is at least a thousand feet. Were another vehicle to arrive, heading in the other direction . . . I shake away the notion. In-stead, I round a curve and come upon a herd of two dozen cows milling in the road. They stare at me with blank expressions, with no intention of moving. How did they get up here? I inch forward, and they scatter in slow motion. Returning to my white-knuckling, I spot a peregrine falcon hovering overhead, circling buzzard-like.

I suppose the situation is appropriate. Troy and death are forever linked, as the plains surrounding the legendary city are the setting for some of the most graphic and horrific descriptions of warfare in lit-erary history. The violence in the *Iliad* is enough to make Mel Gibson blanch. Fifty-three Achaean soldiers and 199 Trojan warriors perish in Homer's epic, and the poet mentions most of the ill-fated by name and manner of death. They are killed by stomping horse hooves, by rocks to the head, by arrows through the jaw, by swords through the neck. Spears are thrust into hearts, and they quiver with the last heart-beat. Bowels gush. Brains scatter. Teeth spill out. Marrow spurts out of spines.

Homer is at his most skilled when describing some of the least desirable means of demise. Peneleos stabs Iloneus through the eye with a spear, slices his sword through the man's neck, and then lifts up the severed head "like a poppy head on a long stalk." Menelaus drives his sword into the forehead of Peisandros so that both of his eyes fall "bleeding in the dust at his feet." Soldiers topple "as a mountain-ash is felled on a far-seen summit" and lie "groaning and clutching at the blood-stained dust." Sometimes Homer extends similes for miles, as when Hector downs Patroclus "like a wild boar killed by a lion, when both are angry and both are parched with thirst, and they fight over a little mountain pool, until the lion is too strong for the panting boar."

Often, the poet transitions quickly from the brutality of war to the finality of its intentions, capping a bloody scene with words like "death surging in his eyes took him, hard destiny" or "life and spirit ebbed from the broken man." In the end, the *Iliad* emerges as a sort of existential tragedy in the sense that Achilles, who is at one point almost inhuman in his destruction and desecration, finally comes to realize that his own inevitable death is what binds him to the rest of humanity.

Which brings me back to me. For the past few days, I have been limping. I cannot for the life of me figure out how it happened, but somewhere along the line I injured my foot, so that if I step in the wrong manner I am rewarded with pain sharp enough to make me gasp and nearly collapse. Later, I will receive a diagnosis: calcific tendonitis in the back of my left foot. In other words, remarkably enough, an inflamed Achilles heel.

Of course, I am already well aware of my mortality. I just didn't expect to confront it on the fringes of Troy. Just a few days into my journey, and already I am risking life and limb (all right, not limb—just a sore foot) in pursuit of . . . what? A better handle on life? If I die in the process, the irony would just kill me. So would Amy.

On the other hand, there are worse places to give up the ghost. This ranks among the most stunning scenery I have ever seen. In fact, there is a story, often told in this part of the country, of a man who dies and rises to heaven, where he is surprised to find a group of people under lock and chain.

"Who are they?" the man asks Saint Peter.

"Oregonians," is the reply, "and they want to go back."

Finally, after some sixteen miles and ninety minutes, my world is flat once more. I arrive at a paved bridge over the Grande Ronde River, Oregon's largest tributary to the Snake River, and a sign: TROY 2 MILES. Quails skitter across the road as I come upon a handful of cabins leading to a sort of compound with a main building that looks as though it was constructed from the pines around it. The marquee says, SHILO INN LODGE — CAFÉ — RV PARK — GAS. Isolation is the mother of diversification.

This remote piece of paradise is the end of the road (as Troy was, too, for Hector and Achilles and Patroclus and the rest, although certainly not Odysseus). I want this place to have profound origins, to have been named by an explorer with a poet's soul — a man who arrived here, where the Wenaha River feeds into the swiftly flowing Grande Ronde, and envisioned the Hellespont along the river Sca-mander; a man who saw the great hills rising on either side of this three-thousand-foot-deep canyon and recalled mighty-walled Troy; a man who glanced at the lush pine forests clinging to the sides of those hills and conjured up an image of arrows protruding from Achaean shields.

Alas, the place, originally settled by Mormons at the turn of the century, was most likely named for an early resident. His name was Troy Grinstead.

There are hamlets named Troy in another thirty states, from Maine to California, and most of them have equally pedestrian origins. The Troy in North Carolina was named after a state legislator; the Troy in West Virginia took the name of the city's first postmaster; the one in Montana was actually named for a weight measurement — the troy-ounce — during the gold rush. Several of the Troys were named after the most famous Troy with which the settlers were familiar — that being, of course, Troy, New York.

Even when a Troy is named after the legendary city of King Priam, it still smacks of the unrefined American frontier. The story goes that a Greek railroad worker in Idaho offered a shot of whiskey to anyone who would vote for his choice. Troy received twenty-nine votes. Nine people still voted for Vollmer.

The lights are dim inside the lodge, and a woman saunters in from a back room to check me into the RV park. "Red" it says on her nametag, and in the faint light it looks as if the name might fit.

"Well, that was quite a harrowing drive."

She looks up from her paperwork. "Did you come down from Flora?"

I nod, and she lets out a little chuckle. "It was pouring rain earlier today. If it had still been raining, that road woulda been really slick." She offers a half-grin. "You got lucky."

There are twenty spaces in the RV park; two of them are occupied. I choose lucky number 13 and park the Aspect with its rear bumper almost hovering over the Grande Ronde (French for "big roundabout"). From the window in the rear bedroom, it looks as if I am on a riverboat.

The sun has ducked behind the hills, and the sky has morphed from a robin's-egg blue to an aluminum gray. Above me dozens of tiny swallows — almost Hitchcockian in number — are darting and dive-bombing and gliding in grand arcs. They seem to be moving in

A lonely campground in Troy, Oregon

layers of concentric circles, some flying low and frenetically, others amazingly high and moving in tranquil sweeps of the sky. The birds are hovering, but this time I resist the temptation to think of buzzards. I made it to Troy.

Morning arrives to the sound of the Grande Ronde murmuring, and I opt for breakfast at the café, where I am greeted by a half-dozen antlered animals peering from their mountings on a wall, as well as the torso of a bear, teeth bared, claws sharp, ready to pounce. Such is the attraction for most of the visitors here — hunting for elk in the hills, fly-fishing for steelhead in the river.

Some locals, all in their seventies, invite me to sit with them at a small circular table in the center of the room. Sharon and Del are my neighbors at the RV park. They have a house about fifty miles south in the town of Joseph, but they spend most of their time in Troy, where Del pursues steelhead. Ginger and Harvey, dressed in complementary flannel, have a home on the mountain, having ranched in the area for many years. In all, the four of them have been married to their respective spouses a combined ninety-nine years.

"I remember my first impression of Troy," recalls Harvey with a smile. "I said, 'Wouldn't you hate to live somewhere where you have to drive up and down like that?'" Harvey turns to Ginger. "Didn't I say that?" He leans back in his chair. "We've lived here since 1987."

I tell them my tale of that very drive, and they all react with groans and raised arms, as if to tell me I don't know the half of it. They recount how frightened travelers constantly have trouble getting in and out of Troy. There was that time a frozen food truck plummeted over the bank, and a fertilizer truck, too. And that day when the pickup went over the edge, but the horse trailer — with two horses inside — stayed on the road, saving the truck from falling . . .

The door opens, and in strolls a fellow with longish silver hair and a white goatee, looking a bit like a cross between Kenny Rogers and Kid Rock. He is a good twenty years younger than the rest of them, but he pulls up a chair and slips into the conversation without missing a beat. His name is Dean E. Dean.

"My parents thought I was going to be dean of a college or something," he says, winking. Having retired from the army after two years in Vietnam, one in Korea and a stint patrolling the Czech and German border, Dean is a hunter, fisherman, and occasional river rafting guide. "If I have to work, I work a little," he admits. "I've lived here seventeen years, and I'm going to die here."

Harvey perks up and, to general laughter, asks, "When do you want it?"

Which returns the conversation to the harrowing road into Troy. My breakfast mates start listing the fatalities — that Kessler kid, that couple a few years back, those two folks in the yellow pickup . . .

"And then there's that kid who put that old Pontiac into Horseshoe Bend," says Dean. "That car's still there!"

At this, I have to interject, only half joking, "Now I'm scared to leave."

"It's scarier than that staying here," says Dean, with another wink. His smile stops halfway, and he shrugs, taking the conversation to the other side of the world. "You never think it's gonna be you. We lost twenty-six men once from rocket attacks — from mortars. But it wasn't me."

Del gives a grunt of acknowledgment. He was a gunner's mate in the navy in Korea.

"So maybe," I offer, "the lesson is to make the journey slow and easy . . ."

Dean nods and clasps his hands behind his head. "Down here, anyone who's in a hurry is in the wrong place."

The banter bears that out, its pace slow and steady, meandering without real purpose, occasionally taking an unexpected turn — just a leisurely drive down conversational switchbacks. There is no destination; the goal is simply to pass time and revel in commonalities.

Isn't that what my wife keeps telling me? She wants me to enjoy

the moment. Take pleasure in life's journey. I always seem to be in
such a rush to get to an amorphous Somewhere. Maybe that's why
she was in such a hurry for me to leave for Anywhere. Good thing she
told me to go to Ithaca before she was inspired to tell me to go to hell.

A stooped elderly man shuffles into the café behind a walker.
"That's Bud. We call him the Mayor," Dean whispers. "He's ninety-
five, never been married. He's pretty amazing. He's going in for his last
chemo treatment for bladder cancer, and he just bought a computer
so he can research volcanoes. The man loves volcanoes."

He calls out to the old man. "You still driving?"

"I been drivin' for eighty years without an accident. Couple o'
fender benders, but those don't count," Bud declares. "My driver's license is good till I'm a hundred and two."

"How about Ol' Man Brown," says Sharon, eliciting some knee-
slapping. She turns to me. "I'm telling ya, he doesn't drive more than
five miles per hour. When he comes by here, you wonder how he keeps
the motor running."

This sort of tittle-tattle appears to be a necessity for survival in
Troy, fifty miles from the nearest grocery store, a place so remote that
when the garbage truck makes the trek to town every Thursday, it is
an occasion for the locals to dump their trash at the inn and stay for
a game of cards. So gossip here is sustenance.

"This used to be called the Lesbi Inn," says Dean, stretching his
arms toward the rafters. "It used to be run by two gals and a guy. He
was gay and so were they."

"Remember when that he/she pulled into the RV park?" Sharon
asks. "We spent days trying to figure it out. We kind of determined
he/she was male. He was strange."

Here, our waitress, a curly-haired woman named Mary, who has
been hovering around the edges of the conversation, hands me a muf-
fin and interjects a recollection. "He had a set of legs I'd kill for,
though. That was what pissed me off."

"It's interesting," I say, as the laughter subsides. "As isolated as
this place is, as hard as it is to get to, as much as you may come here

to get away from it all, once you're here everybody knows everybody's business."

Everyone nods, and Dean speaks for the bunch. "We have a little saying here: You can't fart at one end of this canyon without someone knowing about it before you get to the other end."

I cross a footbridge over the Grande Ronde and make my way to a one-story building painted periwinkle. A red one would have more satisfied my expectations, because here is the proverbial one-room schoolhouse. I walk inside, where a woman named Marilyn is tidying up, and we chat for a while. It is a Sunday, but Marilyn picks up the phone to dial the teacher, who says she will be right over. She lives just down the road.

There are actually two rooms here, each connected to a narrow hallway in which the students' names are taped above their lockers — Jesse, Clint, Luis, Sophia, Karina, Emily, Big Salvador, Little Salvador. That is the entire population — kindergarten through eighth grade — of the Troy School.

One room is Troy's library, brimming with books. The garbage truck drivers, my breakfast companions had informed me, volunteer to transport boxes of books to the canyon on their regularly scheduled pickup days. Posted throughout are the fruits of the students' scientific labors — poster board summaries of experiments about exploding vinegar and a hypothesis that noncarbonated drinks freeze faster than carbonated drinks. Several dozen books sit on a cart, ready to be reshelved. I can't help but notice that one of them is a volume about mythology.

Through a doorway is the single classroom, anachronistically adorned with eleven computers — more than one per child. There are drawings on the walls to accompany haikus created by the students. A poster of the solar system implores them to "Reach for the stars!" Through the window, I can see a playground and a couple of basketball hoops, each set at a different height, and a couple of grazing cows.

"The good thing about this being a one-room schoolhouse," says the teacher when she arrives, "is everything is a science project. Everything is history. Everything is an event. If I cook something, I'll make everybody try it. I'm making sushi at home right now. Or we have killdeer eggs hatching out on the playground, so we're turning it into a hypothesis of the eggs — when they were laid, how many do they think will hatch, how many will survive . . ."

Like the computers in the classroom, Stephanie Haggard upends expectations, and not only because she is making sushi in rural Oregon. Only a few years older than I, broad shouldered, with her blond hair drawn tightly back from her face, she cuts an imposing figure. She is no matronly schoolmarm. Indeed, she tells me that she didn't set out to be a schoolteacher at all; back in Texas, she wanted a job with Border Patrol. But the children of Troy can thank whoever left some Betadine surgical scrub bottles on the steps of a medical clinic at Yellowstone National Park.

"I was working at Mammoth Clinic in Yellowstone, and I went downstairs to get some insurance papers. I stepped on a bottle, hyperextended, and fell down on concrete. I was in tremendous pain. I went to the Texas Back Institute in Plano, Texas," she says. "I had some surgery. I'm titanium from the bellybutton down."

Which, of course, makes her even *more* imposing — the bionic teacher, the Terminator educator.

"I got hired by Border Patrol, and I was hoping my back would be well enough for me to take the position. But the doctor said, 'You can either go in for the operation or take the position with Border Patrol. Not both. It's just going to get worse with Border Patrol.' And I wanted to go into the FBI. I had all these high hopes for a life of grand adventure." She lets out a barely audible sigh and shrugs. "So I figured I'd go to school in the meantime. I got my gifted and talented certification — differentiating the curriculum and customizing it to specific students. So actually, this fit in perfectly for what I was trained to do."

Stephanie's husband remains in Texas, where he coaches high

school football. Her five-year-old daughter is finishing the school year with him there, while her eleven-year-old daughter is the "Sophia" I saw on one of the lockers. She and her husband aren't separated, Stephanie explains. "After being a coach's wife for thirteen years, I don't see him anyhow during the school year. So this is no big deal."

"So . . . is this an adventure?"

She grins. "Absolutely. The best. And it's good clean living. Sometimes it's surreal. I have to pinch myself. I don't hear ambulances. I don't hear cars going by. I open my window at night, and I hear the Wenaha River. I don't lock my door. I know everybody. I went to high school in California, and I swore I would never raise my children there. I love Texas and the people, but I really wanted to get back to my roots. I lived in the town of Jardine, Montana, which is population twenty-four."

"Which makes Troy about twice as big."

She nods. "I'm used to this type of situation — a very rural community with a certain small-town etiquette where you have to both go with the flow and be your own person." She leans forward to make a point. "It took me one year to get my bearings, to knock down walls. But you know what? Parents today don't know who their children's friend's parents are. They don't know who their kids are playing with. I do. I know all the parents real well."

Stephanie points out the potential for boredom, but I can only envision the pressure. There is no comfort in the support system of fellow teachers and administrators, other than a teacher's aide who primarily focuses on the younger students. Stephanie's pupils range in age from near-toddlers to near-teens, so she doesn't have the luxury of focusing her attentions on one subject or age-group curriculum. She happens to be fluent in Spanish, which must be a godsend to the families of her four Hispanic students. So it is essentially a bilingual, multilevel classroom with nowhere to hide any missteps or conflicts. I imagine it is like trying to play eight instruments at once.

From Troy, the students will go on to normal schooling, if it can be considered normal to take a two-hour commute to high school or to board with a family that houses students from rural areas for four hundred dollars a month. Meanwhile, in only her second year of her first teaching job, Stephanie claims to have learned how to make this system work: Explain the why of things, not just the what. Carve out a routine, especially at the beginning of the year, but be flexible. Let the children help. Allow the more athletic ones to lead a PE class. Let a creative student lead an art class. Take advantage of the maturity of the oldest kids, as most one-room schoolhouses do, but don't go over-board — they have their own learning to do, too.

Stephanie Haggard and the school in Troy

"You can get a good education from one room," she says. "For these kids, my goal for them is to graduate, to be productive citizens. That's why I got into teaching — because I got tired of the way schools were going. It honestly depends on the district policy. Who's making the red tape to cut through? See, they're teaching to a test now. Real learning is not taking place. They're cramming the children for finals. It's starting in kindergarten, and it's making me sick. Children are graduating and passing a test, and they can't diagram a sentence. America is raising idiots!"

She laughs, and then seems to think she should tone down the rhetoric. "That's what I see, and it scares me. That's why I said I would only work for a certain type of school that will allow the children to be creative and grow as much as they need and help where they need it. Our kids will take a test, and they'll pass it. But if you're doing real teaching, learning will take place."

I notice that Stephanie refers to them as her children, rather than her students, and it isn't necessarily just a semantic distinction. She takes them camping and kayaking. She drives all eight kids to Idaho for a week of skiing and to the central Oregon coast for a tour of an aquarium and a lighthouse. The students don't bring an apple for the teacher; they bring a bag of apples because they know she'll bake a couple of apple pies — one for her, one for them. Maybe they'll enjoy a bite or two while they're playing at her house.

"At home, I'm still Mrs. H. I'm not Stephanie. The respect is still there," she says, "but I'll be down on the floor playing games with them."

It is at this point that I hear various voices in my head, my own personal Greek chorus. I suppose I should explain:

A few days earlier, on my way out of Seattle, I drove south for an hour to the state capital, Olympia, and an appointment at the Mud Bay Coffee Company. On the second Wednesday of every month, a group of Olympians gather there to sip exotic coffees and teas and ponder mankind's most vexing questions. They call it a Philosopher Café, and it is one of many such open forums for inquiry that have sprouted up around the country — actually, around the world — in the past decade. People meet in bookstores, libraries, community centers, even homeless shelters and airport terminals. They aim for intellectual honesty by participating in critical questioning, as Socrates famously did. They ask questions like: What is patriotism? When is violence necessary? Is human nature constant throughout history? What's wrong with cloning? They talk with each other, not at each other. It is a philosophical jam session — conceptual jazz.

Having discovered Olympia's version, I asked a favor of the participants. Would they be willing to consider the question that propels me toward Ithaca: What, exactly, is a hero? In contemporary America, what is a heroic life?

We gathered at the coffeehouse in a small conference room, its walls the color of hemlock. Most of the Mud Bay Philosophers were in their late twenties or early thirties, but they were an ethnically diverse bunch — John, who has a job at a blood center as he prepares to return to school in pursuit of his masters in philosophy; Kristy, his girlfriend, who works at a day-care center for elderly people with Alzheimer's and dementia; Pasha, an Iranian-American computer systems administrator; Rebekah, a first-grade teacher of Swedish descent; Maki and Keiko, fourth- and fifth-grade teachers who emigrated from Japan; and Ben and Roz, a retired engineer and his wife.

My initial questions begat many more: What is the purpose of the hero? Is it something we strive for? Is it a standard we can't possibly reach? It is an overused term? Is it about physical courage or moral courage? Can a hero still be morally flawed? Can there be a heroic act without heroic motivations? What if you have heroic motivations, but fail terribly? Does it taint the effort to call attention to your own heroic act? Is the hero defined by the actor or by the perceiver? Is each of us the author of our own criteria? Is there such a thing as a universal hero?

Of course, the questions were easier than the answers. Trying to zero in on an absolute definition of heroic achievement is like trying to find your way to the exit of an unworkable maze. Every supposition leads to more possibilities, so the task becomes exponentially more difficult, and you wind up somewhere near to where you began. Still, for a couple of hours I reveled in the nobility of the attempt.

In discussing the spectrum of the heroic with my Greek chorus in Olympia, we worked our way to the subject of heroic professions.

One of the group asked, "What about those people who aren't necessarily at risk of death, but they're constantly, on a daily basis, working toward something greater than themselves? I think when you choose to do something like that, it can be a heroic choice — those things that kind of grind you down, take you piece by piece, that person who gives his or her life away bit by bit until there's nothing left. Isn't that a hero?"

We were talking, in particular, about teachers, and one of the teachers in the group gave a terse reply: "I think we gain more than we give."

Stephanie's dedication to the job in Troy is inspiring to me, and not just on an educational level. It instills much the same warm feeling I get on those rare occasions when I encounter a doctor who takes phone calls at home or a contractor who puts in overtime but doesn't charge for it. For some people, a job is merely a means to an end; for others, it is a means of achieving self-actualization. Call it what you want — conscientiousness, commitment, dependability. But I am convinced there is a heroic quality to not just doing something but doing it to the best of your ability. Individually, it is an affirmation of spirit. Collectively, it furthers humanity. Karma, and all that. It is a driving philosophy of mine, but one to which, I must admit, I don't always adhere.

The students of Troy put on a play last Christmas — *The Legend of the Poinsettia*. It is the story of a poor Mexican girl who had no gift to present the Christ Child at Christmas Eve services. But her cousin tells her that surely even the most humble gift, if given in love, will be acceptable in His eyes. So as she walks toward the chapel, she kneels by the roadside and gathers a handful of common weeds, fashioning them into a tiny bouquet. As she lays the bouquet at the foot of the nativity scene, the weeds suddenly burst into blooms of brilliant red — a Christmas miracle.

I wonder if the actors in the drama — or even their teacher — fully appreciated how the story applies to them.

• • •

After returning along the footbridge, I stop by the lodge and notice a flyer on a bulletin board: WANTED: DEAD, NOT ALIVE . . . JOIN THE IN-VASIVE WEED PATROL. It implores folks to get rid of a particular weed that crowds out native plant species. Its name is the medusahead. More irony.

Moments later, I am confronted with an equally impressive co-incidence when I stop and chat with another local couple, who over-heard me explaining the premise of my journey over breakfast. The man, a fellow named Ralph, informs me that his father was a native of the Aeolian Islands, off the north coast of Sicily. The islands were colonized by the Greeks about two hundred years after Homer's day and named after the mythical figure Aeolus, who kept the winds bot-tled up in a cave on an island and released them at the bidding of the gods.

When Odysseus happens by on his long trip home, Aeolus of-fers him hospitality for a month and then a farewell gift consisting of the blustering breezes tied up securely in a leather bag. But he leaves the west wind free to blow, so that it may carry Odysseus's ships home. And home the weary travelers go, actually to within sight of Ithaka, only to be undone by their own covetousness. Odysseus falls asleep, and his men get to talking. Suspecting that the leather bag must con-tain a gift of treasures, they open it. Immediately, the winds rush out, driving the ships all the way back to the isle of Aeolus.

Astonished at their return, Aeolus is in an unforgiving mood. "Get off this island at once, you miserable sinner!" he shouts at Odysseus. "It is not permitted to comfort the enemy of the blessed gods!" Odysseus and his crew are to sail on, disheartened, with no wind to help them now.

If the scene is to be taken as a sort of fable within a legend, the moral might be that while no man can control the winds, we are the authors of our own decisions. Our choices point us in one direction or another, for better or worse. And, to echo Robert Frost, that can make all the difference.

At some point, Ralph's father decided it was time to set off from a Mediterranean isle toward a new world. Sometime, perhaps during a mortar attack in Southeast Asia, Dean E. Dean came to some conclusions about where he wanted to spend the remainder of his days. Somewhere along the line, maybe even at the bottom of a stairway in Yellowstone, Stephanie came to realize that she had it in her to climb higher. They opted for the road less traveled — a life-changing decision for all. And is there not a heroic element to seeing it through?

Odysseus had no desire to leave his wife and family for war, but he remained true to his word, fought valiantly, even conjured up the idea for the Trojan horse. Then he wanted nothing more than to leave Troy and go home.

The folks in Troy, Oregon? They seem to want nothing more than to stay. THANKS FOR VISITING TROY, says the sign, as I set off on the next leg of my journey. Y'ALL COME BACK AND VISIT US SOON. DRIVE CAREFULLY.

V

may the dogs be with you

Unlike Odysseus after the war, I have the comfort of leaving Troy via a far less circuitous and precarious route than the one by which I arrived. I steer north along the Grande Ronde—"up the river," as the locals suggested — and into the far southeastern corner of Washington, where a spectacular series of switchbacks sends me high into the Blue Mountains. But the road is paved, and the curves are gentle, and the suddenly gloomy late-afternoon sky is not yet sobbing. Down now, into the grasslands of tiny Asotin County, where the highway meanders around huge green foothills with ink-black cows standing halfway up their slopes. Again, how do they get up there?

There is weather in the distance — a curtain of rain half a mile long. The road teases and threatens, sometimes leading me straight for it, then wandering away. I follow the river into Clarkston, a city of some 7,500 at the confluence of the Snake and Clearwater rivers. After my trip to Troy, it feels like a dizzying shock of civilization. The rain soon arrives in earnest, so I find a parking lot and batten down the hatches for the night. Or at least, I make sure the windows are closed.

When morning comes, I set off for points east. Clarkston, named for the legendary explorer William Clark, sits across the Snake River from the Idaho city of Lewiston, which is, perhaps appropriately, the more impressive of the two. U.S. Highway 12 connects them, and — as I am setting off from Lewiston and Clarkston, along the Lewis and Clark National Historic Trail, through Idaho's Lewis

County (site of Lewis-Clark State College), on a riverside trek that will take me past establishments with names like the Lewis and Clark Café — I make the only appropriate move, opening the Aspect's CD slot, removing the Allman Brothers, and slipping in *Undaunted Courage.*

It is an odd feeling to listen to excerpts from the journals of Lewis and Clark while piloting a twenty-first-century vehicle eastward through countless entities bearing their names. I can almost picture a couple of pirogues traveling with me, but I am moving upriver alongside the Clearwater, and I already know how the story ends. The majesty of the expedition's achievements is evident in the very language of the geography. It is a bit like reading a book while living it in reverse.

The Corps of Discovery, of course, is the true American version of the *Odyssey,* a defining epic about aspirations as much as exploration. Led by a charismatic yet flawed soldier, the travelers undertake an arduous journey through uncharted territory and survive encounters with strange and unknown creatures — not hydras and Cyclops and giants but mountain lions and rattlesnakes and grizzly bears. They encounter a series of natives, some accommodating, others decidedly not. The success of their journey is predicated on navigating not only unfamiliar waterways but also the pitfalls of cultural clashes. To get home with their heroic bounty they must rely not on might but on insight, their adeptness at negotiation, their instincts, and a bit of luck. The journey lasts so long, so far exceeding the expected time frame of their return, that all are feared lost.

The big difference is this: Odysseus starts out with twelve ships and loses all of his men — every one of them. Meriwether Lewis and William Clark set off with a keelboat and a couple of pirogues (carrying thirty-two men, one young woman, and a baby) and lost only a single member of the expeditionary force — a young soldier who succumbed to appendicitis, which could have happened in Philadelphia.

Although they never did find a direct water route to the Pacific, as Thomas Jefferson had hoped, there is no debating the success of the expedition. To all but perhaps the natives whose way of life was later

Lewis, Clark, and Sacajawea in Benton, Montana

devastated by the Pandora's box of manifest destiny, Meriwether Lewis has to rank among the heroes of the highest order. Yet, as I retrace his journey in mind and body, I feel a kind of kinship to him — not as a leader of men but as a man haunted by aspirations unmet. Two hundred years earlier and only a few hundred miles away, Lewis penned the most melancholy entry in his journal, a sad and oft-misspelled bit of reflection on the occasion of his birthday:

> This day I completed my thirty first year, and conceived that I had in all human probability now existed about half the period which I am to remain in this Sublunary world. I reflected that I had as yet done but little, very little indeed, to further the hapiness of the human race, or to advance the information of the succeeding generation. I viewed with regret the many hours I have spent in indolence, and now soarly feel

the want of that information which those hours would have given me had they been judiciously expended. But since they are past and cannot be recalled, I dash from me the gloomy thought and resolved in future, to redouble my exertions and at least indeavour to promote those two primary objects of human existance, by giving them the aid of that portion of talents which nature and fortune have bestoed on me; or in future, to live for mankind, as I have heretofore lived for myself.

If a man can admit to a midlife crisis in the midst of preparing to portage over a mountain range, having been handpicked by the president to lead a crew known as the Corps of Discovery, having just become the first American to cross the Continental Divide, having already survived frostbite and relentless heat and mudslides and starvation and stampeding buffalos and grizzly attacks and various confrontations with the natives, well then, can you blame the rest of us — we who aren't en route to having cafés and colleges and counties named after us — for taking stock of our lives and musing on a dearth of accomplishment?

I dash from me the gloomy thought.

Halfway through Idaho, the highway switches allegiances, shadowing instead the Selway River. Here I stop for lunch at the Syringa Café, located next to a wilderness outfitter called, I shouldn't be surprised to notice, River Odysseys West. My waitress has long black hair and a shy smile. She is from Turkey, she tells me, and having spent the winter in Hawaii, she has just embarked on a summer in the wilds of Idaho. Friends of her family apparently own the restaurant.

"Hawaii and Idaho. You chose two spectacular parts of the country."

She smiles. "What I really want to see is San Francisco."

Just as I'm leaving, a pair of hunters bound in. Florida natives, they are shacking up in a friend's cabin near Missoula and desperately hunting for the nearest gas station. Funny how peoples' lives intersect. Later, with the road now traveling alongside the Lochsa River, I find myself musing on the confluence of events that led a writer from California, a dreamer from Turkey, and a couple of hunters from Florida to meet up at a sleepy café in the Idaho outback.

For most of the drive it has been drizzling, but the scenery is stunning—"beautiful," as Lewis once wrote in his journal, "in the extreme." Mist hugs the mountains and the tops of the centuries-old ponderosa pines, so that it all looks like smoking ash. One hundred miles past Syringa, I leave the whitewater of the river for a climb into the mist, up and over Lolo Pass. WELCOME TO MONTANA. By now, it is raining so hard that it is coming in sideways, the drops forming racing stripes across my driver's-side window. Lewis and Clark arrived here on June 29, 1806, and encountered, according to the journals, "hail, thunder and lightning that lasted about an hour."

So it rained on them, too.

The motto of PondeRose's Restaurant, a tiny, low-ceilinged café alongside the Moose Joose Saloon in Lincoln, Montana, is WE TREAT YOU LIKE FAMILY. So as I take my seat in a booth that seems to have been carved out of the surrounding forest, I expect the waitress to tell me to keep my elbows off the table and call my sister. After spending the night in Missoula, I have driven through the morning along Montana Highway 200, playing peekaboo with the rain, the Blackfoot River, and snow-dusted peaks swirled in light clouds, as if ghosts are dancing in the mountains.

I order a pastrami and cheese on rye and a Lewis and Clark Lager, choosing the latter solely because this is Lewis and Clark County, and besides, it sounds a lot better than their dark beer option — Moose Drool.

"So," I clear my throat, as the waitress sets down my sandwich, "do you get tired of travelers popping in here and asking only about the Unabomber?"

She has a lined face, a nicotine voice. "All the time."

Named for the fact that there was a gold strike here at approximately the same time President Lincoln was assassinated, Lincoln is just a typical Montana mountain town — some motels, an RV campground, antique stores, several hole-in-the-wall casinos with names like Bootlegger and Wild Jacks. But Lincoln earned a measure of infamy as the place where Ted Kaczynski figured he could remove himself from society. Most folks knew him simply as the Hermit, the guy who rode his bicycle into town for groceries on occasion, a straw hat covering his scraggly hair. The FBI knew him as a former Berkeley professor and a suspect in mail bombings that killed three people and injured another twenty-three over the course of a decade and a half. In 1995, when the Unabomber, as he became known, threatened to send another bomb "with intent to kill" if his thirty-five-thousand-word diatribe about the evils of technology weren't published, the *Washington Post* and *New York Times* complied.

But when Kaczynski's family turned him in as a possible suspect, agents converged on tiny Lincoln. They tried to go undercover, but the locals could tell the difference, their suspicions raised when they spotted tourists out of season, postal workers who were far off their routes, prospectors who were a bit too tidy, and cars pulling snowmobiles that were conspicuously pristine. In the end, however, the FBI used technology — satellite imagery, electronic surveillance — against the man who so despised it. When Kaczynski was finally arrested, one FBI agent described him as smelling "like warm dirt."

Kaczynski's infamous ten-by-twelve-foot shack was removed from the Montana outback and is now on display at the Newseum in Washington, D.C., along with items like John Dillinger's death mask and Patty Hearst's coat. But that hasn't stopped curiosity seekers from snooping around Lincoln.

"His mailbox is still here, about three miles off Main Street," says my waitress, no emotion in her voice. "People stop and take pictures."

I have zero interest in doing that, particularly because, as I return to the road, the clouds are low, the winds are high, and it has grown so cold that the rain is turning to sleet. About twenty-five miles up the road, a sign at a highway turnoff announces that THE COLDEST OFFICIAL TEMPERATURE EVER RECORDED IN THE CONTINENTAL UNITED STATES OCCURRED AT A MINING CAMP NEAR HERE JAN. 20, 1954, WHEN THE TEMPERATURE DROPPED TO 70 DEGREES BELOW ZERO. A half mile later, I reach Rogers Pass and the Continental Divide. As is my custom, I jump out of the Aspect and straddle the imaginary line, shivering and feeling like a fool.

And I'm thinking: It's all downhill from here.

Soon, the rain stops, and I arrive at a vision of rolling hills and ranchland. Here, for the first time, I notice the big sky for which Montana is famous. More than that, it is big space. The pale green landscape, speckled with ink-black Angus cows on each side of the highway, looks like a massive bowl of mint chocolate chip ice cream. Black mountains rise in the distance, along with a lone broad-shouldered butte. The ribbon of road stretches in front of me, empty and endless. And above it all is a sky so immense that I feel as if cresting the next hill will instead take me plummeting off the end of the earth. I am reminded of how John Steinbeck once described Montana — that it looks like how a small boy would picture Texas, upon hearing a description from Texans.

When Meriwether Lewis arrived at Great Falls, he marveled at the opportunity "to gaze on the sublimely grand spectacle, the grandest sight I ever beheld"—five separate waterfalls making up the Great Falls of the Missouri. But I arrive in the city named for that wondrous sight, and I find my entrance into it dominated by rusting freight trains, seedy motels, strip clubs, currency exchanges, and pawn shops. Two hundred years, and we have gone from the "grandest sight I ever beheld" to the Pawn-a-Rama.

When I finally arrive at my campground, about a mile past the city, I am treated to a view of the high plains, bare and unsettled. It is a vivid illustration of the edge of things and the evolution of things, what the frontier was and what it has become.

• • •

East of Great Falls, the Missouri River starts to burrow into the prairie. Upon reaching the town of Fort Benton, about fifty miles downstream, it begins carving a deep canyon through the terrain, transforming itself into the Wild and Scenic Upper Missouri River. This protected section of the Big Muddy most resembles what the Corps of Discovery experienced two centuries ago.

My arrival in Fort Benton the next morning happens under a cloudless sky. Rumbling along Highway 87, I descend from an expanse of barren nothingness into a little oasis where the trees are mature and the buildings are historic and the Missouri is eighty yards wide. The oldest known settlement in Montana, dating to 1846, Fort Benton was the western terminus of Missouri River traffic for several decades — the "New York of the West" — until the railroads arrived and river traffic all but disappeared.

Today, it is a sleepy old town, charming and intimate. You can purchase a souvenir at Steamboat Shirley's Station, grab a meal at Bob's Riverside Restaurant, and douse your thirst at Jack's Bar. I make my way to the river's edge, the north bank, and saunter along the levee, my pace as languid as the current. Here, over the course of a quarter-mile stroll, I am able to take a trip — by way of statuary and signage — through the history and legend of Fort Benton. One sign trumpets the Bloodiest Block in the West, lined with BARROOMS, CATHOUSES AND GAMBLING DENS — SO LAWLESS THAT IT HAD TO BE CIRCLED BY A CAVALRY TROOP SO A U.S. MARSHAL COULD SERVE WARRANTS ON FIVE OF ITS RESIDENTS. There is a sort of mythological tint to the narration — truth tinged with Old West expectations, as if Homer wore spurs instead of sandals.

At the east end of my stroll is a re-creation of the Corps of Discovery's sixty-two-foot-long keelboat, and alongside that a twenty-foot-tall statue that serves as the official state memorial to the expedition. Lewis holds a telescope to his eye. Clark carries a gun. Sacagawea sits barefoot with her infant son leaning on her shoulder. All three peer toward the south bank of the river. But it is a bronze statue at the western end of the historic levee, in the center of a park nestled between the 123-year-old Grand Union Hotel and the 122-year-old original Fort Benton firehouse, that most intrigues me. It depicts a dog, both front feet on a train rail, peering down the track, as if in anticipation. "Shep: Forever Faithful," says the inscription.

Shep memorialized

In the summer of 1936, a sheepherder in Montana fell seriously ill, and Shep, his faithful Australian shepherd, joined him on a trip to Fort Benton for treatment. When the herder died a few days later, his body was loaded onto a baggage car and sent back east to relatives. Shep followed the casket to the train depot and watched as it rolled slowly away from the station. For the next five and a half years, the dog maintained a vigil at the depot, waiting for his master's return, inspecting the passengers who disembarked from each of the four trains that arrived daily. When one of the train conductors figured out the genesis of Shep's devotion, the dog became famous. Rail travelers would detour to Fort Benton just to catch a glimpse of him. He was featured in *Ripley's Believe It or Not*. He received fan mail, Christmas gifts, and countless offers of adoption. When he died in 1942, slipping on an icy track before an incoming train, his obituary was carried on both wire services. Hundreds attended his funeral. There was an honor guard. There were pallbearers. Of course, nobody quite remembers the name of the sheepherder.

Meriwether Lewis had a faithful dog, too, a 150-pound black Newfoundland named Seaman, whom he purchased for twenty dollars in Pittsburgh while waiting for his keelboat to be constructed. Seaman was a hunter, catching and killing squirrels, geese, even a deer and a pronghorn antelope. He was a sentinel, barking to cause a charging buffalo to change course, saving his master from being trampled in his tent. He was an object of attention from the natives, once drawing an offer of three beaver skins from a Shawnee. Although he is mentioned a couple dozen times in Lewis's journals, there is no revelation of Seaman's reaction to the fact that the Corps of Discovery was forced to eat some two hundred dogs along the way.

I should admit that I am not a pet person. Never have been. I understand the appeal, to some extent. But I have always suspected that when people adore their cat or dog, it is less about the animal being lovable than about the person longing for unconditional affection. Devotion without complication is a powerfully attractive concept. And now that I am a father, I believe that the folks who claim to love their dog "like a child" are devaluing the profundity of parenthood.

So, no, I have never had a pet, other than a couple of goldfish, which I won at a school carnival and which were lucky to survive a week. But these stories of heroic dogs (who have been the subjects of entire books) fascinate me. They seem to represent paragons of devotion on two sides of a behavioral spectrum — the commitment of a fellow adventurer and the fidelity of one who lingers in waiting. It may be that I find it interesting because I seem to reside on both sides of that spectrum, paradoxically, as a homebody/explorer.

I suppose I might be described as a binge traveler, staying in the house for days at a time and then hitting the road for weeks. My cross-country excursions — and I take annual two-month summer RV trips with my family — are akin to my coming up for air, allowing me to play the part of intrepid adventurer as an antidote to my usual role as a sort of high-functioning hermit. On a good day, I can imagine this as part of a grand heroic journey, an element in the departure stage of Joseph Campbell's monomyth — a trek into the unknown. "The usual person is more than content, he is even proud, to remain within the indicated bounds," he wrote, "and popular belief gives him every reason to fear so much as the first step into the unexplored."

Indeed, usually I prefer to be at home. I have been like this for most of my life. As an adolescent, I would concoct various excuses to avoid school, due not so much to a disdain for going but rather a preference for staying. At the university in Ithaca, I would go several days without making it to campus. Instead, I would immerse myself in the textbooks — traveling between the pages and accruing the necessary knowledge but missing out on much of the college experience. And now I spend most of my days in front of a computer keyboard, cocooned in a detached office in my backyard, content to remain removed from the chaos. I live eight blocks from the Pacific Ocean, and I may go a couple of weeks without seeing it.

But I was discussing the dogs. So let me phrase it like this: Sometimes I seek out life, sniffing out unfamiliar terrain like Lewis's frantic Newfoundland. Much of the time I explore instead the life of the mind, waiting — like Shep — for something special to come to me. Or to put it another way, despite all the admiration I have for the exploits of Meriwether Lewis, part of me understands the reclusion of a Ted Kaczynski. Of course, the stories of Seaman and Shep are tales of loyalty, which is an element of the heroic, to be sure. But it is one of those virtues — like pride or decisiveness — that can prove ugly and harmful if taken to an extreme.

Anyway, both devoted pooches were really only manifestations of a Homeric icon. Before he left for Troy, Odysseus bred a great hound who used to join the young men of Ithaka when they went hunting. But in the ensuing two decades, Argos, as he was called, was neglected and abused and grew too old and weak to do anything but lie on a heap of mule dung and wait for his master's return. When Odysseus does finally arrive in Ithaka, disguised as a beggar, Argos is the first to recognize him:

"There lay Argos the hound, covered with vermin. When he knew that it was his old master near him, he wagged his tail and dropped both his ears; but he could not move to approach him." And then, moments later, Argos "passed into the darkness of death."

The athletic teams at the University of Great Falls, just down the road, are known as the Argonauts, an homage to that band of several dozen heroes in Greek lore who accompanied Jason in his quest to find the Golden Fleece. Apparently, however, Great Falls fans are prone to shouting "Go, Argos!" Which, without their knowing it, is a hell of an endorsement of fidelity.

VI

dragon bones

Another thirty-eight miles northeast, and I come to the town of Big Sandy, which is as genuinely western as it sounds. A covered wagon sits in front of the high school — HOME OF THE PIONEERS. There is a cemetery on a hill on the edge of the settlement, and there are dirt roads through town. A columned Wells Fargo Bank stands on a corner, looking like the kind of place Butch Cassidy might have scouted. There is a shop called the Tumbleweed Gallery and a restaurant called the Bear Paw Lodge and a bar called the Club and a hotel called, best I can determine, Hotel. Big Sandy is off the beaten tourist path, so the whole place oozes authenticity.

After eating a quick lunch at a city park in the shadow of a gray grain elevator, I stop to fill up my other tank at a gas station at the corner of Route 87 and Judith Landing Road, which extends south into a swath of Montana wilderness. My atlas seems to regard it as an iffy proposition. A well-traveled white Mazda pickup with a canopy over the cab pulls into the station alongside me, and a man climbs out with a grunt and a wheeze. He looks to be in his late fifties, with a red face, a bulbous nose, bushy eyebrows, and an uncombed thicket of brown hair, fringed with white. He wears frayed jeans and a stained gray long underwear shirt, unbuttoned to reveal a thatch of white hairs poking from his chest. The man looks like he hasn't seen a shower in weeks.

"Are you familiar with this road?" I ask, pointing southward. "Doesn't look like too many folks use it."

"Tell me about it. I just spent four hours hitchhiking. I saw four cars," he grumbles. "I was canoeing on the river the past few days, and I had to go get my truck." He climbs into the pickup, which is missing four hubcaps. "Now I'm heading down to the landing to get my canoe. You going that way?"

I hesitate and then nod. "I guess I'll see you there."

According to my map, it is forty-four miles to Judith Landing, where the Missouri River joins waters with the Judith River, named by William Clark for his future wife. The Corps of Discovery camped there on May 29, 1805, which is enough to convince me to follow the white pickup.

Fifteen miles later, I have passed exactly three vehicles going the other way — all of them with horse trailers — and the pavement has ended abruptly, turning to a dirt and gravel mixture that makes me thankful for the dry weather. Come to think of it, Zeus has been kind to me when I have needed him most — while weaving around Mount Rainier, during my zigzag descent into Troy, and now on this dubious trek toward the Big Muddy. Forced to slow down by the road conditions, I can no longer spot the white pickup ahead of me. It has disappeared, as if the cloud of filth it had been kicking up were some sort of magic dust.

I feel very much alone at the moment, my world consisting only of rambling ranchland and big sky. Civilization seems a hazy concept. At a public library back in Fort Benton, I had located a collection of reminiscences, written by the hardy men and women who had tried to homestead these barren lands. Now that I see the landscape for myself, I am awed by their resilience.

Big Sandy had been a cow town of long standing, but in the early twentieth century it became a homesteaders' boomtown. Hopeful immigrants, many of them from Czechoslovakia by way of Chicago, would ride the Great Northern Railroad into Montana, unload their cargo and livestock at the depot in Big Sandy, and then fan out into the countryside. They had names like Jirsa, Tordik, Driga, Pribyl . . . and they were as short on options as they were on vowels.

Often, the men would arrive first. If the fellow was lucky, his neighbors would help him construct a sod house. If he had to wait, he might live in a hole in the ground — quite literally — until it was his turn to get a house built. Provided the family could endure long enough, they would graduate into less humble living conditions. But most didn't last more than a few years before moving to more hospitable locales.

Driving through this treeless expanse, all dry grass and dust, I find myself trying to envision what it must have been like to have been Frank Baldik, hauling water three-fourths of a mile in barrels after discovering that the water in the well he had dug near his homestead was alkaline. Or John Cikrit, mining his own coal for his furnace and making the full-day trip into town only two or three times a year, returning with hundreds of pounds of flour and sugar and coffee beans. Or Julia Fisher, carrying water from a reservoir for a bath night every Saturday, straining out the bugs, heating it on a wood stove, pouring it into a tub, and then using it again the next morning to scrub floors.

In the midst of the tales of desolation, I found a poem, written in 1929, by a local named Nellie McLean. It read, in part:

> We built our humble cabin.
> A place wherein to dwell.
> But of the loads of suffering
> Only ourselves can tell.

Twenty-three miles into my route, I come upon a leaning cabin atop a gentle knoll, long abandoned by the looks of it. The white pickup is parked in front of it. I stop the Aspect in the middle of the road and walk toward the cabin, camera in hand, figuring my fellow traveler had much the same idea. Instead, I find him sitting behind his steering wheel, smoking pot out of an old Busch beer can.

"I thought I'd just stop and pack a bowl," he grins, looking like a red jack-o'-lantern. "Want any?"

I wave him off and offer a handshake instead. "I'm Brad."

He sets down the homemade bong. "Name's Dan," he replies, and he decides to join me in poking around the old homestead.

"Be careful of rattlesnakes," he warns, as we make our way through the tall grass. "There's a lot of 'em in Montana." Not ten seconds later, a tiny white rabbit pops out from hiding. Dan jumps three feet in the air; I jump even higher.

On tiptoes, we peer into the spaces where the windows should be — they look like empty eye sockets. In what used to be the kitchen, the walls are discolored and peeling. An ancient-looking stove sits in the center of the room, as if it were left behind in the midst of a move. A decrepit ironing board leans against a wall. In the bedroom, half of a flaking wooden chair sits next to a rusted bed frame beneath a mattress that looks as if it has exploded.

Dan is saying something, surmising what kind of animals have been at the mattress, but I am lost in thought, wondering if any homesteader would have endured daily sufferings if he had been told it would all lead to *this*.

An abandoned house on the outskirts of Iliad, Montana

Three miles later, Dan and his pickup having once again sped ahead of me, I am surprised to encounter an actual intersection — an east-west dirt path oddly named Five Corner Road. One mile more, and a YIELD sign rises from the roadside, which is a bit like finding a crossing guard at the Bonneville Salt Flats. It is so full of bullet holes that only the *L* and *D* remain. Next to it, a small green street sign: ILIAD LOOP.

This stretch of nothing in the middle of nowhere is Iliad, Montana. There is an explanation for the name. Apparently, a woman named Virginia Donnell and her husband Ade homesteaded in the area in around 1915. Virginia also ran the post office, such as it was, and, according to the history book, "she was a religious lady and named the post office after the book called *Iliad.*"

It seems a banal recollection, but I find it to be an intriguing statement, surely unintentionally so. The account categorizes Homer's epics as religious texts when really religion itself might be described as a subset of mythology. As mythologist Hans Bellamy once put it, "Religion is fossil mythology; mythology is fossil history."

Another mythologist, Carlos Parada, has compared ancient mythology to an egg that once contained "about all that was needed for life." History, philosophy, religion, creativity, cultural biases . . . all were contained in mythological tales. Then, sometime around Homer's era, the egg broke. Its contents oozed into separate fields, and it was impossible to recombine the elements into a single entity ever again.

Just as I am thinking how glad I am to have nothing but unobstructed space around me, if only so that I may ponder these abstractions free of distraction, I notice fencing along both sides of the road. The wide open landscape and the furious winds have turned it into a barbed-wire metaphor: the place where tumbleweeds go to die. There are hundreds of them stacked in piles against the fence like convicts gripping the bars of their prison cells. A mile later comes evidence that this may also be a place where dreams die. A collection of abandoned structures sits among the windblown grass — an old house, a corral, a barn, the unmistakable outline of an outhouse leaning at a precarious angle. It is a haunting sight and a rather beautiful one.

But there is life here deep inside Choteau County. Just down the road, I come upon four magnificent horses, two chestnut and two black, hanging their heads over the fence, staring at me, their manes dancing in the breeze. A couple of miles later, I find the other end of the Iliad Loop and several large, rusted mailboxes bearing the names of families possibly descended from the Czech originals — Drga, Handel, Silvan. An abandoned car — an AMC Eagle with a "Veterans of Foreign Wars" bumper sticker — decorates the roadside, a tumbleweed wedged against one of its wheels. Prairie dogs have carved out a home four feet behind its rear bumper.

I push on, and the ranchland begins to roughen into badlands. The land rises into modest hills, which soon become angular ridges. The road gouges a trail. I spot a lone tree, about one hundred yards to my left, its barren branches reaching at all angles, and I realize it may be the first I have seen in about forty miles. I suspect it could tell its own stories. And then a herd of cows, their ears tagged, roaming through the sagebrush, one of them inexplicably and obliviously on the wrong side of the fence.

Finally, Judith Landing and another glimpse of the fabled Missouri, only this time it is burbling between majestic limestone formations.

It was here, at the confluence of the rivers, that myth and history intersected as well. In 1855, fifty years after the Corps of Discovery's arrival, twenty-five-year-old American geologist Ferdinand Vandiveer Hayden uncovered the first dinosaur remains in the Western Hemisphere. When the last continental ice sheet retreated nearly twenty thousand years ago, it exposed broad expanses of fossil-bearing rock in eastern Montana, and Hayden's party came across what was later determined to be a small collection of fossilized dinosaur teeth. In recent years, an outfit called the Judith River Dinosaur Institute has made equally dramatic discoveries in the area, including one brachy-lophosaurus considered by many to be the world's best-preserved dinosaur.

Hayden's big find occurred barely a dozen years after the term "Dinosauria" was even invented — by a fellow named Richard Owen, who combined a couple of Greek words that roughly translated to "terrible lizard," although most dinosaurs were neither. But this was not the first misinterpretation of the prehistoric beasts. Today's dinosaurs, in a manner of speaking, are yesterday's dragons.

Nearly every culture has dragons as part of its mythology. Apollo, Hercules, Perseus . . . all were said to have slain dragons. In Norse mythology, there are tales of the dragons Nidhogg and Farnir. The Egyptians told stories of Apep; the Aztecs spoke of Quetzalcoatl; the Huron Indians feared Angont. As late as the early seventeenth century, the uncharted regions in various maps of the world would include drawings of dragonlike creatures — representations of the unknown, yet a concept based in reality. Like the basis of all mythology, dragons were merely history misconstrued and made vivid. In fact, dinosaur bones may be the most obvious example of how mythology is fossilized history. After all, humans are pattern seekers and storytellers. So when the ancients happened upon buried bones suggesting creatures of uncommon stature, they sought explanation for such fossil evidence and found it in fantastical stories.

But it could be that mythology allows us a glimpse into prehistory, preserving a lost past — much like this protected stretch of the Missouri River. There is a recent and remarkable illustration of this notion. It concerns a legend of long standing in the South Seas. Myths regarding the Indonesian island of Flores, about 350 miles west of Bali, told of a shy and diminutive race of people who would accept gourds of food from the Floresians and then return to their limestone caves. "South Seas leprechauns" is how they have been described, and folktales suggested that they survived on the island as recently as five hundred years ago.

In an evolutionary sense, there is some logic to the tales. On islands without big predators, undersized individuals don't have to fight
off attackers and are more likely to survive on limited resources, so
large mammals tend to evolve toward smaller sizes. Still, most scientists dismissed the myths as fanciful legends — until 2004, when a
team of paleoanthropologists discovered seven tiny adult skeletons in
a cave on Flores. The oldest dated back 95,000 years; the most recent was from 13,000 years ago. One adult female skeleton was nearly
intact — and no more than three feet tall. The scientists nicknamed
her the Hobbit.

So in some cases myths may be defined as misinterpretations of
phenomena, a naive effort to replace the fear of the unknown with a
satisfactory explanation, but they cannot be dismissed as mere fan-
tasy. There is likely a kernel of truth in there, but this truth is hidden
beneath layers of sentiment, transformed over the millennia in the
telling and retelling and by the psychosocial biases of the tellers themselves. In this way, mythological tales are much like the traditional
telephone game in which every time a word or phrase is passed on, it
moves further from its original construct. As much as mythology is a
manifestation of the human psyche, if you strip away the emotional
stratum of myths, you often can find historical reality — causes, origins, seminal events.

So it is with the *Iliad* and Troy. In the early 1870s, German ar-
chaeologist Heinrich Schliemann used Homer's epic as his guide and
found the ancient city called Hisarlik in western Turkey, which has
been widely accepted as the probable location of the legendary forti-
fied city. Interestingly, he found layers there, too — about nine levels
of ruins, indicating nine different versions of Troy over the years —
nine historical truths discovered through one largely fictional piece
of mythology.

I suppose the point is this: mythology is history obscured. But
we can't escape our history, even subconsciously, no matter how hard
we try.

•   •   •

One of the heroic elements of the Corps of Discovery is the fact that the expedition pointed itself toward a cartographic void. The region west of the Mississippi River was essentially a blank space on a brand-new map. Naturally, many in the early nineteenth century filled it with myth — rumors, for instance, about a race of redheaded Indians who stalked prehistoric beasts roaming the countryside.

One suspects the explorers may not have been much disappointed. Meriwether Lewis arrived in the vicinity of Judith Landing to find "scenes of visionary enchantment." One hundred ninety-nine years and 354 days later, I find instead my fellow traveler Dan.

"I got nothing to hide," says Dan, as we settle on each side of a picnic table a few dozen yards from the river. At one time, Judith Landing was a bustling community. There was a hotel here, a saloon, a blacksmith shop. But now it is merely a three-acre mini-campground, and it is just the two of us here, although a couple of park rangers make sporadic appearances. They seem to regard Dan with suspicion.

I point to his license plate. "Do you live in North Dakota?"

He rubs his bloodshot eyes and looks skyward, as if he were Oedipus being asked to solve the riddle of the Sphinx. "That's a tough one. I don't really live anyplace. The two toughest questions to answer are 'Where do you live?' and 'What do you do?' For the past year, I've been in North Dakota. Before that, Seattle . . . It's pretty interesting, because you're talkin' to someone who's been doing this all my life. All my life! People ask me what I do, and I say, 'I don't know. It just comes to me.' "

A few miles back, as I was snapping photos of the horses, I experienced the highlight of my day when I was nearly knocked senseless by a bouncing tumbleweed. As Dan's tale unfolds, I realize that might perfectly describe my random encounter with him. Here I am, traveling alone cross-country, yet between the two of us I am very much the fixed object. Dan is a beer-drinking, pot-smoking tumbleweed. He was born in Bottineau, North Dakota, about a dozen miles south of the Canadian border. Nearly six decades later, he is sitting in a self-inflicted fog along the Big Muddy. Everything in between begins to sound equally cloudy.

"I think our mothers are the ones we gotta watch out for. They're the ones who steer us in a direction," he begins. "My mother was a very controlling, dominating person. She used to say, 'Your father fought in World War II so that you could be free. Get out there and see what's going on in the world.' Then I became a hitchhiking hippie and Mom would say, 'Your ribs are showing! Stay home for a while!' She just died a couple of months ago and . . . boy it's tough to think of anything good to say about her."

Since the heroic archetype is someone who undergoes a dramatic transformation and returns with a lesson learned, Joseph Campbell claimed that motherhood could even be construed as a heroic act. I would very much agree, but I base this conclusion primarily on the efforts of my own mom, about whom it's tough to think of anything *bad* to say. Yes, she can be as subtle as a flashing neon sign. But really, Oedipus aside, what hero doesn't adore his mom?

Meanwhile, Dan is still trying to dredge up some compliments about his. "She cooked good. She never beat me or anything like that. But boy oh boy . . . You think of a mother as a person who's supposed to nurture you and help you along, but she was a troublemaking, conniving person." He stops himself, sits up, belches. "Still, I loved her right to the very end, goddammit."

After an uncomfortable pause, I steer him back to the road. "So you were a hitchhiker . . ."

"Yeah, I spent seven years hitchhiking in my twenties. I would sleep anywhere. If I didn't have a tent, I would sleep under a bridge. And then one day, I walked out of a bathroom, and I was going across the parking lot, and I totally freaked out because I didn't know where I was. I had no clue. I didn't know what city. I didn't know what state. I didn't know what highway. . . . Then I decided to stop."

Stop, as in not really. There was a chimney sweep business in Seattle, dirtbike trips to Baja, a few months in Hawaii . . .

"The soil there was so fertile. It was like 'Jack and the Beanstalk' kind of shit. So I thought, goddammit I sure would like to grow somethin'. So I went to Seattle, hopped a freight train to North Dakota, and bought an eighty-acre farm. I cleaned up my act. I didn't smoke pot. . . ." He pauses and shakes his head vigorously. "No, wait . . . I must be stoned to say that. I stopped drinking. That's what it was. But I was horny. And I couldn't get a date because I wasn't hanging out in the bars. So I started a dating service. They would write me, and I would give them a code number, and they would enclose money. Did it for about six years, and then I met this woman who was a bitch from hell . . ."

Somehow, his face grew even redder. "She was a pathological liar — I mean, literally. She and I had gotten into an argument over her kids because I thought she was neglecting them. And anyway, she turned me in to the police for growing pot on my farm. I lost my farm and went to prison for a year — North Dakota State Penitentiary."

He reaches into a bag and removes a small black case, keeping his hand on top of it. "When I had my farm, one day I'm sitting on my porch, sampling my product," he says, making a toking motion with his free hand, "and I'm looking around at some goddamn gophers. They're tearing up my garden, and I figured I oughta start farming the fucking gophers. I went out and blasted away about twenty of 'em, and I started experimenting with them — you know, tanning the hides, doin' stuff with the tails, shit like that. I couldn't really come up with anything. So when I got out of prison, I ended up in Seattle again, and I started experimenting with one of the hides again, and I ruined it. The only thing left was the damn feet. So I made a pair of earrings out of the feet."

There are times throughout this conversation when I wonder where reality stops and Dan's THC-fueled imagination begins. But he opens the black case to reveal some two dozen earrings, each consisting of a tiny gopher's paw. I would have been no more surprised if he had revealed to me a belt made of Minotaur hide.

"Pretty clever," I mutter, but I can't help myself, "and creepy at the same time."

He grins. "I sold nine thousand pairs of 'em. I was a traveling gopher-foot salesman for a few years."

"Who buys them?"

"Oh, just about anybody. Grandma and Grandpa would look at 'em and say, 'By golly, I used to hunt gophers as a kid.' And other people will say, 'My God, that's disgusting! How much are they?' One guy on an Amtrak train said to me, 'Oh, fishing lures, huh?' I said, 'Yep.' He said, 'You catch trout with them?' I said, 'Bass, too.' He was drunker'n I was. Anyway, I had a distributor who would buy about two thousand pairs a year, and that would give me a trip to Mexico every year."

"What'd you do in Mexico?"

He slaps his forehead. "Oh fuck, we haven't even touched on Mexico! I spent every winter there for ten years. What did I do there? Well, I didn't go to jail. That's important — for a life like mine. And I didn't shed any blood. That's important, too. It really is." He shrugs. "I did different things. A couple of years, I got a boat and did the tourism thing — go to a bar, get drunk, and hustle people out of the bar . . . 'Hey , wanna go fishing tomorrow?' And for a couple of years, I was a treasure hunter. I invested in about five thousand bucks' worth of treasure hunting equipment, diggin' big holes . . .'"

"Find anything?" And as soon as I ask, I wish I hadn't.

Dan laughs so hard he nearly falls off his bench. "Does it look like I found anything?" He looks around him, mockingly. "Where is that damn treasure anyway?"

I suppose I deserve it. "What else did you do?"

His face reddens again. "For a couple years, I fell in love with this Texas oil heiress, a very, very wealthy woman who was living in Mexico. It was a fuckin' nightmare." Dan says "fuckin'" with a drunken slur, so that it sounds almost Yiddish. "She was an awful person, and I would have gotten away from her if she had been just a normal person. But she was very wealthy, and the greed made me want to stick around. I liked the Jeep. I liked the lifestyle. I was her boy toy. I liked the sex, too. She was a total alcoholic." He smirks, suddenly realizing he has stepped in a steaming pile of hypocrisy. "I mean, I'm a drunk. But she was a fuckin' alcoholic, man. That lady passed out every fuckin' night by nine o'clock. A total goddamn drunk, a mean fuckin' Texas loud-mouth fuckin' rich bitch." He literally spits this last part out.

"My whole life has been full of stories, Brad," Dan continues. "But I've never been shot, and I've never shot at anybody. Of course, I've been shot at a lot of times . . ." He straightens his shoulders. "I don't rob. I don't cheat. I don't steal. I might tell a few tales, but I don't lie . . ."

Those tales continue for a better part of an hour, stories about how he brought a rock to a knife fight with a biker, how he hitched a ride with a fellow who happened to be driving a stolen car, how he sat in jail for a week after a case of mistaken identity, how he has been arrested "more times than I can remember," usually for public intoxication and disturbing the peace.

"Another time was for statutory rape," he says. "I didn't know she was that age! She was fifteen or sixteen, but I was like nineteen!"

This sparks another synaptic segue, and Dan whispers conspiratorially, "I'll tell you another side of me that you probably didn't realize." He pauses for dramatic effect. "I've become a sex addict. When I hitchhiked and traveled, there was always a woman at the end of the fuckin' line somewhere. It seemed like I had a string of women all along the United States — Seattle, North Dakota, Omaha, Texas. And then when I got too old and stopped hitchhiking and all that kind of shit, then the Internet came along . . ."

He raises his voice. "Aw, fuck! I'm an Internet predator! I am an Internet . . . fuckin' . . . predator!" He looks at me, and perhaps he notices that that the color has suddenly drained from my face. Where are those park rangers anyway?

"I'm fifty cyber-years old. That means I don't get any older on the Internet. But I'm not a pedophile. Christ, if I fucked a twenty-five-year-old, I'd feel like a pedophile. Forty is probably the bottom limit for me. When I'm on the road, I go to libraries, Internet cafés, that sort of thing. Hell, it was a problem for me to take three days off to canoe the river. Really!"

When Odysseus returned to Ithaka, he told his swineherd, "There is no worse life for a man than to tramp it." But could Homer have possibly imagined this version of the modern-day tramp, on the road and online? Then again, Odysseus had his libido issues, too.

Dan points a finger at me. "I have more sex than you do. I'll guarantee you that."

"I'm sure you do," I reply, deciding that humor is the best means of deflection. "I'm married."

Dan nods his head toward the Missouri, a faraway look in his scarlet-streaked eyes. "It moves nice." And then, "Would you like to go for a little paddle?"

"I don't know." A thousand thoughts scull through my skull. "Upstream?"

"Well, I don't think we should go downstream. It's too easy," he says. "Yeah, let's go upstream for a ways."

And here is the proverbial head-versus-heart dilemma. The cautious thinker in me is saying: *Don't you dare. You don't know this guy. He's stoned. He has a temper. He's been behind bars more often than most bartenders. He knows you're alone. And you are so deep in the middle of nowhere that even the vultures won't hear your cries for help.*

But the devil on my other shoulder is whispering: *Lewis and Clark.* Will I ever again have another opportunity to paddle the Missouri? Is it not fate to receive such an offer almost precisely two centuries after the Corps of Discovery did the very same thing at the very same spot?

"Is it safe?" I ask, basically thinking out loud.

He tilts his head at me. "Can you swim?"

Moments later, he hands me a paddle and tosses me a life jacket. Then, as I'm climbing into the bow of his canoe, pushing aside some filthy clothes and a couple of beer cans, he cautions me, "No matter what you do, don't turn around and look at me, because we'll tip over. That's what happened to me and my friend Ned."

He says it again. "Don't turn around and look at me."

He says it a third time. "Really, don't look at me."

And as he does so, my mind is talking to me, too, saying, "You are about to die."

I pride myself on my judgment of character. I can usually tell within moments of meeting someone where the relationship is going. Maybe it is because I observe for a living. Perhaps it is a talent developed through years of extrapolating insight from brief peeks into peoples' lives. Whatever the reason, I am usually right. And in Hobo Dan, as I came to think of him, I perceive a harmlessness, even a glimmer of goodness.

But for a split second, I think perhaps I am wrong. Dead wrong. I picture myself turning around in the canoe just in time to gasp at my last earthly sight — Dan swinging his paddle like a baseball bat, aiming for the back of my head. I envision a headline a few weeks hence: "Man's Body Washes Up in Bismarck: Reported Missing in Montana." I imagine Dan trading in his beat-up pickup for a shiny new Winnebago Aspect.

"All right," I hear myself croak, "let's do it."

The plan was to paddle a few hundred yards upstream and then float back down to the landing, after which I would climb out of the canoe and revel in my pitiable approximation of Meriwether Lewis.

Instead, I come away feeling more like Jerry Lewis.

I am certainly an adequate canoeist. I have paddled through the Boundary Waters Canoe Area in northern Minnesota. I have canoed the Russian River in California and the Brule River in Wisconsin. Hell, I used to teach canoeing at summer camp. But — and this is a statement with many implications — I have never paddled upstream. The Missouri River moves a lot faster than it looks.

Almost immediately, we find ourselves a couple hundred feet downriver. We try paddling hard for several strokes, but we have only drifted farther downstream. Dan doesn't seem much bothered by it.

Then again, he is in a state of mind where he isn't much bothered by anything. Meanwhile, I nearly panic. My paranoia no longer focuses on thoughts of dying; instead, I have visions of drifting helplessly to the next landing some ten miles downstream, arriving just in time for the sun to go down, leaving me to share a sleeping bag with Hobo Dan, his head resting against my shoulder, his beer-fueled snores echoing in my ear. Then my imagination has me spending the following day hitchhiking in vain, wandering under a searing sun like the ill-fated astronauts in *Capricorn One*, stumbling toward mirages, grabbing at hallucinations.

So now I paddle twice as hard, and I implore Dan to do the same. We dig at the water like a couple of prospectors who sniff a strike. We maneuver toward the riverbank where the currents are slower, and, inch by inch, we move forward, finally making it back to the landing. I place my paddle on my lap, bow my head, and chuckle.

"Well, that was fun . . ."

But I swallow the sentence. Because I look up to discover that Dan has steered us back to the middle of the river. So we do it all over again.

"I have traveled all over the world," Odysseus reports toward the end of the *Odyssey*, "and this is what I have come to."

When we finally return to the picnic bench, I hear shades of this in a monologue from Dan, as he seems to be in a reflective mood. "I could have been a responsible human being. I could have been a bread-winner. But I'm still doing the same thing I was doing when I was twenty-one years old . . . ," he says, letting his voice trail off. And then he starts again, aiming a finger at me. "When you get old, you'll have grandkids and security and family and insurance and all that sort of thing. Now that I'm old . . . I have a better tent."

Campbell figured the hero as a sort of progressive force—"the champion not of things become but of things becoming; the dragon to be slain by him is precisely the monster of the status quo." Transformation is at the heart of the heroic journey, but the adventure is incomplete until the hero's return, which Campbell suggested may be

Hobo Dan stands proudly alongside the Missouri River

the most difficult task of all: "The returning hero, to complete his adventure, must survive the impact of the world."

Meriwether Lewis returned as the quintessential American hero, and two centuries later he is all but canonized. But he couldn't cope with the impact of the world, the transition from adventure to ordinariness and, as newly appointed governor of the Louisiana Territory, numbing bureaucracy. He became an alcoholic and an opium addict. Only three years after his triumphant return, at the age of thirty-five, he killed himself. "Regrets," Campbell wrote, "are illuminations come too late."

On the other hand, Hobo Dan — addicted to his lifestyle, as he puts it — has simply refused to heed the call to return at all. Dan is convinced that his autonomy represents a grand heroic adventure, and as I chat with him I can't help but think of the classic children's story *Fish Is Fish* by Leo Lionni, which I have read to my boys. It is the story of a pond, where a minnow and a tadpole get along swimmingly until they realize the differences between them — specifically when the tadpole sprouts legs. Having achieved froghood, he heads off to explore the world and returns with gleeful stories of land-based wonders. Naturally, the fish is envious and curious. So one day he flops himself onto land, realizing too late that he wasn't meant for the air up there. Fortunately, his old friend happens upon him and nudges him back into the pond.

The story is about friendship and self-awareness, but to me it is also a tale about aspirations. Some people are fueled by ambition. They long to be princes. Others crave freedom. They just want to be frogs.

"I'm not homeless." Dan says with a wink. "I'm an outdoorsman."

He is also a product of his past, as we all are. Everything is prologue — as history was to mythology, as dinosaur bones were to dragon tales, as the Corps of Discovery was to manifest destiny, as the homesteaders of Iliad were to the sprawling ranches, as the *Iliad* is to the *Odyssey*. Even the *Odyssey* itself is primarily prologue. Homer enters the story at the tail end of Odysseus's wanderings, revealing some of the most famous encounters in literature — from the one-eyed Cyclops to six-headed Scylla — merely in a few lines of flashback revealed through the protagonist's storytelling. Odysseus has been gone for nearly two decades; the *Odyssey* takes place over the course of only about forty days. But the book is really about a new chapter in its protagonist's life.

The lesson may be that while a man is a product of the myriad forces that formed him — his ancestry, his achievements, his fears, his regrets, his battles, his buried skeletons, his mother — the measure of him is where he paddles from there. Are we anchored to our past? Do we turn our personal histories into self-styled mythologies? Do we start to believe them?

It is time for me to move on. Dan accompanies me to the

Aspect. We shake hands, and I climb behind the wheel. As I begin to drive away, Dan motions for me to roll down my window.

"You know what?" he says, holding a canoe paddle like a banner. "I like to think of myself as the last free man."

I rumble over the Missouri and onto another uncertain stretch of highway, musing that we all make our own legends.

VII

oblivion

Unlike most of the heroic characters who came after him, the man who served as their ancient template is not given much of a hero's entrance. When we first meet Odysseus, he is sighing and weeping. After Zeus destroys the last of his ships with a well-aimed thunderbolt, drowning all of his shipmates, Odysseus is washed ashore on the remote island of Ogygia, home of the nymph Calypso, daughter of Atlas. Calypso receives Odysseus with loving kindness — lots of loving — and is so enamored of him that she keeps him on Ogygia for seven years. Odysseus is imprisoned, albeit with a lovely nymph on an island paradise. But when Athena finally convinces Zeus that such exile is an unkind fate for the hero of Troy, the king of the gods sends a messenger to inform Calypso it is finally time to send Odysseus home.

Hermes, messenger of the gods, arrives to find a blissful scene. A soft meadow thick with violets leads to Calypso's great cave, which is surrounded by sweet-smelling cypress trees and draped in grapevines with clusters of ripe fruit. Inside, a magnificent fire burns in the hearth, sending the aroma of cedar and juniper logs wafting over the island. And Calypso, her beautiful hair flowing over her shoulders, weaves on her loom and sings in a lovely voice. It is, says Homer, "a sight to gladden the gods." And yet Odysseus isn't there. Instead, he is "sitting in his usual place on the shore, wearing out his soul with lamentation and tears."

Calypso tries to convince Odysseus to remain on the heavenly isle as her immortal husband. She offers him a life of eternal youth and ceaseless physical satisfaction. "But," as Odysseus would later explain, "she could not win my heart."

Here is the moment when Odysseus accepts the hero's call to return. Here — at a point when, in the words of Joseph Campbell, "the hero . . . is swallowed into the unknown, and would appear to have died" — Odysseus chooses rebirth. For him, a life without end would also mean a life without struggle, without closure, without meaning. Which is to say no life at all. Brokenhearted, Calypso allows Odysseus to build a raft and provides him with a fair wind to speed him home.

It is significant to note that the name Calypso comes from the Greek word for "concealed." What Odysseus is really choosing is an escape from oblivion. The Greeks had a goddess of such things — Lethe was her name, or simply Oblivion. According to Hesiod's *Theogony*, which fused a variety of Greek traditions to explain how the gods came to be, at the beginning of the world there was a baby boom of personified abstractions. Oblivion was one of the children of Discord; her siblings included Pain, Famine, Illness, and Anarchy. Discord was spawned by Night, who sprang from Chaos. It is a dark pedigree, and it must have made for one hell of a family portrait.

Lethe was also the name of one of the principal rivers of the underworld. According to the Orphics, who were essentially ancient Greece's version of New Age cultists, the befuddled and thirsty soul of the dead would arrive in Hades and be tempted to drink from the spring of Lethe. But one drink would cause complete forgetfulness. The soul would not recall the lessons of past lives and, upon reincarnation, it would be no wiser than the rest of humanity. So the Orphics were trained to endure thirst and to distinguish between the rivers Mnemosyne and Lethe, between memory and oblivion.

Not only does Calypso ask Odysseus to disconnect himself from the happenings of the world, but she would also have him disregard memories of his faithful wife, his son, and his own island of Ithaka. Odysseus refuses immortality, but in doing so he actually conquers death. Widely believed to have died, he reappears, as if reborn. "The hero would be no hero if death held for him any terror," wrote Campbell.

We all have our reasons for fearing our demise. As with most (I assume), mine is a considerable fear. I often confront this prospect with a dose of irony, or at least verbosity. For instance, I may purposely joke about the horrific possible outcomes of flight while en route to the airport. My rationalization: it would then be intolerably unjust for the airplane to go down. Certainly I have no death wish. If anything, I have before-I-die wishes. Like Odysseus, I cannot bear the thought of an eternity apart from my family. But I also fear a sort of cultural and historical oblivion. I wish to be remembered.

By this, I don't mean to say that I am consumed by ambition. I long ago sacrificed a heap of frantic wannabe-ness for a healthy dose of serenity in my daily life. But I dread the prospect of walking into the sunset and leaving no footprints. If possible, I would like to depart this life knowing that my efforts furthered the course of humanity in one way or another. Frankly, I aspire to a legacy — yes, even a sort of immortality. Which is funny, because I am headed toward a place called Calypso.

In October 1896, a child was born in Wolverhampton, England, a boy named Arthur Jordan. At the age of fourteen, he ran away from home and stowed away on a ship to America. When he was in his early twenties, he and his new wife made their way by wagon to eastern Montana and the banks of Big Dry Creek (they name things as they see them in Montana — Big Muddy Creek, Granite Peak, Big Hole). The Jordans built a cabin, which soon became a way station for cowboys, who referred to their host as the English Kid. The town that sprang up became known as Jordan — "the most tough and vicious little town in the Northwest," and that's according to Arthur Jordan himself.

After twenty-six years in Jordan, he picked up and left, taking his wife and two sons, and headed for the mountains. But the town remains, and the sense of seclusion that drew the original residents is preserved there by simple geography. Jordan is still the American frontier. It is the only surviving town in Garfield County, a region nearly as big as Connecticut yet home to fewer than 1,300 people. Seventy-five years ago, there was approximately one person per square mile in the county; today there is roughly one person for every four square miles. Jordan is so remote and serves such an enormous area that for many years the high school actually made use of a dormitory.

Jordan seemed destined to live out its existence in anonymity, a tiny hamlet tucked between two swells of a rolling prairie amid an afterthought of a county in a nearly empty region of an oft-ignored state. But exactly one hundred years after its founder set down roots, the town made national headlines.

Montana-based author Walter Kirn has suggested the state motto be: "Better Feared than Ignored." To many Americans, Montana has come to represent rebel territory, a place so empty and sprawling that it either spawns or lures gun-toting enemies of the state — über-libertarians looking to avoid the reach of law enforcement. In other words, people craving a sort of oblivion — or at least total separation. The state's reputation may be undeserved, but in 1996 the poster boys for such things were the Montana Freemen.

Drawing from a jumble of philosophies — some Old Testament, some Magna Carta, some selective reading of the Constitution, some gobbledygook about Jewish conspiracies — the Freemen refused to acknowledge the legitimacy of the federal or state government, believing that the highest level of valid government was the county. They disposed of their driver's licenses, discarded their social security numbers, refused to pay taxes, stopped making mortgage payments, and defied foreclosures. When a tax delinquent and anti-Semite named Leroy Schweitzer went recruiting for like-minded members, he found a receptive audience in the folks who lived on the margins amid eastern Montana's unforgiving plains. The group gathered at a Garfield County ranch, renaming the location Justus Township. They raised an inverted U.S. flag on one of the buildings in their compound, claiming it symbolized a nation in distress

Here we have a modern-day approximation of Homer's Cyclops, whom the poet describes as "a violent and lawless tribe." The Cyclopians, says Homer, "have no parliament for debates and no laws, but they live on high mountains in hollow caves; each one lays down the law for wife and children, and no one cares for his neighbors."

The Freemen were after more than just individual sovereignty, however. They tried to form their own shadow government for a white Christian republic, acting as their own central bank, issuing arrest warrants, invading courtrooms to hold mock trials of government officials, even threatening to kill a federal judge. Over the course of two years, according to federal indictments, the Freemen defrauded banks, public agencies, and private businesses out of nearly two million dollars.

In the spring of 1996, the movement culminated in the longest federal siege in U.S. history — an eighty-one-day standoff at Justus Township between the separatist group and federal officers. It ended peacefully with Schweitzer surrendering and receiving a twenty-two-and-a-half-year prison sentence. He continued his antigovernment rants from his cell. As for tiny Jordan, it was overrun by FBI agents and national news media and nearly torn apart by the confrontation, because everyone in town either was acquainted with or related to one of the Freemen. And they had their share of sympathizers.

"They had some good ideas. They just got off on a tangent," a nice old lady explains to me, as she hands me a phosphate from an actual working soda fountain inside Jordan's drugstore. "We've known them all their lives, so they're not hardened criminals or anything. A lot of them just got misled, or people were foreclosing on their ranches."

I arrive in Jordan after a morning of driving through the Big Lonely — a stark stretch of sagebrush and shortgrass surrounding Highway 200 as it slices the state into northern and southern halves.

Eastward from Lewiston, the exact center of the state, I outpace the rain, leaving ominous clouds behind me and heading toward blue skies of scattered fluff. The handful of settlements along the way — Grass-range, Winnett, Mosby — are mere hiccups. I see nary a sign of human life for the 130 miles into Jordan. Hence the various names of this region, scarcely populated even by Montana standards: Big Dry Country. The Big Open. The Big Empty. The Breaks.

My stop in Jordan is only a lunch break, after all. I stroll around town for a few minutes, watching the dust devils dance down Main Street, a dirt thoroughfare wide enough to allow a chariot race. This is a no-frills kind of place, where the business district, such as it is, consists of boxy, low-slung buildings with minimalist marquees that say only JORDAN DRUG and MAIN HARDWARE and FIRE HALL. No need for hyperbole here; there is no competition for hundreds of square miles.

At the Hilltop Café, on the crest of a swell on the edge of town, I savor some curly fries and watch a man enter to a small-town greeting.

"How ya doin', Bill?"

He scratches his head. "Ah, fair to partly cloudy," he says, and then he announces that some loose cows are running down the high-way just west of town.

A couple of families walk in and share a table. The kids are whin-ing, talking loudly, fighting over crayons. One little boy is pulled out to the parking lot and admonished. God, I miss my kids.

I have to push on. The storm is still pursuing me, and I have set myself the task of locating an elderly woman named Mary Haughian. I spoke to her on the phone a few days earlier, and she invited me to her remote ranch along the Yellowstone River.

"This is where the train wrecked," she told me. I want to see it for myself.

On June 19, 1938, a locomotive described as "the crack passen-ger train of the Chicago, Milwaukee, St. Paul, and Pacific Railroad" was speeding through eastern Montana on its way from Chicago to

Tacoma, Washington. As the train reached a 180-foot-long steel and concrete trestle over tiny Custer Creek, which had always merely trickled toward the Yellowstone River, a confluence of events coalesced into one of the worst tragedies in Montana's history. For several hours, a frightening storm had passed through the area, and Custer Creek swelled to flash flood conditions. Sometime just after midnight a wall of floodwaters — some estimates describe it as much as thirty feet high — washed over the trestle, weakening it considerably. Moments later, the train arrived.

The steam locomotive, tender, and baggage cars made it over the bridge before the supports sagged and the trestle gave way. *Life* magazine would later describe what happened next: "[The cars] were jerked back and up like the tip of a lashing whip, the locomotive falling on the baggage car. A mail car toppled across the locomotive. A smoking car, day coach, and tourist sleeper piled up behind. Another tourist sleeper was at once submerged. A third plunged in a few minutes later." In all, eight of the train's twelve cars plunged into Custer Creek. The Fates snipped the thread on four dozen lives — instant oblivion for forty-eight souls.

The train was called the Olympian. The last town it passed safely? Calypso.

Southwest now on Highway 59, an even lonelier highway that eventually feeds into the interstate at Miles City (population nine thousand, which makes it the biggest city in all of the eastern third of Montana). The drive consists of eighty miles of emptiness, broken up midway by a frenzy of activity when I am forced to a dead stop by cows being herded across the highway by two men on motorbikes. I pass up the chance to turn onto Dead Man Road and opt instead for a road called Kinsey. Eighteen miles of pavement, then three miles of gravel, then a one-lane dirt road and a sign: HAUGHIAN RANCH — 6.1 MILES.

I rumble past a parched creek, a fleeting thicket of forlorn trees, bales of hay stacked in pyramids, a junkyard of rusted implements and automobiles, a cluster of free-ranging cattle, and a mosaic of rocky outcroppings and sandstone formations. This is badlands ranchland. Six miles on, and I arrive at a ranch entrance made of iron and brick, the words HAUGHIAN LIVESTOCK atop it. From my vantage point, it looks as if the letters have been branded into the sky. It is only now that I realize that all of this has essentially been the Haughian family's driveway. Just as I pass under the gate, a woman driving a horse trailer rumbles up and stops alongside me, facing the other direction. Her name is Jan. She is Mary's daughter-in-law.

The beginning of a very long driveway near Calypso, Montana

"It's another eight miles to the home place," she says. "You can't miss it."

The Haughian ranch is decorated with all the vehicles and equipment and outbuildings that one would expect from a sprawling operation. The home place rests alongside the north bank of the Yellowstone, and apparently William Clark camped here — in what is now the bull pasture—in the summer of 1806. Slightly more than a century and a half later, the Haughians constructed a tram to transport the Haughian children over the river so that they could walk to the highway and be picked up for school.

"We've had seven years of drought here," Mary explains, as she motions toward the badlands. "This is the first green we've seen in a long while. We had ten inches of snow last week!" I check my calendar. It is the nineteenth of May.

Although Mary is in her early eighties, her hair has a remarkable burgundy hue. It may be an homage to her mother-in-law, a feisty, red-haired Irish lass whom the *Saturday Evening Post* once profiled as "The Cattle Queen of Montana." Her name was Susan Quinn, and she was the youngest daughter of a successful Irish businessman. Susan's oldest sister had been engaged to marry a chap named Dan Haughian, but in 1890 Dan had skipped to America in search of free land in a place called Montana. A decade later, after finding some success as a sheep rancher, he sailed back to Ireland to retrieve his beloved, only to find that she had grown tired of waiting and had married someone else. So Dan married Susan instead and dragged her back to Big Sky Country.

When Susan stepped off the train in Miles City and saw nothing but dusty shades of brown, she exclaimed, "Good lord! What have I done?" Her new home was a log cabin at a place Dan called Big Sheep Mountain, some forty miles into the Montana outback.

They started with forty acres and perhaps a mule or two. But over the years, they gradually bought land that other homesteaders had abandoned—anything they could afford. When Dan died suddenly in 1931, leaving Susan with ten children and an expansive ranching operation, she was devastated. According to Haughian family mythology, she spent a year in mourning, barely leaving her room. But when she finally emerged, she vowed to turn the ranch into an empire. She purchased abandoned ranches, transitioned into raising cattle, took on the U.S. government in a dispute over grazing rights, formed the Haughian Livestock Corporation, and ran it until her death in 1972, by which time there were some 240,000 acres of Haughian land.

Mary's trip to the Haughian ranch is less of an epic tale. Born about thirty miles east of here in the town of Ismay, she completed one year of junior college, which was enough to get her a job teaching at a country school in the Big Lonely. There she met Dan and Susan Haughian's son, Dan Jr., at a dance. She married him in '45, moved down to the ranch, and has been here ever since.

The land has been divided several times — between Dan Jr. and his four brothers (Dan died in 1993) and then again between Mary's three sons, each of whom raises about five hundred head of cattle. One son lives in a house next to Mary's. His name is the same as his grandmother's maiden name — Quinn.

Mary and I sit at her kitchen table, beneath a squeaking fan suspended from a very low ceiling and surrounded by the various accoutrements of Mary's hobbies. Isolation breeds diversions, and she has many. She collects agate rocks, paints in oils, reads voraciously. And Mary is an amateur historian who has self-published several books — accounts of her early years, a family history, even an homage to soldiers from Prairie County who fought in World War II.

"I don't know why," she says, nearly whispering. "I just like the good old days. Life was simpler."

When I had spoken with her by telephone before my arrival, I had asked if there was any sort of cell phone service in her area, figuring it might come in handy if I got lost en route to her ranch. Her response: "I don't know. And I don't care." So Mary has immersed herself in what used to be.

She pulls out a scrapbook filled with newspaper clippings from various sources, and a piece of paper falls out. It is a horrific photograph of the wreck of the Olympian, its cars facing every which way in Custer Creek, as if tossed mercilessly from Mount Olympus. It used to be that the Haughian ranch was right along the beaten path. The passenger trains ran right through it, never slowing down until that fateful night in 1938.

"They were supposed to go to a dance in Kinsey that night," she says of her late husband and his siblings "but they decided to stay home because they saw some terrible black clouds coming in. Believe it or not, they never heard anything till morning. Then Dan got up to irrigate at about four in the morning, and he saw little airplanes flying around. That was the Associated Press."

Leafing through Mary's clippings evokes a range of emotions. Sometimes I find a terrifying poetry in the reporting: "Cries, screams, groans and curses mingled with the hiss of steam from the broken boilers and the shouts of rescue crews, as flashlights and locomotive lights slashed into the dawn." But the pictures also speak volumes: as powerful as it is to see bodies being carried from the wreckage, it is doubly so to come across a photo of three children orphaned by the accident.

Sometimes there is a sense of detached reportage: a passenger list revealed travelers from Spokane, Missoula, Minneapolis, Detroit. A "Latest Train Wreck Death List" shouted from above the fold in the *Seattle Daily Times*. But there frequently seems to be a morbid fascination with titillating details: one body was reportedly found floating in the Yellowstone River at Sidney, Montana, 130 miles from the crash scene.

Sometimes I am inspired by heroic example: the *Montana Standard* told the story of a "Negro Pullman porter" and a navy midshipman who tied together several hammocks and rescued passengers from a coach that had plunged into the creek. But I am also disheartened by the indignity of death: one headline asked "Does Anyone Know These Train Victims?" and mentioned a 175-pound male, a woman with short gray hair, and a twenty-year-old woman with a ring on her right hand bearing the initial L.

Sometimes the Fates appear magnanimous: a nineteen-year-old woman's coattail caught on some wreckage, suspending her just high enough to keep her head above the raging waters for three hours until a railroad employee spotted her golden hair in the darkness. But most of the time the Fates are cruel: among the dead were a soon-to-be bride, a mother and her two small daughters, and one half of a set of twins.

I ask Mary if I can see the site of the crash, and her son, Quinn, offers to lead me there. I follow him in his pickup truck just a short drive east along the old gravel railroad bed that parallels the river, past a bright yellow sign that warns NOT A COUNTY ROAD. TRAVEL AT YOUR OWN RISK.

About a mile on, we reach what used to be the town of Saugus, located just west of the ill-fated railroad trestle. There were once a few buildings here, Quinn tells me, but the handful of residents were so traumatized by the train wreck and so fearful of forever being associated with the tragedy that they changed the town's name. They opted for Susan, in honor of Quinn's legendary grandmother.

This seems to be a trend in this part of the country. Ismay, where Mary was born, is best known for temporarily changing its name during a particular NFL quarterback's heyday. It became Joe, Montana. It strikes me that this is one way to assure at least the prospect of immortality. Get some folks to name a town after you. I wouldn't be the first author to try it. The community of Thurber, Utah, was founded in 1875, honoring an early explorer named Albert Thurber. Forty-one years later, Thomas Bicknell, an educator and author from Rhode Island, offered one thousand books to any town that would name itself after him. Thurber's residents agreed; it remains Bicknell to this day.

It may be that name changes are only permanent, however, if the namesake needs help achieving immortality. The town of Joe is back to calling itself Ismay. And Susan? Nowadays the settlement consists only of a collapsed wooden structure and a barbed wire fence on which is nailed a small white sign with uneven black lettering. SAUGUS, it says. The sign was made by Mary herself.

Moving on, I approach the crash site, and two thoughts dominate. First, I don't think I can squeeze the Aspect between the raised sides of the one-lane bridge. Not to worry, says Quinn, and he leads me on an off-road shortcut around the trestle (ironically) and actually through the shallow waters of Custer Creek. Second, the bridge is so low, the creek so meek, that I wonder how a tragedy of such proportions could have occurred. I step out of the Aspect and walk to the center of the bridge. The slow-moving creek looks like chocolate milk.

Some of the Haughians' cows are lazing on one bank. Birds are chirping. The sun, for a moment, is shining. And forty-eight people died here. There is no memorial that I can see, except for Mary's scrapbook.

I bid farewell to Quinn and continue along the railroad bed, now closer to the river, where I notice a trio of stately swans floating with the current. The ancients might have interpreted this as an omen from the gods. In fact, Zeus was said to have disguised himself as a swan, oddly enough, when he raped Leda, Queen of Sparta. She later gave birth to a child who would come to be known as Helen of Troy. More ominous to me, however, are the storm clouds once again racing up behind me. I am rumbling as fast as possible along this NOT A COUNTY ROAD, which translates to about twenty miles per hour.

Finally, another of Mary's signs: CALYPSO.

Strangely, there are two other homemade markers here, announcing that a couple of boys — Andrew "Joe" Sullivan and Richard Wallace Skeel — were born here in 1915. And there is a Montana license plate, only a few years old, wrapped around a fencepost, the word *Calypso* visible between the bullet holes that I have come to expect. Other than that, Calypso is nothing, just grassland leading toward the Yellowstone, abandoned and mostly forgotten. To my thinking, it is a suitable representation of oblivion.

When I said my good-byes to Mary earlier, she told me, matter-of-factly, "I don't like many people to visit." It was her way of explaining that while she may have enjoyed my company, she prefers her relative isolation on the ranch. Mary seems to crave oblivion, not in

the sense of forgetfulness, but rather as it suggests a separation from the bedlam of the world. Certainly, the high-functioning hermit in me can understand. We share an affinity for simplicity and silence. But maybe oblivion is an impossibility.

Consider the paddlefish of eastern Montana. For much of the twentieth century, these prehistoric-looking creatures — almost grotesque in appearance, without scales or bone skeletons and bearing a snout as much as two feet long — were considered extinct in America, found only in China's Yangtze River. But in 1962, when a fisherman landed one at a lake near a dusty Montana hamlet called Intake, it became clear that the paddlefish also lurked deep in the bowels of the upper Missouri River drainage.

Remaining in the depths of the river, never rising to bait, they are removed with dumb luck and brute force. An angler uses weights to send his line to the bottom of the river, then jerks it along blindly, hoping to snag an unwitting ancient who only wishes to be left alone in the murky nowhere. The fish puts up a tremendous fight to stay there. Paddlefish, it seems, are not meant to be caught, not meant to be turned into whitefish and caviar. The battle is not man against fish, but rather man and fish against fate.

So maybe there is no such thing as absolute oblivion, no possibility of utter detachment. Like the Unabomber, you can hide from civilization and fidget with your bomb-making tools in a Lincoln shack. Like the Freemen, you can retreat with your antigovernment delusions to a Jordan compound. Like Mary Haughian, you can live out your days on the fringes of the Big Lonely, looking backward in time for comfort. But then you write a manifesto or raise an anarchist flag or publish a book to capture history. And you reveal yourself. You don't want oblivion; you want immortality. And maybe you get it when someone like me comes along, with rod and reel or gun and badge or pen and paper, angling for something.

VIII

on time

Chaos came first.

According to Hesiod's *Theogony*, Chaos was the first of the gods to grace Olympus. He was followed by Gaia (earth), whose firstborn was called Uranus (heaven) and was conceived immaculately. But Gaia and Uranus then coupled (the gods were nothing if not incestuous), and this was essentially the Greek version of the Big Bang. The last of their twelve children was Chronus, the god of time, from whom we derive our words chronometer and chronology and chronic. He was, claimed Hesiod, "a most fearful child who hated his mighty father."

Here's why: Uranus foresaw that one of his children would overthrow him, so he simply thrust them back into the darkness of Gaia's womb as soon as they were born. Naturally, nobody much enjoyed that, particularly Gaia. So she came up with a vengeful plan. She crafted an enormous, sharp-toothed sickle of iron and gave it to bold Chronus. When Uranus next "lay stretched out upon her," Chronus seized his father's genitals with his left hand and swiftly sliced them off — somewhat Bobbit-like — with his right hand, tossing them into the sea. The blood that was spilled formed creatures like the Furies and the Giants. Meanwhile, the severed organ bobbed in the waves, forming a white foam, from which emerged the goddess of love, Aphrodite, who became "fond of a man's genitals, because to them she owed her birth." I'm not making that up. Hesiod wrote it.

Anyhow, castrated Uranus was understandably miffed, although he seems to have resorted to calling his children names. "Titans," he called them, meaning "overreachers." And he said their deed would be avenged someday.

The Titans made a king out of Chronus, who was said to have three heads and a serpentine tail that was perpetually entwined with that of his consort Ananke, the goddess of inevitability. So Time and Inexorableness were always together. But Chronus continued the cycle of abuse. In fact, he may have been even more of a tyrant than his father. The same fear drove him — a prophecy that his own children would turn on him. So when his wife Rhea (who, of course, was also his sister) bore five children, Chronus immediately swallowed each of them whole — a vivid representation of the notion that time devours all things.

But when the sixth child, Zeus, was born, Rhea gave Chronus a large stone to devour instead of the baby. Apparently, Chronus didn't discover the deception until it was too late. Zeus was kept out of sight until he was grown, upon which he promptly returned to ambush his father, causing him to regurgitate Zeus's siblings — Hestia, Demeter, Hera, Hades, and Poseidon. An attempted coup ensued, with the grateful siblings making Zeus their leader and each claiming a portion of creation as their dominion. They declared war, leading to a protracted battle that shook the cosmos, and eventually Zeus and Co. imprisoned the Titans in the underworld.

So that's how the Olympians came to reside on Olympus. And that's how Chronus was overthrown. Time may devour all things, heal all wounds, march on, stop for nobody, and fly when you're having fun. But apparently, at least according to the genealogy of the gods, Time can also be conquered. And that is a notion I can embrace.

In fact, in North Dakota it is a virtual certainty.

Several years ago, I was asked to write a magazine article for an in-flight publication. In fact, it was for an airline named after the fourth letter of the Greek alphabet. The article was about life on the boundary of time zones, and I found myself captivated by the concept of malleable time. It has been said that time is an illusion proposed by the manufacturers of space. Einstein said much the same thing, I think. Best I can tell, his theory of relativity says that neither time nor space is absolute, and each is sort of dependent on the other. I have no understanding of space-time curvature and electrodynamics and inertial reference frames. But time zones I can do. They constitute my relative theory regarding the theory of relativity. I don't think it's what Einstein was trying to say, but it works for me.

For most of us, time zones are hardly a daily concern. They may be a pause before a long-distance telephone call, maybe a wristwatch adjustment after a four-hour flight, perhaps a brief moment of awareness on New Year's Eve. We may go days, even weeks, without giving the change in hours a second thought. But I would think that the folks who live on the edge — the people, say, in Riggins, Idaho, who can close down a bar there at 2:00 a.m. and then cross a bridge spanning the Salmon River and drink until 2:00 a.m. at another watering hole — well, I would think there would be a sense of power over the one dimension generally regarded as immutable. Or at least, a sense of humor about it.

Historically in the United States, time zone lines often zigged and zagged according to the whims of the powerful railroads. The federal government officially became involved with the Standard Time Act of 1918, which essentially codified what the railroads had created. Today, Congress and the U.S. Department of Transportation are the keepers of the clocks. Despite the government supervision — or perhaps because of it — the intangible lines that form the boundaries of time seem to have been drawn by a drunken cartographer. The swerves and dodges can make for some strange pairings (sections of Florida and South Dakota share a time zone), bizarre juxtapositions (part of Oregon is on mountain time, while northern Idaho is on Pacific time), and suspect divisions (El Paso seems to have been abducted from the central time zone).

In North Dakota, it means confusion. The boundary line between the central and mountain time zones cuts right through the heart of the state. It follows the course of the Missouri River — except at Sitting Bull's burial site, which it swerves around. And except at the city of Mandan, where it makes a sharp westward turn. And except at sparsely populated Oliver County, which it detours to avoid completely. Then there is the point where the time-zone line leaves the Missouri River and follows the Little Missouri instead. A boundary line that entered the state going due north leaves it heading west.

The result is widespread bewilderment on the wide-open plains. Consider, for instance, an attempt to schedule a simple meeting among representatives from the affiliate sites of Theodore Roosevelt National Park, which I come upon a couple dozen miles east of the Montana border along I-94. The south unit of the park, along the interstate, is located comfortably in mountain standard time. The north unit is just forty miles away, but it is bisected by the Little Missouri. Because the visitor center and facilities are located on the north side of the river, the entire north unit is managed as if it is in the central time zone. Thus many scheduled meetings leave the staff wondering: Did they mean central or mountain time?

Forty miles northwest of the north unit, along the North Dakota–Montana line, is the Fort Union National Historic Site. The fort is on central standard time, but its parking lot is in the mountain time zone. While researching the article, I chatted with a ranger there who was able to look out his office window and see an hour into the future. Just south of there are the adjacent hamlets of Fairview (Montana) and East Fairview (North Dakota), each in a different time zone.

But my favorite anecdote concerns the chemical processing plant in the city of Beulah, North Dakota. Beulah goes by mountain time. But the Dakota Gasification Company, which covers one square mile just outside of town, conducts most of its business east of the Missouri River. So the plant chooses to go by central time. The fellow I talked to there — the company's community representative — changes time zones more often in a day than most of us do in a year. So he simply wears two wristwatches.

Thus I came to the understanding that time-zone boundaries aren't really boundaries at all. They are more like suggestions. For people living on the edge of the hour hand, it is whatever time they say it is. Time is simply a state of mind, depending primarily on where one's attentions are focused. And they aren't going to let silly things like absolutes get in the way of life.

I drive into Theodore Roosevelt National Park, past rodent sentinels in prairie dog towns and into North Dakota's Badlands, an expanse of ravines and buttes carved more than half a million years ago by the Little Missouri River. As Roosevelt once said, they "seem hardly properly to belong to this earth." I park at a turnoff and hike a ways until I reach the Wind Canyon Overlook, where I marvel at a graceful bend in the river surrounded by the wind-sculpted sands of the canyon. A sign here shows a photograph of someone etching their name into a rock and says, "These forces built up over thousands of years are being destroyed by man right now."

Whenever I find myself in a place of great beauty — whether I am looking at a gorge relentlessly gouged out by a river or a giant sequoia patiently grown to otherworldly heights or a collection of hoodoos and pinnacles chiseled by the winds — my awe is bred of humility. I am humbled by the disparity between geological and human time, humbled by the fleeting nature of my existence. I don't have the luxury of changing my shape over the epochs. Life is short. Time is of the essence. But if I am going to make the most of my life, if I am going to strive for some heroic contribution, then it may take a while. I may need all the time I can get

So the notion that we can simply lose a few hours — time vanishing while we snooze on a flight from California to New York, for instance — is, I must admit, a moderate source of stress for me. Frankly, I am glad I wasn't alive in 1582 when the Catholic countries of the world switched to the Gregorian calendar. In an effort to correct the Julian calendar's flaws, which resulted in the vernal equinox coming too early, folks decided to just skip a week and a half. One day in Italy and Spain and Portugal, it was Thursday, October 4. The next day it was Friday, October 15. Pretty mind-blowing if you think about it.

Apparently, time — or at least, the means by which we mark it — is somewhat open to manipulation. And I resolve to make the most of it, one way or another. Who knows? Those three hours I save when I fly from New York back to California may be the time I need to make my mark — my case against irrelevance and oblivion. Of course, I'll probably just spend the time reading the in-flight magazine.

There has long been a name for the intersection of time and space, as the former moves along and the latter emerges as accessible. We call it the frontier, and it is the arena where we tend to locate our iconic heroes. The town of Medora, North Dakota, gateway to Theodore Roosevelt National Park, aspires to that vanished setting on the edge of the unexplored.

All tourists are welcome in Medora, North Dakota

It is a *restored* western town, and it seems like a hodgepodge of re-productions. There is a Rough Riders Hotel, a Sacajawea Trading Post, an Iron Horse Saloon, a James Gang Java. The town is gearing up for tourist season, so there are men on ladders repainting exteriors of buildings, women unpacking goods in gift shops, people trimming trees and beautifying the ground around a statue of Teddy Roosevelt. In the center of town, shining like a temple, is the gleaming white North Dakota Cowboy Hall of Fame — which, I am disappointed to discover, is scheduled for a grand opening a month after my visit.

The fifteen-thousand-square-foot museum honors all aspects of the region's cowboy culture — trail drivers, homesteaders, ranchers, rodeo stars, Native Americans. But what interests me is the cowboy as metaphor, as a sort of western heroic ideal.

The Greek myths are where the ideal first took shape — Jason harnessing flame-breathing bulls to plow fields, Theseus ridding the highway of various ancient serial killers, Odysseus navigating his ship between Scylla and Charybdis, Hercules doing battle with Nemean lions and eight-headed Hydras. The typical American of valor has long followed this historical template — rugged, determined, independent, taking on all tasks, usually somewhere in the inhospitable hinterlands. Daniel Boone qualifies. Meriwether Lewis, as well. Davy Crockett. Sam Houston. Wyatt Earp. Audie Murphy. Chuck Yeager. Alan Shepard. They are all, in a sense, cowboys, though some of them may never have herded a heifer in their lives.

Louis L'Amour, who may have done more than any other person to reinforce the icon of the cowboy hero, was from North Dakota. He was a hero himself, earning four Bronze Stars during World War II, and he boxed professionally before that. But I am most impressed by his prolific output — 118 books written, and more than 300 million in print worldwide. The man makes Stephen King look like Harper Lee.

Like me, he wrote about rugged individualists, perhaps even lionized them. But he was the Homer to their hero. If destiny had placed me along the frontier in the waning days of the Old West, I would have been the one telling the stories — about Wild Bill Hickock and Calamity Jane. But I wouldn't have earned the nicknames. At best, perhaps I would have been Mild Brad Herzog. Or Mishap Brad. I probably would have appeared much like Teddy Roosevelt did when he first arrived here — a four-eyed, Ivy League–educated pretender with an eastern accent, as out of place on the plains as a teddy bear at a rodeo. Back in the days before contact lenses, I would have had everything but the accent. After Roosevelt's young wife and mother died on the same day in 1884, he moved to the Dakota Territory to start a life as a lawman and rancher near Medora. He was in search of what he called the "strenuous life," and if by that he meant grasshopper plagues, drought, and a disastrous winter that wiped out his herd of cattle, well, he got it.

Roosevelt later said he wouldn't have been president if not for his experiences on the frontier, and it might be argued that, by earning the grudging respect of the Dakota cowboys, he learned that he possessed the kind of character that would one day propel him to greatness as a Rough Riding, Nobel-winning, trustbusting icon. He carried a big stick like Hercules. He hunted big game like Theseus. He charged into battle like Achilles. As Odysseus did, he took on myopic giants, albeit the corporate kind. And he was blind in one eye, perhaps like Homer. So he wound up on Mount Rushmore, our modern-day Olympus.

Teddy Roosevelt was our first cowboy president, but not our last. In his few Halloweens on earth so far, my oldest son has dressed up as a unicorn, a dinosaur, a robot . . . and a cowboy. In this day and age, when the frontiers are more intangible and life's challenges have become more cerebral in nature, that is largely what the cowboy ideal has become — a sort of anachronistic costume.

George W. Bush certainly wore it. Like Roosevelt, Bush was an Ivy League–educated son of a wealthy East Coast family who moved west and entered into a nomadic period in his twenties. But you don't simply become a cowboy by cultivating a Texas twang, clearing some brush periodically at your ranch, and saying things like "You are either with us or against us." It is all about authenticity — about *being* yourself rather than having to *sell* yourself. This is true regarding places as well as people. Big Sandy, Montana? Now there was a real western town. But from my point of view, Medora is merely playing dress-up. A real western town isn't self-aware. It just is. It doesn't have business establishments with names like Teepee Tanning and Pitchfork Fondue. A true cowboy would spit tobacky juice in disgust.

So Dubya and Medora have taught me a significant lesson. You can't adopt a heroic mantle like a costume, as if trick-or-treating in a ten-gallon hat. Audacity is not the same as courage. The myth does not make the man; the man earns the myth.

IX
white buffalo

I detour north a bit, planning to make a stop at Fort Mandan, a re-construction of Lewis and Clark's winter quarters in 1804–5. So I am once again hurtling east on Highway 200, and soon the tedium of the level prairie gives way to the intrigue of gently rolling hills. North Dakota has a reputation for relentless flatness — fodder for countless one-liners about being able to see your dog run away for three days or being able to stand in your front yard and see the backs of polar bears in the Arctic. The state even used to post tongue-in-cheek billboards welcoming visitors to NORTH DAKOTA: MOUNTAIN REMOVAL PROJECT COMPLETED. But between the Badlands and now these unexpected un-dulations, it seems to be a case of false advertising.

I roll past Killdeer and Dodge and Golden Valley, until finally I come to one of those signs that make me reflexively stop for a quick look around. ZAP, says the billboard. QUIET COUNTRY LIVING. There is a tiny white post office here — ZAP, ND 58580. And a gray featureless town hall with CITY OF ZAP affixed over the doorway. And a lonely, squat water tower on a hill, ZAP emblazoned on its side in big, black letters. Zap is named after a Scottish coal mining town named Zapp. But of course, naming a town Zapp with two p's would have been silly. This town of a couple hundred diehards appears to be a pious, placid place these days. But once it was primed to be the center of the countercultural universe.

It all started in the spring of 1969, when a fellow named Chuck Stroup, the student body president at North Dakota State University, placed a classified ad in the school newspaper, the *Spectrum*. He couldn't afford to go to Florida for his spring break, so instead he planned to have spring break come to him — specifically to a tiny town in his native Mercer County. He called his theoretical shindig the "Zap In," and it wasn't conceived with any political or social agenda in mind. It was just to be a party in the Plains, some flatlander frivolity. People would simply "Zip to Zap."

But it grew bigger than he ever imagined. A front-page article in the *Spectrum*, soon picked up by the Associated Press and disseminated nationally, touted the beauty of the region and predicted that people from all over the Midwest would converge on the weekend of May 10–11. This would be a "Grand Festival of Light and Love." Sparsely populated Mercer County would be reinvented as the "Lauderdale of the North."

The plans began in earnest. Student organizers hired some regional bands to play and obtained permission from local landowners to allow camping in their fields. Zap stocked up with beer, and a local café ordered fixings for Zapburgers. As the mayor later explained, the citizens of Zap believed this gathering — and the resulting economic boom — would be a way to "put ourselves on the map."

But the publicity outgrew the ability to prepare. By May 10, a few thousand revelers showed up — hardly a mass pilgrimage, but still about a dozen times Zap's population. As the town's resources were depleted, so was the patience of both the locals and the visitors. Soon the beer was gone, the café had to close, the temperature had fallen below freezing, students were using wood from a demolished building to start a bonfire on Main Street, and partiers were puking, pissing, and passing out in the center of town. Eventually, it escalated into a full-fledged riot.

By Saturday morning, five North Dakota National Guard companies had surrounded Zap, and two hundred guardsmen moved in with fixed bayonets, dispersing a few hundred revelers who were still on their feet and another thousand or so who were sleeping anywhere they fell. The fiasco was Walter Cronkite's lead story that evening. *Newsweek* reported about how Main Street was strewn with charred furniture and broken glass. "They wrecked the whole town," the local sheriff lamented.

Three months later, at a farm near Woodstock, New York, nearly half a million people gathered peacefully, despite the fact that the weather was equally imperfect and the accommodations just as uninviting. Why the gods allowed one gathering to become a debacle while the other emerged as an iconic moment in American history is either a matter of destiny or, more likely, a case of it being the wrong place at the wrong time. Maybe, if things had turned out differently, the "Zap In" might have come to exemplify the harmonious counterculture of the sixties. Maybe Joan Baez and Jefferson Airplane would have hitched a late ride to the love-in. Maybe baby boomers would be impressing Gen Xers these days by saying, "You know, I was at Zap."

Alas, it is just another example of what North Dakotans seem to fear most — bad publicity.

CBS newsman Eric Sevareid once described North Dakota as "a large rectangular blank in the national consciousness." And he was born and raised there. Such is the state's public perception. Of course, it doesn't help when the news media trumpets a study by two Rutgers University urban planners, as it did a couple of decades ago, suggesting that North Dakotans be relocated and the lands be returned to the buffalo. They pointed out that the region boasts "the nation's hottest summers and coldest winters, greatest temperature swings, worst hail and locusts and range fires, fiercest droughts and blizzards." It doesn't help either when Rand McNally accidentally leaves a portion of your state out of the atlas, which it did in 1989. Or when an article in a 1995 issue of the *New York Times Magazine* asks, "Is North Dakota necessary?" Put it this way: the situation is so bad that Montanans tell North Dakota jokes.

Small wonder that a "state of the state" study of a few years ago revealed that many in North Dakota suffer from a lack of self-esteem. The state wallows near the bottom of most national lists, including the one under "Population." North Dakota has only a few thousand more people than Alaska and half as many as Maine. There are actually fewer people in the state today than there were seventy-five years ago, even though the U.S. population has nearly tripled. The few folks who do live there are plenty tired of the gibes and barbs directed at their state, so every once in a while a movement begins in North Dakota that is premised on a simple idea: Ditch the "North."

North and South Dakota were born on the same day — November 2, 1889 — weighing in at slightly more than 70,000 square miles each. The region had been called the Dakota Territory (from the Dakota tribe, which means "alliance of friends"), and when it was divided along the forty-sixth parallel each new entity laid claim to the name. Neither side would yield, so each was given a directional modifier. Unfortunately for North Dakota, it was the northern one.

The thinking seems to be that the word *north* conjures up images of igloos and ice floes — when really it has never been colder than 60 degrees below zero in North Dakota. And that was way back in 1936. Of course, less than five months later, the state reached a record high of 121 degrees. But hey, who doesn't like the change of seasons? Perhaps this is why Exit 1 in North Dakota directs you to a town called Beach. Who could be cold in Beach, right?

Still, there is this movement — spearheaded by an alliance of politicians, businessmen, and reporters — to change the name to simply Dakota. The anti-North faction rationalizes that the state is north only in relation to South Dakota, but not when compared to, say, Saskatchewan. They claim that a name alteration would bring national attention — positive attention for a change. They also predict that South Dakota would be to Dakota as West Virginia is to Virginia — a pretender to the name.

Frankly, I can empathize with North Dakota's predicament, because we have something in common: I happen to be a twin, too. My brother Brian arrived twelve minutes before me on a late summer night in 1968. Yes, we are Brian and Brad. In the realm of wince-inducing twin monikers, it ranks slightly ahead of Mike and Ike, and Jack and Jill, and North Dakota and South Dakota. But not by much.

We are fraternal twins, no more genetically alike than any two brothers. I am occasionally asked what it is like to grow up as one of a pair, but all I can say for sure is that there is no singular twin experience. Some are attached at the hip (in fact, as I write this, doctors in — yes — North Dakota are separating conjoined twins). Other twins are yin and yang personified. Personally, I find eminently creepy those types who room together in college, dress in matching outfits, marry a couple of brothers named Larry and Gary, and serve as queens of the annual Twins Days festival in Twinsburg, Ohio.

Not that I minded my twin-ness back then. Those were the days before the widespread use of fertility drugs made multiple births commonplace, so we were always showered with attention — the kind that feeds self-esteem. It was nice to be noticed, nice to never want for company, nice to have a peer around to join me in tossing around a Frisbee or playing a set of tennis. We shared a bedroom. We shared a baseball card collection. We shared myriad life experiences at the same time and the same place and the same age. But there are challenges to being regarded as one half of a whole, and that notion seems to have been part of the human psyche for several millennia. In ancient tales, at least, twins were often an ill-fated lot.

The alpha twins of Greek mythology, of course, are the divine siblings Apollo and Artemis, son and daughter of Zeus and residents of Olympus. But an oft-repeated mythological theme concerns the story of siblings with simultaneous births, yet widely divergent destinies — twins, yet not at all. Usually the legend has Zeus acting in his usual capacity as Philanderer-in-Chief, descending to earth in disguise and copulating with some queen or another. Often, the king of the gods fathers one twin, while the other twin is spawned by a mere king of mortals. How that happens is anyone's guess. Of course, by then we have already accepted the plot point that Zeus has decided to shape-shift into, for instance, a shagedelic swan.

Anyway, such was the case with Iphicles and his more gifted brother, Hercules. Such, too, was the tale of mortal Castor and immortal Polydeuces. When Castor was killed, Polydeuces volunteered half of his own immortality so that his twin could live again. Zeus agreed, provided they spend one day in the underworld for every day on Mount Olympus. He placed their immortal souls in the sky as the constellation Gemini, one star shining slightly brighter than the other.

Lest you think this was merely a quirky notion of the ancients with no real or modern equivalent, consider this: Jim Thorpe, Ed Sullivan, Liberace, and Elvis Presley were all twins. Thorpe's brother died at the age of nine. Sullivan's brother perished at age one. The siblings of Liberace and Elvis died at birth. The survivors went on to become the greatest athlete in the world, the Great Stone Face, Mr. Showmanship, and the King.

Still, for the Greek myth-builders, the tragedy was often compounded by the fact that fratricide was a frequent plot device. Consider Acrisius, king of Argos, and his twin brother Proetus. They began their lifelong quarreling while still inside their mother's womb. Or Eteocles and Polyneices, the twin sons of Oedipus, who killed each other over political power. Then there's the tale of Aegyptus, king of Egypt, and his twin brother, Danaus. Forty-nine of the latter's daughters murdered forty-nine of the former's sons.

And what about Odysseus? Well, apparently he had twin issues, too. According to legend, only the warrior Helenus rivaled him in intelligence and cunning, so much so that Greek solders referred to him as the "Trojan Odysseus." So Odysseus didn't much care for Helenus (who was himself a twin), and when he later captured him, he tortured the Trojan prophet until he told him under what circumstances the Greeks could take Troy. So here we have spiritual twins as sworn enemies, much of it caused by circumstance and outside perception. And maybe that's the crux of the matter — comparisons that rankle.

Being a twin was a boon for childhood attentions, but it was a bit of a bane when it came to adolescent intentions. What do teenagers want most? Their own identity. And what do twins get least? Same thing. So I began to tire of being viewed as a tandem when friends called for social plans. I grew weary of having to explain to distant relatives or acquaintances that, no, I'm Brad, and he's Brian. I became frustrated at having my personality and behavior interpreted in a dual context, as if we were a two-headed entity with one brain and one life path. There came a time when our levels of individual success began to diverge. Sometimes he would shine; sometimes I would. But often the achievements would tend to be diminished by a small but significant sense of guilt.

So I began to rebel against my twin-ness. I moved into a separate bedroom. I gravitated to a sort of clique within our high school clique that allowed me to have the same group of friends as he, but different best friends. I began to cultivate character traits of my own, trying to stay true to myself but still keeping one eye on his personality for good measure. We would join our peers for some party or another, and people would joke that my brother and I never said a word to each other. There was some truth to it. I think we were both hoping for a temporary reprieve from the Brian-and-Brad Show.

When it was time to choose a college, the divide was nearly fully realized. Brian was bound for the University of Michigan, following in the footsteps of our father and joining about half of our closest friends in a maize-and-blue stampede. I wound up with a choice between two futures — one in Ann Arbor, the other in Ithaca. I can admit now that I was eager for the opportunity to reinvent myself as an individual instead of as one of a set. Many of the friends I found at Cornell didn't know that I was a twin at all, and that was fine with me. I wanted to exist, achieve, perhaps even aspire to the heroic without it being compared or contrasted or combined or confused.

Brian (left) and Brad, age four and not really conjoined

Eventually, we became recognized as two largely dissimilar people who happen to possess a few brotherly similarities. He is an accountant by trade and now a business owner — a number cruncher. I am a right-brained wordsmith who can spell *budget* but can't actually adhere to one. He lives with his wife and four kids in a grand house in suburban Chicago, a few miles from our childhood home. I live in a modest house in a quiet California town a few blocks from the ocean. I think the only comparisons these days are probably made by ourselves. I will admit that I envy his financial comfort; I suspect he is occasionally jealous of my lifestyle. But I think we're genuinely happy for each other — and perhaps glad to be rid of each other, too.

Of course, the gods have a sense of humor. For one thing, we both married women named Amy. In fact, both Amy Herzogs are from the same high school class (one year behind us) in our hometown. My Amy and I fell in love in high school; Brian started dating his Amy in college. But our weddings — on Memorial Day and Labor Day — bookended the summer of '93. People tend to find that funny. But, to be honest, I find it annoyingly twinlike. And I suspect our wives, who bristle at being called Amy No. 1 and Amy No. 2 (in whatever order), feel much the same way. Welcome to my world, I say.

Essentially, in my proximate world, I am not a twin — in the sense that nobody really knows it. Even our close friends in California have to be reminded on occasion. Most have never met my brother and know him only as the guy I point out in my family photos. Yet somehow, I still get confused for him all the time. It's eerie, actually. I'll pick up a prescription at a pharmacy and the bottle will say "Brian Herzog." I'll leave a work-related phone message and the person will call back asking for "Brian." I'll be introduced to someone at a cocktail party, and the next time they see me that evening they'll mistakenly call me . . . well, you know.

Somewhere Artemis and Apollo are having a good laugh.

I am now one hundred miles east of Bismarck, which John Steinbeck considered the midpoint of the American map, contending that each side of the Missouri River here may as well be a thousand miles apart. Geographically, I suppose I am nearly halfway through my expedition, but it doesn't seem that way. I feel as if I am gaining insight in small chunks — parts of the whole. But the sum of it all still eludes me and seems a long way off.

Talking to Amy on the phone the previous evening, I sensed a certain resignation in her voice, as if she was growing accustomed to being a single parent, as if she was beginning to realize that not having me around might be preferable to having both me and my periodic black cloud. I could hear voices in the background — my sons' high-pitched squeals — and I envisioned a horde of suitors come to court Penelope while Odysseus meanders. Neither could possibly fully understand the other's travails. So it is with Amy and me.

She wants to vent about the daily parenting gauntlet — about bedtime challenges and tantrums and allergies — while I search for ways to convey my mini-epiphanies about expectations and dedication, leadership and legacy. But we are immersed in such different worlds at the moment, and we each seek answers that the other can't possibly provide. I am fourteen days into my thirty-one-day challenge, and all I seem to have done so far is worry her. I shouldn't have told her about my precipice-hugging drive down to Troy and my comical paddle up the Missouri. So our phone conversations seem to include a lot of sighing.

"I love you," she said, in a voice that seems to suggest the need to remind both of us. And then she adds, "Don't do anything else stupid."

"You started it," I told her. "You married me."

I can't imagine that I might find many answers where I stand at the moment — beneath boulder-sized cement testicles. The testicles belong to a sixty-ton sculpture — twenty-six feet tall, forty-six feet long — standing atop a grassy hill in the city of Jamestown. It is the World's Largest Buffalo. Built in 1959 by a fellow named Harold Newman, a local merchant who envisioned an eye-catching tourist trap, it overlooks the comings and goings on I-94 like a sleepy-eyed version of the Colossus of Rhodes.

You can't blame North Dakota for trying some attention-grabbing tactics. Maybe the "Zip to Zap" would have worked if there had been more beer and blankets. Perhaps the rock obelisk marking the town of Rugby as the geographic center of North America might be a must-see landmark if it were someplace more appealing than the parking lot of a Conoco station in Rugby, North Dakota. And Lawrence Welk's birthplace near the hamlet of Strasburg could be a destination on par with Elvis Presley's Tupelo — if only the accordion were to make a comeback.

So why not the World's Largest Buffalo? The sculpture is part of an attraction featuring the National Buffalo Museum, as well as a herd of a few dozen bison transplanted from Theodore Roosevelt National

The World's Largest Buffalo in Jamestown, North Dakota

Park in 1991 and roaming some two hundred acres of pasture on either side of the interstate. Apparently there used to be a restaurant here that served buffalo burgers, which is a bit like offering deep-fried terrier at Westminster. It brings to mind the time when Odysseus's crew sealed their doom by feasting on the sacred cattle of Helios, god of the sun. After all, at least one resident of this buffalo herd is, indeed, considered sacred. Her name is White Cloud, and she is a rare albino bison with a snow-white coat and pink eyes. She was born in 1996 on a ranch north of Jamestown and has been leased to the museum nearly all her life.

Legend has it that long ago a traveling native war party happened upon a wide valley containing thousands of grazing buffalo (from the Greek *boubalos*, by the way, though *bison* is technically the proper term). In the midst of all this brownness they spied a beautiful white beast standing somewhat separate from the herd. This was interpreted as a sign of reverence for the creature, and the white bison became a symbol of peace, prosperity, and hope.

The animal's rarity alone is remarkable. Back in the days when the buffalo herds numbered in the tens of millions, the chances of spotting an albino calf were estimated at about one in ten million. Only a few thousand bison remained by 1925, and it was generally assumed that the recessive gene for a white coat had gone the way of the great herds, never to appear again. After all, half blind and conspicuous in a shiny white coat, they were predator magnets. I am reminded of a *Far Side* comic from several years ago, the one in which one buck points to a target-shaped mark on another buck's belly and says, "Bummer of a birthmark, Hal."

But by my way of thinking, conspicuousness isn't necessarily a bummer at all. As an adult, I have devoted a good portion of my energies to being a white buffalo. Emerson said, "Whoso would be a man, must be a nonconformist." I think I have adopted that as my mantra, probably to a foolish extent. It's not that I want to go live in the woods like Emerson's pal Thoreau. My life is hardly one of extremes. Still, I hold in high regard the idea of taking the road less traveled, and I occasionally even travel it. A therapist would likely attribute it to unresolved issues associated with being a twin. But as I examine my attitudes and search for an underlying motivator, I can only conclude that many of my choices stem from an occasionally fanatical fear of being just one of the herd.

It is said that White Cloud tends to stand alone, too, much like the original white bison of native legend. But I wouldn't know. I can't find her. A sign tells me, "The National Buffalo Museum is pleased to have White Cloud join the herd, which is not confined, but allowed to roam freely in the pasture as their heritage would dictate. That is why, on any given day, visitors may or may not be able to view White Cloud or the rest of the herd. We believe their heritage is sacred as is their right to roam."

Mine, too. It is why I went east to college instead of opting for a midwestern institution. It is why Amy and I spent that year on the road as newlyweds, embarking on what became a forty-eight-state home search. And it is why we went west, all the way to the Pacific, to launch a new phase in our lives amid entirely unfamiliar but spectacular surroundings. Hell, everybody I knew from high school seemed to be returning to Chicago to lay down new roots over old ones. How was I going to carve out an exceptional existence? So the Golden State shined like a seersucker suit amid a sea of khaki.

But if I am being honest here, my disdain for conformity tends to manifest itself primarily in petty, silly ways — mini rebellions against trends and traditions and accepted norms. So I shave only once a week, as if announcing my civil disobedience with stubble. And I keep odd hours, doing my best writing deep into the night, when the rest of the world seems asleep and I have a monopoly on inspiration. I tend to be the most underdressed person in any room, and I like to think that I am striking a blow against a fashion-obsessed society. But mostly it's because I prefer comfort over style — and because I am pretty sure that the one sport coat I own comes from the *Miami Vice* era.

If I see a group of people standing in line, my initial reaction is almost always scornful. They could be selling the Meaning of Life for ten cents per insight, and I would probably scoff, "Aw, it couldn't possibly be worth the wait." I do my best to stubbornly refuse the latest fads, rolling my eyes whenever I see someone endlessly fiddling with their wireless gadget of the moment or fighting for position to grab this year's hottest toy or doing Sudoku or the Macarena or whatever inanity has elbowed its way to the forefront of the public consciousness. And yet I love my TiVo, I bought my kids a Tickle Me Elmo, and I have seen nearly every episode of *American Idol*. And hell, I actually told a national television audience, "That's my final answer."

So I am a hypocrite. While I like to consider myself a bit of an antiauthoritarian maverick, maybe I am all talk. Maybe I am an iconoclast without a cause. You can't be truly revolutionary if you can pick Ryan Seacrest out of a crowd. In fact, if you ask my wife, she would probably tell you I am really not much of a rebel at all. She just considers me quirky. But at least that makes me special.

It is a terrifically blustery day, by far the windiest of my journey. After heading east about seventy miles on the interstate, I exit north onto Highway 18 and realize just how windy it is. Gusts of nearly fifty miles per hour are blowing from the west, and they had been giving me a good tailwind. But now they pound the sides of the Aspect as if directed by an angry Zeus himself. This makes me uneasy, mostly because of my destination.

I first get a glimpse of it from about ten miles away, a thin red-and-white-striped behemoth rising like a gigantic peppermint stick into the cement-colored sky. It is a TV tower — the KVLY-TV mast — and at 2,063 feet it is the tallest man-made, land-based structure in the world. I know, that sounds like a lot of qualifiers, but trust me: this thing is tall. It is taller than the combined height of the Great Pyramid, the Washington Monument, and the Eiffel Tower. It rises more than three times as high as the Space Needle. Supposedly, the only structure taller is the Petronius Platform in the Gulf of Mexico, 85 percent of which is underwater. Completed in 1963, the KVLY mast was assembled in thirty-three working days by an eleven-man crew. It contains two million feet of steel and cable — a true marvel of engineering. And all of this in North Dakota, where even four-story grain elevators are called prairie skyscrapers.

Even more remarkable is this: it isn't a tourist attraction. I see no signs directing me to the very thing that makes North Dakota stick out — quite literally. It is a nonpromoted superlative, an exclamation point without a sentence to lead you there. So I navigate by sight, the way Odysseus must have, only they didn't have TV towers in his day, which is probably why the ancient Greek Olympics got such poor Nielsen ratings. I veer onto an unmarked dirt road, past a nondescript farmhouse, and into a one-lane entranceway, stopping before a concrete block of a building fronting the massive antenna. Like life itself, this thing is simply too immense to take in from up close. Only distance brings perspective.

In fact, for me at least, standing beneath it brings only fear, mostly because of two pieces of information of which I am aware. The first is this: if an ironworker on the antenna dropped his wrench, it would be traveling at a speed of 260 miles per hour when it hit the ground. So immediately, I am tempted to search for wrench-shaped indentations in the muddy field around me. Although, really, wouldn't

it be wiser to search for ironworkers instead? The second factoid reveals that this antenna wasn't always the world's tallest. In 1974, eleven
years after the KVLY-TV mast was constructed, a radio mast was
built in Warsaw that surpassed North Dakota's landmark by fifty-
seven feet. But the Polish version collapsed seventeen years later, killing
three people, and thus it has been deservedly banished from the record
books.

So as I tilt my head toward the heavens and squint at the top of
this transmitting Titan, which seems to be swaying precariously in the
wind, only one thought comes to mind: These things fall down. I picture myself trying to outrun the calamity (a dubious proposition,
given my still-aching foot) or trying to guess in which direction it will
collapse, and it is an image that would only be fully realized if accompanied by the whimsical chase music from the old *Benny Hill Show*.

But maybe there is a lesson here, too: Even Titans get toppled.

X
deluge

Rumbling along Interstate 29, on North Dakota's eastern edge, I spot a large bird — a crow perhaps — on the shoulder of the road. As I pass, it launches itself skyward, and I notice that it has a large snake in its beak. From my late-night forays into the pages of Homer's epics, I know that this is nearly always a portent of things to come. Whether that is good or bad remains to be seen.

In the *Iliad*, the Trojans are about to burn the Achaean ships when they spot an eagle flying high above, holding in its talons a struggling serpent. The serpent curves its back and strikes the eagle in the breast, causing the bird to drop its prey among the crowd of soldiers. Polydamas, a cool-headed young Trojan commander, interprets this as a bad omen indeed. But Hector, Troy's mightiest warrior, scoffs at him for obeying the advice of a bird. Turns out Polydamas is right. Within days, Hector's lifeless body is dragged through the dirt behind Achilles's chariot.

In the *Odyssey*, as Telemachus (son of Odysseus) and Menelaus (king of Sparta) are saying their good-byes, an eagle swoops down with a white goose in its talons. Menelaus's wife — the incomparable Helen, herself — interprets this omen favorably, predicting that Odysseus will return home and conquer his wife's suitors as easily as the eagle has caught the goose. Later in that same chapter, Telemachus catches sight of a hawk carrying a dove, which is again construed positively. But still later, when Telemachus returns to Ithaka, his mother's suitors are musing on how best to eliminate him. Again, an eagle swoops down while holding a dove in its claws, and this is interpreted by one of the suitors as a sign that their scheme will not succeed.

So imagine my confusion upon seeing the bird-and-snake thing. Either my journey (however defined) is destined for completion (whatever that may mean) . . . or my grand plan is doomed to failure. It seems to me that it all depends on whether the gods are on my side. Meanwhile, the wind continues to gust furiously as I arrive in Grand Forks, and it does so all night, rocking the Aspect back and forth while I try in vain to sleep.

The people of Grand Forks know well the power of nature. In April 1997 the city was all but consumed by it — specifically by the Red River that gave it life in the first place. With the wind still blowing mightily the next day, I drive into the city, which seems nearly empty on this late Sunday morning. I stop at the corner of First Avenue and Third Street, where there stands a brick monument to the Great Flood of 1997.

The monument is 96.8 inches tall, which represents the record snow accumulation of 1996–97. Eight blizzards blanketed the entire Red River Valley, bringing three years' worth of snow in one winter. The National Weather Service warned of possible heavy spring flooding, so Grand Forks and East Grand Forks (in Minnesota) began raising the levees on each side of the river. Thousands of volunteers filled 3.5 million sandbags and expected the river's waters to be contained. But an early April blizzard brought heavy snow, subzero temperatures, and seventy-mile-per-hour winds. Sandbags froze. Power lines fell. Tens of thousands of residents lost electricity. As dire warnings continued, evacuations began — all of East Grand Forks and most of the 50,000 residents in Grand Forks, in what was then the largest evacuation of an American city since the Civil War.

Then the floods came. There are five flags flying over the Grand Forks monument. The city flag flies at 28 feet, marking the height of the flood stage of the Red River. Two state flags fly at 42 feet, the level when a flood emergency was declared. American and Canadian flags fly at 54.35 feet, the height of the river's crest. By April 19, 1997, all of East Grand Forks and half of Grand Forks were underwater.

Then high water descended into hell. Amazingly, at the height of the flood, a massive fire broke out, engulfing the Grand Forks Security Building, which is now the location of the monument. Firefighters did their best, but the hydrants were submerged, and floodwaters stalled fire trucks. The blaze burned for two days, destroying eleven buildings in the heart of Grand Forks. In all, the flood and fire severely damaged 80 to 90 percent of the city, leaving a stew of mud, sewage, oil, and animal carcasses in its wake. Schools were canceled for the rest of the semester. The building that housed the *Grand Forks Herald* was gutted, including the 120 years of history recorded in its archives. Not a single life was lost in the city. No one was even injured. Yet it was as if Grand Forks had the task — or perhaps the opportunity — of starting over from scratch.

Many of the world's ancient cultures tell stories of a Great Flood, a deluge of unprecedented proportions, perhaps associated with the melting of Ice Age glaciers before recorded history. Noah's Ark in the book of Genesis is only one of several such tales. In Hindu scriptures, Manu is the hero, having been cautioned (by an avatar of Vishnu in the shape of a fish) to build a boat. In Mayan mythology, an irate storm god named Huracan tries to wash away impudent humans. And in the Babylonian *Epic of Gilgamesh*, Utnapishtim is the lone survivor of a deluge. He is sought out by the wandering Gilgamesh, who believes the old coot knows the secret to immortality.

Of course, the Greeks had their legend, too. Like most flood myths, it begins with an irritated god. Zeus is so appalled by the cannibalism of the Pelasgians, the original inhabitants of Greece, that he lets loose a deluge to wash everything clean. What this story also has in common with the many others is a creature who represents a kind of mediator between the immortals and the earthbound. In this case, the Titan Prometheus (meaning "forethought," after all) has warned his son Deucalion to build and provision an ark. After a nine-day flood, Deucalion and his wife, Pyrrha (daughter of the infamous

Pandora), land safely on Mount Parnassus and commence repopulation — only they do it by throwing stones over their shoulders. His
rocks become men; hers become women.

These deluge tales are mythological markers, each Great Flood resulting in a blank slate — an opportunity to tell the tale of man's
modern genesis as apart from the story of creation. Joseph Campbell
described the deluge hero as "a symbol of the germinal vitality of
man, surviving even the worst tides of catastrophe and sin." But he also
wrote this: "The tendency has always been to endow the hero with extraordinary powers from the moment of birth. . . . The whole hero-
life is shown to have been a pageant of marvels with the great central
adventure as its culmination. This accords with the view that herohood is predestined, rather than simply achieved."

Nevertheless, catastrophes like the flood along the Red River
seem to turn the entire notion — the idea of a preordained heroic
mantle — on its head. I stroll ten yards from the monument to the
Great Flood and stare at a sculpture depicting people being helped

Part of the Grand Forks flood memorial

into a rowboat amid swirling waters — a metallic metaphor for the heroes of Grand Forks, most of whom were normal folks, not born to a higher calling yet answering the call when it came.

They were the volunteers who arrived in church vans and school buses and military vehicles. The utility workers who poured in from surrounding states, trying to keep the power on before the flood. The soldiers from Grand Forks Air Force Base who made eight thousand sandbags per hour, twenty-four hours a day, for nearly a week. The firefighters who battled the blaze and rescued forty apartment tenants who had not evacuated Grand Forks. The crew of nine US West Communications office technicians who barricaded themselves in the company's building, just one block from the raging fire, and worked tirelessly to maintain phone communication with federal, state, and local emergency officials. The National Guard troops who delivered food, clothing, and cots to them by boat. The anonymous "Angel of Grand Forks" (later revealed to be McDonald's heiress Joan Kroc) who donated $15 million to the flood victims. The editors and reporters of the *Grand Forks Herald*, who lost their building but realized that their newspaper was a lifeline for the community. Their coverage of the disaster would earn them the 1998 Pulitzer Gold Medal for Meritorious Service.

Heroes all, I say, including Mrs. Kroc.

I had discussed this sort of situational heroism with my Greek chorus in Olympia, and one member insisted that the quintessential hero is one without responsibility or societal expectations: "It's tougher for, say, a police officer to be a hero than for some citizen leaping into the breach. . . . It has to be something you do entirely voluntarily, where you could walk away from the situation and no one would say anything because they have no expectations. But if in those circumstances you did something extraordinary, then you would be a hero, at least in my book."

My book demands a bit less purity of motivation. I contend courage can be heroic, whether it's part of your job responsibility or not. However, if there were a sort of antithesis of Dante's circles of hell — call it gradations of heroism — I do agree that the innermost circle would be reserved for men and women who are gallant unexpectedly. So while the Grand Forks firefighters and soldiers did their jobs, and did them bravely, among the other standouts were newspaper editors, office technicians, and the wife of a guy who sold billions and billions of burgers. They all stepped up to the plate.

Not long ago, a fellow in New York City was celebrated nationwide for saving a teenager who suffered a seizure and fell onto a subway track moments before a train arrived. The hero, Wesley Autrey, a fifty-year-old African-American construction worker who was waiting with his two young daughters, jumped down and rolled with the young man into the trough between the rails as a southbound train roared in. Although the train's operator put the emergency brakes on, two cars passed over the men — with about two inches to spare. Unequivocally and entirely selflessly, he sacrificed his own well-being to save a stranger's life.

Up until then, Autrey's life had not been, in Campbell's words, a "pageant of marvels." He was not predestined for greatness at every turn. But his instincts would put Achilles to shame. And we love him for it. New York City breathlessly praised its paragon of virtue. Donald Trump handed him a $10,000 reward. TV talk shows booked him. But it wasn't fame or fortune that motivated him. And it wasn't any societal expectations. In fact, the expectations were his own. "I don't feel like I did something spectacular," he told the *New York Times*. "I just saw someone who needed help. I did what I felt was right."

I recall one member of my Greek chorus fearing that I was leaning toward defining our term too broadly: "If ten percent of the population is heroic, or twenty percent, what do we call that one person in a million who does something really extraordinary?"

His wife answered: "A superhero."

So it is that the press dubbed Wesley Autrey "Subway Superman."

A third chorus member continued: "It's pretty fascinating that we had to create a concept of a person who is so beyond what humans can do. Because I think the purpose of a hero is to inspire the rest of us jerks. We make a person a hero so we have a sort of idea of what we should aspire to."

I am no Superman, just the fellow who gushes about him. Mine is hardly a selfless profession (I am not averse to fame and fortune). I didn't necessarily make a heroic career choice. Still, I believe that if the situation were to arise, I would be up to the challenge. I feel that I have it in me. In fact, I *know* it. If heroism can be defined as the intersection of courage and circumstance, just give me the circumstance.

And maybe a life constructed out of heroic instincts — the Everyman with the potential for Superman surprises — is truly a heroic existence after all. It may simply be a matter of semantics, but I note that Campbell seemed to prefer the word *herohood* to *heroism*. To me, this implies not an active state, but a passive one. It is a state of being, not necessarily doing. He may have been implying that the hero is in the eye of the beholder. I mean, some misguided simpletons view Trump as a hero, which doesn't necessarily make him the least bit heroic. But I like to think that the state of being is a state of mind. You cannot be courageous in deed without first being courageous in thought, even if you are unaware of it until it happens.

XI

currents

I cross the Red River into Minnesota and set off east on Highway 2. The dark clouds above me are crowding each other. Northwest Minnesota calls itself the Land of the Dancing Sky, a nod to both its Native American history and the northern lights. But at the moment, the sky is brooding. It may be my mood, but there seems to be a gray tint to everything I see — the worn road, the fallow fields, the faded hay bales, the bark on the trees, the dirty roofs of barns and farmhouses, the mud mounds at construction sites, the telephone poles like a procession of leaning crosses. It is midday, and it looks like dusk. Spring in these parts is a recovery from winter.

Fifty miles on I reach a town called Mentor, a quiet hamlet of some 150 Minnesotans, most of them of Norwegian descent. The men who owned the land around here had names like Orval Sveningson and Gust Hangsleben. Why the town isn't named Odin or Loki or Thor is unclear. Mentor is a word that first appeared in the *Odyssey* as the name of an old friend of Odysseus, to whom he had entrusted his household when he sailed to Troy. Mentor is also one of several forms that the goddess Athena takes in her quest to assist both Odysseus and his son Telemachus through their journeys, so the word has come to mean a counselor or teacher. He is a hero's guide.

Campbell theorized that while earlier generations were guided by mythological symbols and spirits in their quests, contemporary unbelievers like myself essentially have to adventure alone. "This is our problem," he explained, "as modern, 'enlightened' individuals, for whom all gods and devils have been rationalized out of existence."

I decide to stop for lunch at the Lakeview Restaurant, about a mile south of the Mentor town center, along Maple Lake. As I chew on a cheeseburger called, regrettably, the Tidal Wave, I peer through a filthy window at a lake transformed by wind gusts into a froth of whitewater. Lugubriously, I am thinking about fate and chance and choices.

South for a spell, and then east again through the White Earth Indian Reservation and the county seat of Mahnomen, where the Shooting Star Casino beckons like a weary, middle-aged prostitute. This is an option for which I know the right decision but always make the wrong one. I choose to stop at the gaming tables for an hour, and as usual I am rewarded with lighter pockets and smoky clothes.

Back in the Aspect, and it seems as if I am surrounded by forest for the first time since western Montana. I had forgotten how beautiful the lakes and pine trees of the upper Midwest can be. This sort of landscape leads you to a totally different state of mind — in some ways, a more tentative one. The road no longer stretches out before me. There are sudden twists and curves. The way ahead is blind.

As I head east, the sun is growing late behind me, throwing long shadows in front of the Aspect — shadows that move from the shoulder to the center of the highway with every bend in the road. Just before I reach the town of Zerkel, a tiny bird crashes into my windshield, scaring the Hades out of me. Minutes later, a deer darts out in front of the Aspect, not ten feet ahead of me. I slam on the brakes, and somehow the animal manages to cross the highway without being fricasseed by an oncoming truck. Fate. Chance. Choices.

I finally arrive at my campground just before sundown. But before I set up camp, I follow the signs to a specific turnoff and walk about a quarter-mile until I come to a pine-ringed lake feeding into a tiny stream. Amid the Land of Ten Thousand Lakes, this is actually one in a million — Lake Itasca, generally accepted as the headwaters of the Mississippi River.

After Hernando de Soto discovered the great river in 1541, it took nearly three centuries for someone to find its true source. Henry Schoolcraft Rowe is credited with the discovery, although he relied on a Chippewa guide. As often happens in such cases, the guide's name — anyone ever heard of Ozawindib?—has been all but lost to history. Meanwhile, Rowe didn't much care for the Chippewa name of the lake (Omushkos), so he named it himself. He combined parts of two Latin words — *veritas* (meaning "truth" and *caput* (meaning "head") — to form Itasca. Which, if you think about it, is a pretty strange thing to do. Frankly, I would much prefer visiting Lake Caput.

Lake Itasca State Park was created in 1891, but even forty years later the park superintendent described it as "a swampy, muddy and dirty sight . . . not becoming to such a great river." So the Civilian Conservation Corps stepped in, filling in swamp areas, constructing parking lots, planting trees, building a rock dam, and turning the Mississippi's headwaters into the kind of gently gurgling wonder most of us would hope to find. Though by the looks of it — I am standing before a stream perhaps twenty feet wide, gurgling as best it can — calling this a river is stretching it a bit. Still, this is a momentous beginning, the start of a ninety-day, 2,552-mile journey to the Gulf of Mexico.

Here, in fact, there is a choice. A log bridge laid across the stream allows visitors to cross the Mississippi in ten easy steps. But I have something else in mind. I remove my shoes, roll up my pants, and cautiously make my way from one side to the other across a series of slippery rocks. Admittedly, it is a silly thing to do, sort of like yelling "Echo" in a canyon. But it is immensely satisfying.

If it is a somewhat childish act, it is also an apt one. Upon first discovering the Mississippi, de Soto named it Rio de Espiritu Santo — River of the Holy Spirit. And it is an allegory for life, no? Emerson once wrote that "the river makes its own shores, and each legitimate idea makes its own channels." Life is so easy to navigate at the beginning. As youths, we go largely on instinct. But as adults, we are forced to make choices. Challenges that could have been met

Where the Mississippi River begins—at Lake Itasca

much earlier become fed by great torrents of doubt and grow into something overwhelmingly imposing. We launch our journey as innocents — heroic, perhaps, in our purity. But our innate goodness is muddled by tributaries of fear and pride and greed and insecurity, mixing with morality and responsibility and other streams of higher consciousness. We encounter obstacles — the metaphorical equivalent of eddies, rapids, obstructions barely submerged. At times, we change direction, though often at a glacial pace. Often, we loop back on ourselves, revisiting decisions. We develop depth (and width) gradually. By the time it is all over, Zeus willing, we are figuratively broad and impressive, if tired and murky.

All of which is to say I took great pleasure in crossing Old Man River in its infancy. Why? It is a reminder of simplicity. As Mark Twain once wrote, in *Life on the Mississippi*, "Plain questions and plain answers make the shortest road out of most perplexities."

In the morning, the winds are gone, and so are the gray skies. Southward on Highway 71, I am drenched in sun and serenity and surrounded by great fields of dandelions. They gather in clumps and convene in odd geometrical patterns like floral constellations. *There's Perseus and Pegasus and Orion.* They curve around driveways and crowd the highway. They circle collapsed barns and peek out from beneath farm implements. The beautiful weed is everywhere, like a magnificent yellow explosion.

I imagine myself in the land of the lotus-eaters, the race of people whom Odysseus and his crew encounter, probably on an island near North Africa. The island is brimming with lotus fruits and flowers, which have a narcotic effect, causing Odysseus's men to want only to munch some more and linger forever in a blissful haze. However, Odysseus forces the men back to the ships, just in time to encounter the land of the Cyclops. Talk about a buzz-kill.

At the intersection of Highway 29, a choice. I have heard of a town in west-central Minnesota that sounds like something out of a drug-fueled dream, where there are watermelons as big as Volkswagens and insects as large as poodles and bathtub-sized coffee cups suspended in midair. The detour will take me a couple dozen miles in the wrong direction, but I wager it may be worth it.

A half hour later I arrive. WELCOME TO VINING, DOORWAY TO THE LAKES, says the sign. POPULATION 68, says another. I stop to fill up at Big Foot Gas and Grocery, which is fronted — the tales were true!— by a sculpture of an enormous cup suspended by a stream of coffee. It looks as though it is being poured by an invisible giant. Next to the gas station is Nyberg Park, which I can only describe as a sort of psychedelic sculpture garden. There are about a dozen oversize creations here — an immense watermelon being sliced by a knife as big as a canoe, a colossal set of pliers, a massive square knot, a giant elk, a huge potted cactus. There is also a green alien scratching his head, as if to say, "Where the hell am I?" Two sculptures actually stand out precisely because they aren't bizarre. One, in the middle of the park, depicts a man welding. The other is a life-sized astronaut planting a flag. There is a sign: VINING HONORS KAREN NYBERG, ASTRONAUT.

A quarter-mile up the road, not far from the twenty-foot-tall

clothespin looking down on the tiny Vining post office, I realize that
the Big Foot gas station wasn't named after the elusive Sasquatch.
Rather, I come upon a truly big foot — with a slightly raised and apparently swollen big toe. Here, a sign explains all: "Ken Nyberg built
this 1,200-pound, 12-foot-high human foot out of ten-gage steel in
1988. 'I just thought Vining should have something different,' he says.
Nyberg, a welder and former construction foreman, creates his unique
sculptures from leftover scrap metal he hauls from job sites to his
workshop. . . . Why does he do it? 'It's fun,' Nyberg says. 'I get to
choose what I do and when and how long I work on things. What
can be better than that?'"

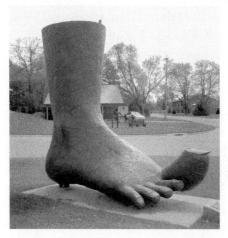

Ken Nyberg's first completed sculpture in Vining, Minnesota

Amen, I say. I ask around where I can find this Hephaestus of the
Heartland, and I am directed to his workshop about a mile up the
road, the one featuring a one-ton doorknob mounted on an equally
large door remnant. As I meet sixty-seven-year-old Ken Nyberg, now
retired, he is putting the last bit of primer on an only slightly oversize sculpture of a raven. He turns out to be an amiable fellow with
a fringe of white hair and smiling eyes.

"Nobody knew what I was doing for a few years," he tells me. "I was working still, then I'd come here for an hour or two. When I was finished, I'd cover it up."

I nod, but I wonder about the inspiration for his first creation. "Why a huge foot?"

He wipes his hands on a rag and shrugs. "Why not?"

This is more of a hobby than a business, he explains, though he has been commissioned to produce a handful of creations through-out the region — a huge stethoscope at the clinic in Henning, an otter in Ottertail, even (to my delight) a Spartan warrior on the grounds of Minnesota State Community and Technical College, "Home of the Hustling Spartans."

"I'm still curious," I admit to him, "how you wake up one day and say, 'You know, today I think I'll start work on a twenty-foot clothes-pin.'" And then I realize it's like asking Picasso why he put the nose over there.

He shrugs again. "I can't really explain it. Right now, I don't know what I'm going to make next. When the time comes, it's whatever feels good that day."

Ken appreciates the great gift of retirement — the fact that life presents him with options now, instead of responsibilities. The choices are his. So if he chooses to spend his days constructing the World's Largest Doorknob, who is to say the effort isn't a superlative of its own? Certainly not Vining, which is now on the map — or at least in the pages of Roadside America guides — thanks to Ken Nyberg's for-ays into whimsy.

Among Ken's proudest creations, however, is the astronaut. Not the one in the park — the real one, his daughter. As children, many of us announce we are going to be astronauts — a term derived from Greek words meaning "space sailors." Karen meant it. In high school, where she excelled in science and math, her classmates would sign her yearbook with phrases like "Good luck in space" and "See you on the moon!" She went to college in Grand Forks, graduating summa cum laude with a mechanical engineering degree from the University of North Dakota. She earned a master's degree and a Ph.D. from the

University of Texas and became an expert in human temperature reg-
ulation in space suits. Soon after earning her doctorate, Karen made
the cut as a mission specialist in NASA's 2000 class of astronauts,
one of only three women among the group of seventeen.

"It's kind of a funny feeling really," says Ken, who can't quite put
into words his boundless pride. "It's just so rare. You can think of a
pro football player, for example. Very few of them make it. But it's still
many compared to . . ." He lets his voice trail off and then tries to explain that since the first woman cosmonaut in 1962, there have been
only fifty-four female astronauts. "That's a pretty small percentage of
the world population," he says, and there seems to be awe in his voice
that a welder who has spent nearly all of his life in Otter Tail County
could raise a daughter who plans to explore beyond the stratosphere.
No wonder Ken made that astronaut sculpture in Nyberg Park to
scale. In his mind, she is already larger than life.

"It's a pretty dangerous endeavor," says Ken, "and the speed
they're traveling is absolutely unbelievable. They say that a bullet
coming out of an MI rifle goes about three thousand feet per
second. That thing," says Ken, pointing skyward, "is about eight times
faster — five miles per second."

My generation knows well the perils. Every generation has its
horrific historical touchstone, its where-were-you-when moment. Pearl
Harbor. JFK. September 11. For men and women of a certain age —
say, late thirties and early forties — the explosion of the space
shuttle *Challenger* was a jolt of reality. I was not yet eleven months old
when Neil Armstrong made his lunar leap (my mother claims she
plopped my brother and me in front of the TV, so we could say we
saw it). I was only four when NASA abruptly cancelled the Apollo
program, sending the last pair of astronauts to the moon. Over the
next decade and a half space exploration faded from the forefront of
public perception. Say "historic moonwalk," and people my age tend
to think of Michael Jackson busting a move on a Motown twenty-fifth
anniversary television show in 1983. NASA was still moving onward
and upward. But somehow, the notion of rocketing into the heavens

became anachronistic, almost quaint. Astronauts? Those were the guys who made occasional appearances on *Brady Bunch* reruns, along with the likes of Davy Jones and Don Drysdale. And they were most certainly guys.

Then in January 1986, they were sending a teacher into space — a lady teacher! She was exactly as old as I am now. But back then, I was seventeen and smitten by the possibilities of new frontiers, by the marvel that a simple science teacher from New Hampshire could be part of a crew aiming for the stars. Only CNN carried the launch as it happened, but NASA had arranged a special broadcast of the mission into television sets in schools. So a good portion of the people who were viewing it live consisted of students. I watched the launch at my high school. I saw the rocket blast off and blaze into the late-morning sky. And then a flash and that sickening split and arcs of flame, and for a moment all was confusing and surreal. I recall Christa McAuliffe's parents, standing on the viewing stand, pointing heavenward, as yet unaware of the tragic implications. I remember a pause, followed by a numb announcement: "Obviously, a major malfunction . . ." And the image of that Y-shaped smoke plume is burned into my brain.

For me and many in my generation — too young to remember the Apollo 13 drama or the Apollo 1 fire — this was our first confrontation with disaster in the pursuit of physical and intellectual frontiers. For those of us on the cusp of adulthood for whom a rocket launch was a metaphor for our aspirations, it was a confidence-shaking moment. Later, when we were young parents, the September 11 attacks would lead us to question what kind of world our children were entering. But as teenagers, the fate of *Challenger* suggested that our greatest challenge might be to avoid a cruel fate. John Lennon aside, this was really our first public encounter with the death of a hero. Indeed, when I consider some of what might be considered heroic archetypes — let's call them the Innocent, the Seeker, the Sage, the Caregiver, the Cowboy — I realize that Christa McAuliffe was all of them rolled into one. "I touch the future," she said. "I teach."

Karen Nyberg was a teenager then, too, fascinated by space exploration. I can only imagine how her heart must have raced when she saw a female high school teacher blasting off and how her heart must have broken in the aftermath. But maybe, while I was staggered, she was somehow inspired. Indeed, Karen was inspired enough that in June 2008, she was part of a seven-member crew on a fourteen-day mission aboard NASA's space shuttle *Discovery*. Perhaps someday she will visit the McAuliffe Crater on the moon.

On Ken Nyberg's desk is an autographed picture of Karen in her NASA uniform. "I guess I probably wasn't a real good example," Ken says. "I just worked construction, just worked all the time." Ken was helping to raise six children. He seems to be apologetic about his parenting, but minutes later he admits he took Karen flying as a child, soaring above Otter Tail County in the calm early morning, usually in a Cessna 150. I can imagine a little girl's epiphany above the lakes of rural Minnesota.

And this is my mission, my thoughts turning to my own children as they launch their own journeys. My goal as a father is to fuel passions — to enable their inspiration. They don't have to yearn for the stars. Maybe they will want to be forensic pathologists or firefighters or sports historians or robot designers or cartoonists or ice cream inventors or — may the muses be with them — storytellers. I don't care what their passion is, as long as it is something. And my hope is that, instead of falling into a career, they will pursue one — eagerly, resolutely, perhaps even heroically.

Again, it comes down to choices. I want them to choose a life, rather than life choosing for them. I want to serve as a mentor in the Homeric sense of the word — guiding them in their journey, whether they recognize that I am or not. And if I can't be a source of such inspiration, at least maybe I can manage to not screw it up.

When Campbell suggested that perhaps motherhood could be construed as heroic, he may have been talking about the actual act of giving birth. Still, I would add fatherhood, too. Parenthood is nothing if not an act of courage and selflessness and devotion to something greater than oneself. Campbell pointed to five elements generally found during the heart of the heroic journey: the Challenges, the Abyss, the Transformation, the Revelation, and the Atonement. To me, that sounds like a typical weekend with a couple of preschoolers.

Those who suggest that responsibility precludes heroism would argue that a parent is only doing what society expects. But there are plenty of people who aren't good parents. In fact, lots of folks aren't parents at all. And maybe *that* was my heroic choice. I guess what I am saying is this: Ken Nyberg may have constructed a monument to his daughter, who has told reporters, "I was born to be an astronaut." But someone raised her with an understanding that she could shoot for the moon.

XII

silent siren

One of the most ubiquitous characters in the Homeric epics is Dawn — the goddess Eos, daughter of Earth and Heaven. She is mentioned more than a dozen times in the *Iliad* and at least four dozen times in the *Odyssey* — nearly every morning, in fact. Dawn rose from her bed . . . Dawn of the saffron cloak . . . Dawn of the yellow robe . . . Young Dawn . . . Divine Dawn . . . Fair-haired Dawn . . . Rosy-fingered dawn . . .

Not long after daybreak I am camped on a stool in the Pour House, a sports bar and café in the center of Siren, Wisconsin, some twenty miles east of the Minnesota border. Settled by Swedish immigrants in the 1880s, the town was originally named for the abundant flowers in the area. It was called Syren, the Swedish word for lilac. And in fact, there is a Lilac Festival here every spring. But as so often happens, Old World sensibilities were Americanized. The spelling was incorrectly corrected.

"Before I ever moved here, I remember seeing stories about Siren on the Weather Channel," says the bartender, a young fair-haired woman who moved here only a couple of months earlier. She hands me a BLT, then climbs onto a step stool to retrieve a framed newspaper clipping hanging high above the bar. "Tornado Anniversary Edition," it says. June 17, 2002. "A year ago," the article begins, "terror came out of the sky. . . ."

The photos are startling. A street brimming with toppled and decapitated trees. A snapshot of the Pour House, its roof opened like a sardine can, a wall caved in, a car upturned on the front walkway. There are "after" pictures, too — not after the storm but after the rebuilding effort, and you wouldn't know that terror had visited at all. I look around me — at the pool tables and dartboards and pennants and forlorn-looking men nursing beers — and the scene looks timeless, eternal. But this is apparently version 2.0. According to the newspaper clipping, the actual bar in the (new, improved) Pour House is constructed of cross-sections of trees downed by the tornado. As I scribble notes into a tiny notebook, the bartender keeps glancing over at me.

"What're ya doin'?"

I sigh, never quite sure how to respond. "I'm on a bit of a journey." Then I embark on a long-winded account of Homer's epic stories of original heroes. I tell her about the Sirens, those minor goddesses whose seductive singing lured sailors to their deaths on the rocky shores of their tiny island. And when I finish, I am confident that my small-town bartender has found some enlightenment amid the dim tavern.

She smiles. "I just finished reading the *Iliad*," she says, and then she moves down the length of the bar, running a wet rag over the dark wood, leaving me to sit there with my mouth slightly agape and my preconceptions askew.

"What's your name?" I call after her, wondering if perhaps the coincidence might be cosmic. Helen, maybe? Penelope?

"Dawn," she shouts over her shoulder.

I should have figured.

Welcome to siren: a place for all seasons, says the highway sign, in pretty lavender and green lettering, followed by another: siren: pop. 988.

"There's actually one thousand and seventy-nine," says Sheriff Dean Roland, as we rumble over the town line in his squad car. And then he chuckles. "They don't have enough money to pay for a new sign."

Dean was chief of police when the tornado hit and has since been elected sheriff of Burnett County. He has offered to take me on a tour of the region and the twister tale. This is my first time in a police cruiser, and it is a relief to be in the front seat.

"No one was working that day because I was on vacation," he says. He is in his early fifties, with a sheriff's badge over his heart on his short-sleeved uniform shirt, a pen in his breast pocket, and a thick mass of white hair on his head. "I had just come back from seeing the movie *Shrek*. It was hot, humid, muggy. I went home and turned on the news while I paid my bills and said, 'I've got to go to work. I've got to let people know.' Then when I heard it was on the ground, that's when I started going nuts, telling people to take cover."

The Siren tornado arrived several years before me — on June 18, 2001 — but it took much the same route into town, along Highway 70, starting in Minnesota. In Wisconsin, it first touched down just east of the St. Croix River, which serves as the state border, in the hamlet of Grantsburg (whose most famous citizen, a seven-foot-six fellow who served as the town marshal and lamplighter a century ago, was ironically known as "Big Gust"). The tornado then roared through the unincorporated hamlets of Alpha and Falun, reaching Siren just before nightfall.

In the *Odyssey*, Homer describes the wicked Sirens, "who bewitch everyone who comes near them. If any man draws near in his innocence and listens to their voice, he never sees home again, never again will wife and little children run to greet him with joy." Forewarned of the danger, Odysseus orders his men to tie him to the mast of the ship, allowing him to hear their song while being unable to leap to his death in pursuit of it. So it is a passage about Sirens and forced inaction.

The town of Siren experienced much the opposite. Remarkably, although there is a warning siren here, mounted on a pole in the center of town, it had been struck by lightning and severely damaged a few weeks earlier — more proof that Zeus is a sardonic bastard. The broken siren was so old that replacement parts weren't available. An appointment with a representative from FEMA (to discuss funding for a new warning system) had been scheduled for June 21 — three days after the tornado struck. So it was left to people like Dean Roland to sound the alarm.

"I used my PA system, lights, siren, yelling, telling everyone there was a possible tornado coming. I had about a twenty-minute warning," he recalls. "The tornado was rain-wrapped. You couldn't see it. And when I finally did see the tornado coming out of the dark cloud, and I heard what sounded like the roar of a jet, I was only about a quarter-mile away. I tried to get to my house, but I couldn't make it. So I went around the corner and parked beneath an awning at the center of town." He shakes his head and rubs his hand through his thick hair, as he pulls the car to a stop at that exact spot. "At the time I remember thinking, 'Oh, my God, I forgot to take care of me.'"

It sounds like an Emersonian moment, in the sense that Ralph Waldo claimed that a hero is no braver than an ordinary man — he is simply braver five minutes longer.

"Two big Dumpsters came flying at me. I watched a church pulsate — I mean, the whole building was pulsating. Trees were exploding. Roofs were coming off. And I just sat through it. There was a brief calm when it was right in the eye of the tornado. I went from total fear, saying, 'God, don't let me die' to 'Wow, this is beautiful.' And then it picked up again."

All around him, there was chaos. A bartender in the Pour House stepped outside the front door and was immediately swept off his feet, spending the next several minutes horizontal, having grabbed a man in front of him, who in turn had grabbed something secure. Another fellow would later tell of clutching a pole in his yard, the winds pulling him straight out as if he were a flag in a stiff breeze. He hung there and watched as his barn exploded and his cows flew over his silo.

In just over an hour on the ground, the tornado, swirling at speeds upward of two hundred miles per hour, left behind a path of devastation as much as a half-mile wide and forty-one miles long — an estimated $17 million in damage. As one local student later described it in an essay, "It looked like a T-Rex came through Siren." In recent years, the town had made significant efforts toward recasting itself as a tourist destination, building two new hotels, gift stores, an indoor ice rink, a movie theater. Then it was gone. The skating arena was destroyed. The movie theater collapsed. Trees that had survived a century were snapped to pieces in seconds. Whole sections of forest were sheared off like so much stubble. Boats were tossed and flipped and twisted into unrecognizable shapes.

A memorial to the tornado's power in Siren, Wisconsin

The sheriff drives me to a spot near the corner of highways 70 and 35, where one boat remains wrapped around a tree in the heart of town like a grotesque memorial.

"As soon as it cleared, I went to my house to see if my wife was okay," Dean says, and we drive a couple of blocks farther, stopping in front of a large white Dutch colonial, neat and tidy and once surrounded by a dozen and a half mature trees. The Roland home, which also serves as Lilac Village Bed and Breakfast, run by Dean and his wife, Shelly, received more than $50,000 in damage. But he arrived to find his wife at the back door, on the phone with her frightened mother, whose house had also been hit.

"How's the town?" Shelly asked.

"I think it's gone," Dean replied.

"Then I took off. When I got to the Holiday gas station, I could see total devastation. That's when I said to the dispatcher, 'Send ambulances, fire, police, paramedics, national guard. I need all the help I can get.' And then I started grabbing people who had come out of buildings. I said, '*You* go set up a command post at the grocery store. *You* go to the doctor's office. *You* go to the clinic. *You* go to the pharmacy . . .' With everything that was down, I anticipated dozens dead. They were my neighbors, my friends," he says, and then he shakes his head in wonder. "But they just started showing up. They would hop out of buildings that were devastated. We had a triage set up at the market, and I would come back every forty-five minutes and ask, 'How many injured? How many dead?' They would say, 'None. Just a couple of minor injuries.' So we searched all the houses and everything three times that night. And everything was fine. We didn't lose a single life."

Three people did perish that day — all outside the village of Siren. Two died during the storm; a third was in a fatal ATV accident immediately following it. About a dozen people were injured in all. Siren lost its village but not its villagers.

"It was truly a miracle," says Dean. "There were a number of people at the Dairy Queen who were herded into the freezer. And at the last minute, they got taken out of the freezer and into the cooler. We've never found the freezer. Never found it."

The challenge of leadership in a time of crisis, of course, is that the decisions are yours. It sounds paradoxical, actually — the risks of control. And in the midst of calamity, the risks are far more than just the threat of appearing incompetent. You can save lives, yes. But what if you fail?

"Before the tornado hit, during the warnings, I had sent six people into the Auto Stop gas station," says Dean. "And it was just gone. It was as flat as a pancake. I started crying. I thought I'd killed six people. There was just one bathroom standing, and I yelled, 'Is anyone in here? Is anyone all right?' And the bathroom door opens, and six people say, 'Can we come out now?' I hugged every one of 'em."

Stories that emerged in the tornado's aftermath merely added to its legend. Records from the Siren Dental Clinic were found more than twenty-five miles east in the town of Spooner. The sign from the Auto Stop was deposited in Trego, some thirty miles away. One young student's school picture — which had been in a frame on the family's piano — was discovered eighty miles away in the hamlet of Cable. More than 175 buildings were destroyed, turned into piles of rubble and scattered possessions.

The sheriff takes me along a back road to a large house — about a mile outside of town — that hasn't yet been repaired. "This was a gorgeous place. There used to be a barn, a wrap-around porch, fruit trees," he says. "The family was in the little root cellar, and as the guy went to shut the door, the wind came up and blew the door right out of his hand. He just held on so he didn't get sucked out."

The house that I see now is a shell of a place. An entire side of the building has collapsed, so that it looks a bit like an open doll-house. The floors are covered with chunks of ceiling plaster. Every window is blown out, shards of glass still clinging to the frames. And there are nails everywhere, hundreds of them, long spikes popped from the walls and discarded into sad piles. "That was the biggest problem after the tornado," says Dean. "Punctured tires, people stepping on nails, nails everywhere."

But as we drive back into the center of town, you wouldn't know disaster had struck here. It feels whole, a normal smattering of supermarkets and day-care centers and pizza parlors and body shops and mini golf courses, as if the tornado left a scar that was once red and raw but has faded so much that it has become nearly imperceptible.

"Right after the tornado, you could see the path quite nicely,"

Dean explains. "But it's pretty much grown back up now. Everything's pretty much cleaned up. Another year or two, and you won't be able to tell anything happened." He pauses for a moment before adding, "And that's okay. The first couple years, on the anniversary, we celebrated it. We all got together and had a community dinner. Last year, we didn't. We're moving on. You never want to forget it, because that's history. It's who you are. It's what shaped you. But you don't want to live in the past. You want to take that foundation and build on it."

"I had every intention of being a music teacher," says Dean, as we roll into a lakeside park in the center of town, where there is a memorial to the tornado. Dean grew up in southern California, the son of a landscaper, and earned a degree in music education, singing and playing drums to pay his way through college. But then he joined a cop, an old high school friend, on a ride-along over Thanksgiving weekend. "I just got hooked," he says. "Every day is different. No two calls are the same. You have to use creativity, imagination, self-reliance. I've just been fascinated with this job for twenty-nine years. What I love most about this is the sense of pride when somebody gets their property back or when somebody who was beat up or raped gets justice — that sense of being able to restore their dignity."

The sheriff will tell you that the tornado brought out the best in people. Indeed, anecdotes about fortitude and rectitude abound. Siren experienced the same stampede of volunteers that had followed the Grand Forks flood — youth groups from Minnesota, a dozen members of the St. Croix tribe who arrived with chain saws, two dozen folks from the city of Comfrey, Minnesota (which had itself been devastated by an earlier twister). An eight-year-old boy arrived at the Salvation Army distribution center with sixty-five dollars in a white envelope marked "donation money." The town buoyed itself with an air of hopefulness, evident in the graffiti scrawled on boarded-up buildings ("We'll be back — but better") and in the T-shirts that sprouted up, announcing, "We've Spun Forward."

"There was one guy in town who hated his neighbor, always

fought with him. I was there for domestics all the time," says Dean, as he drives me through the countryside, where the tornado dipped lower and where the oaks and poplars and birch trees are shaved off closer to the ground or uprooted completely or tilted eastward like a parade of commuters leaning against the wind. "When I got to this guy's house, it was flattened. He's about six-foot-four. He came out, gave me a big hug. He was crying, and he said, 'Dean, I've lost everything.' Then he picks up his chain saw, starts it up, and says, 'Well, I gotta go help my neighbor. He's lost a lot, too.' "

So this is the cliché about tragedy eliciting virtue, how an innate sense of righteousness rises to the top when life is suddenly prioritized and made precious. Surely this is why heroic tales tend to sprout from the rubble of calamity. Then again, in the storm's aftermath, Siren's former chief of police also watched the vultures descend — the people looting stores for videos and cigarettes, the bogus cleaning operations, the insurance scams. Such is the dichotomy of the life of a cop. Your day-to-day existence is peppered with the extremes of human behavior — the grateful and the hateful, the blameless and the shameless. And the interactions with bad eggs far outnumber the good, which is why I believe law enforcement is, in general, a valiant choice.

Dean deservedly received several awards for his efforts. But I wonder if evaluation of such actions is dependent on results. Is it enough to simply answer the call to run into a burning building or pull the trigger of a gun? Or is it the outcome that defines heroism? Dean says he ran into a burning building once. He was overcome by the smoke within seconds of entering the door and wound up being rushed to the hospital. His appraisal: "Well, that was dumb." And what if you shoot your gun once in your career, as Dean admits he did, but it is aimed at an attack Doberman during a drug raid . . . and you and your partner go back and forth, like some comic Starsky & Hutch banter, about who should pull the trigger . . . and you finally screw up the courage to do it . . . and you are inches away . . . and . . . "I missed," says Dean, allowing a smile.

Sheriff Dean Roland

I again recall the contention from a member of my Greek chorus: "It's tougher for, say, a police officer to be a hero than for some citizen leaping into the breach." It isn't exceptional, he claimed, if it is your job. But isn't there gallantry in the choice — the decision to handle the lowlifes that *somebody* has to deal with, to never quite be off duty, to have all eyes turn to you at a time of crisis, to wear a uniform that elicits the gamut of visceral responses?

"The majority of cops say they get into it to help people, and I think that's pretty sincere," says Dean. "But for a lot of them, the cynicism takes over. When you're working dope, for example, you soon start to believe that your family might be involved or your friends or your neighbors. Because that's all you see, day in and day out. That's why the bed and breakfast is a good thing in my life — because I see the good side of people. In law enforcement, ninety-five percent of our time is dealing with three or four percent of the population. We forget that ninety-six percent of the population is good."

He says this, and I wonder if my career choice has been one of selective encounters. I began my career as a straight journalist — a newspaper reporter — but left the fold quickly, largely because I didn't want to be beholden to someone else's agenda. I wanted to pursue my own stories, inject my own sensibilities. To some extent, I wanted to chronicle a world of my own making.

So now I can decorate my days comfortably, choosing, if I so desire, to live in a rose-colored bubble where every subject I pursue possesses a glistening subtext of inspiration or perseverance. I can shine a spotlight on the deserving and the overlooked. And I have the luxury of balance. For every serious issue I tackle, I can follow it up by setting a course for whimsy. So after writing about civil rights martyrs or medical fraud, I can pen an ode to college fight songs or Pez dispensers. As deep as I may delve into weighty concepts, I can always come up for air.

Dean Roland doesn't get to pick and choose. The world comes to him, for better or for worse, sometimes at two hundred miles per hour.

Back in 1997, when he had only been chief of police for about eighteen months, Dean woke up in the hospital. He figured he had either been in a car accident or had been shot. Turns out he had suffered a grand mal seizure. He had a brain tumor. Doctors gave him less than a month to live unless they operated. They weren't sure he would survive.

"When we came home from the hospital, it was almost midnight," Dean recalls. "I was dead tired and I told my wife, 'Just take me home.' But she said, 'I have to take you through town.'"

Dean's wife, Shelly, grew up in Siren. In fact, she was once named Miss Siren in a local pageant. But Dean was the outsider, the police chief who rode in from the West, having worked as a patrol officer in Los Angeles County and an undercover narcotics detective in Idaho.

"So I didn't think people much cared for me. But Shelly said, 'I want to show you something.' We drove through town, and on every marquee was "Get back to work soon, Dean" and "We miss you.""

Then we got back to my yard, and I have a picket fence. On every single picket was a yellow ribbon—"Get back soon" and "Hurry back"—all around my big oak trees and maple trees. Ribbons, everywhere. It was an emotional thing to me that I had been accepted by this town. So it almost became expected of me to do what I did during the tornado because they knew I cared about them."

It is a moment of which I dream, a George Bailey moment in which a lifetime of endeavor crystallizes into a gathering of appreciation — a confirmation that yours has been a life well lived. Most all of us like to think that our efforts constitute a credit in the universal ledger, that we are on some sort of heroic journey, but on occasion it would be nice to receive a hero's welcome.

The sheriff just shrugs. "People seem to be very pleased with me, but that can change in a heartbeat. Something else can happen, and tomorrow I might be a bum."

XIII

nebagamon

Two counties up from Siren, along a pine-lined ribbon of road known as Highway B, I arrive at what was always one of the most satisfying sights of my childhood — a simple yellow light hanging alongside the highway and flashing intermittently. And next to it, a yellow sign with blue lettering: CAMP NEBAGAMON FOR BOYS.

My friends in California, who never had the opportunity to attend sleepaway summer camp, don't seem to understand the grip it can have on one's sense of self. It is difficult for most of them to conceive of sending their children away for eight weeks, as my parents did every summer for six summers beginning when I was nine years old. And if they do send their kids to camp, they generally choose one close to home — not like my annual journey of a flight to Minneapolis and a three-hour bus ride into the northwestern corner of Wisconsin.

But that was the point. Summer camp was a trip outside my insular box, a paddle away from the mainstream. I was from Chicago, but my cabinmates were from Atlanta, Memphis, Dallas, Cincinnati, St. Louis. I had counselors from Milwaukee and Detroit and Denmark and Northern Ireland. I learned how to put up a tent, chop wood, string a bow, cast a fishing line. Because of this excursion into the exotic, rather than despite it, Camp Nebagamon became, in many ways, my psychic home. My memories of my childhood tend to be rather sparse, but the most vivid of them are set not in the suburban enclave in which I spent four-fifths of my existence but rather during those fleeting but wondrous summers in the North Woods.

The camp began in 1928, when a broad-shouldered fellow named Max "Muggs" Lorber — a former three-sport star at Indiana University — purchased seventy acres of land on the shores of Lake Nebagamon (*nebagamon* is a Chippewa term for "hunting deer from the lake by fire," although my father always told me it meant "peeing over the side of a canoe"). In 1929, forty-seven campers and fifteen counselors arrived.

The land on which the camp was built had previously been the site of a Weyerhaeuser lumber mill, so lumberjack lore has long been a part of its tradition. The four "villages" (age-group cabin groupings) are known as Swamper, Logger, Axeman, and Lumberjack. And the first thing one encounters upon entering the grounds is a twenty-foot-tall statue of Paul Bunyan, his pike embedded in a log, his expression

serene, looking like the American mythological creation that he is —
Hercules in flannel.

Ol' Paul is ubiquitous. A painting of him hovers over the tables
in the dining hall. A cutout of him serves as the gender indicator on
the door of the showers and bathrooms (there is a family camp at the
end of each summer). In the center of the camp, there is even an odd
piece of whimsy in the form of a makeshift gravesite and a wooden
tombstone announcing, "Here is the grave of Paul Bunyan as a boy.
The whereabouts of his grave as a man are unknown." Kind of creepy,
perhaps, and the offbeat humor is probably lost on the younger children. But as I consider it now, I think it suggests the notion that every
magical childhood romp comes to an end.

That was my perspective for the better part of a decade, after
the conclusion of my camping career. While my brother and several
friends extended their adolescence, serving as camp counselors even
well into college, I opted for summer jobs at various magazines. I figured it was time to let go of the past, keep an eye on my future. But
as we age, we begin to grasp at youthful bliss like a life raft in a sea of
harsh reality. So it soon became with Nebagamon and me.

Then, a few years ago, my close friend purchased the camp. I met
Adam Kaplan here in 1978. He was a year older than I, slightly ob-
noxious, with a big mop of curly black hair — one of scores of kids
for whom this place was merely a thrilling summer diversion. He had
no idea it would become his passion and then his possession a quarter-century later. But when the opportunity arose, he and his wife
Stephanie became only the fourth set of directors in Camp Nebagamon's history. A dream job, Adam called it at the time.

Only days before the announcement — which was greeted among
camp alumni with the same kind of giddy speculation that generally
greets the selection of a pope or a Notre Dame football coach —
Nebagamon celebrated its seventy-fifth anniversary. More than two
hundred former campers and counselors and their spouses, ranging in
age from nineteen to nearly ninety, converged for a weekend of respite
and reminiscence. Think about that. There was a fellow there who had

attended in 1929. He made the trek back to Wisconsin to celebrate the same memories treasured by men young enough to be his great-grandchildren. The trees are a bit taller, and the carrier pigeons have been replaced by kayaks, and the campers are wearing Kobe Bryant jerseys instead of crisp white T-shirts. But it is essentially a timeless place, and such is its appeal.

It was over that reunion weekend that I fully realized how significant this place is to me, how it is a personal and family touch-stone — our version, to some extent, of the ancestral homestead. My father spent his childhood summers here and has spent at least a week in the North Woods every summer for the past three decades. My brother and I followed in his footsteps. It is my hope that my sons will follow in mine. You can't live vicariously through your children, but you can try to offer them the experiences that were formative in your life. Maybe I had to distance myself from this place in order to truly appreciate it. Life isn't always linear. Sometimes you have to loop back a little and reexamine where you've been through the prism of where you've gone.

I stroll into the Big House, the century-old three-story building that serves as the camp's summer office, and I start chatting with one of the handful of counselors helping to prepare for the chaos of the campers' arrival. I feel a bit self-conscious, like the college student who returns from campus and hangs out in the high school parking lot, telling anyone who will listen, "Yeah, I used to go here." The coun-selor's name is Spencer, and we try to come up with mutual acquain-tances. It is only when he starts referencing his friends' parents that I realize I am twice Spencer's age. So I am no longer in the I-used-to-go-here class. I am a member of the back-in-my-day genus.

In an adjacent room, I begin leafing through a pile of old photo albums that amount to a year-by-year snapshot of the twentieth cen-tury. Suddenly it is 1958, and everything is black-and-white, and there is my dad — eighteen years old, skinnier than I have ever known him and looking a lot like my brother. He is watching a trio of campers leap down the sand dunes. He is serving as the base of a human pyramid. He is overseeing a group of twelve-year-olds aiming BB guns at targets, looking like a Civil War captain telling his troops to ready, aim, fire.

While he was the air riflery instructor, his good friend taught archery a few hundred feet away. Together, they instituted a friendly range rivalry, a mock war of words between the riflemen and the archers that still reverberates here nearly a half-century later. So it is rather ironic, if somewhat oedipal, that I excelled in the sport of Apollo as a member of the camp archery team.

Apollo Shootafar, Homer calls him in the *Iliad*. "His deadly shafts fell all over our camp, the people fell in heaps," says Achilles, who would later be felled by an arrow, himself. Many years later, when Odysseus finally returns home, his ability to string his mighty bow and shoot an arrow through twelve ax heads is what convinces Penelope that her love has, indeed, returned. And he uses that bow to slay the hordes of suitors who have overrun his house. So it is that I, a would-be Odysseus with a sore Achilles' heel, recall that my greatest feat at summer camp occurred with a bow in my hand.

Mine was not a camping career brimming with achievement. The walls of the dining hall at Nebagamon are decorated with various awards commemorating all manner of heroic accomplishments — lengthy wilderness trips completed, tournaments won, inspiring efforts celebrated. There are plaques carved out of birch branches, trophies fashioned from tin cans, thousands of names painted and etched into immortality. My name appears exactly once — as the winner of the camp horse-and-goggle tournament. You know, the game where you count one-two-three and then throw a number with your fingers. It is all chance, not a smidgen of skill involved. Come to think of it, my only other campwide success — when I caught the largest fish of the summer as a nine-year-old — was equally luck-based. I have no record of it all, just a tale that enthralls my youngest son and grows taller with each telling.

My talents with a bow and arrow were somewhat suspect, too.

There was a rather odd fellow on the archery team whom we called the Professor. He arrived every summer with his own compound bow, a complicated piece of machinery that looked as if it had been designed by NASA. His arrows whizzed toward the target, sounding like giant hummingbirds. Mine traveled in a slow arc, as if I were Robin Hood on Quaaludes. I didn't really aim; rather I pointed my arrow in a general direction and went by feel. Somehow I managed to approximate the center of the target, but I was no Professor.

On one particular day, however, I was better. The long and short of it is that during a tri-camp meet — a multisport competition against two other camps in the region — I closed out the archery competition by hitting the bull's-eye on five of six attempts, which was about five more than I usually recorded. It was enough to win the event and (if memory serves) the whole shebang. For a few fleeting minutes, I was Paris aiming at the heel of Achilles. I was mighty Odysseus. I was Apollo Shootafar.

But while the bow was the weapon of Olympians and kings in the late Bronze Age when Troy fell, four hundred years later, in what was likely Homer's era, it was often considered the weapon of cowards. Homer's account of the siege at Troy has King Agamemnon chiding his soldiers by calling them "long distance champions with the bow" rather than fighting men. Also in the *Iliad*, Homer describes Athena speaking "in words that winged like arrows to the mark." Given Agamemnon's scorn, I wonder if that is some sort of backhanded compliment.

I wonder, too, if that is what I do as an essayist — sling my words from afar, aim my opinions from the relative safety of a distant desktop. Is there a passive-aggressiveness to being a writer, as opposed to, say, a radio or television commentator who is immediately responsible for his observations? Mine are detached from my voice, from my face, often appearing in print many months after their birth. Would I have the courage to shoot from the lip at point-blank range? I don't know. Perhaps it depends on the target.

•   •   •

I wander from cabin to cabin, searching for myself. In Swamper 4, my first cabin, I find our cabin plaque featuring a photograph in which I am wearing a neatly tucked Camp Nebagamon T-shirt. In the photo from the second four-week session, my hair is longer, my posture more relaxed. I am wearing green sweats and a Pee Wee basketball T-shirt and sitting with my legs splayed. The guy sitting next to me in the photo, my pal Bob (he was Bobby back then — it said so on the front of his shirt), recently visited me with his three sons. The oldest is now camp age himself.

I make my way through the chronology of my childhood — Logger 3, Logger 5, Axeman 2 . . . until I reach my final cabin, called Voyager, where I find dozens of names painted in the rafters. Mine is easy to spot, in a prime space above the doorway to the counselors' quarters. Tucked between Jim Mendelsohn '72 and Juan Infantes '91 — and painted with typical neurotic care — is Brad Herzog 1983. It is a rite of passage to leave your mark. By the time you are a ninth-grade camper, you consider yourself a guardian of tradition. Sensing imminent graduation, you understand the profundity of the situation. So you paint your name, as if to say, "My childhood was here." It is bittersweet graffiti.

Bittersweet graffiti, still there decades later

There is an instinctive, sense-memory feel to walking around this place of my youth — the smell of the pine needles after a soft rain, the crunch of the pinecones, the gentle ruffle of the wind through the trees, the chirpy conversation of the birds, the tilt of the land along certain pathways, the varying heights of the railroad-tie steps leading down to the waterfront, the sponginess of the wet sand, the darting minnows in the shallow waters of the lake. It feels comfortable and intimate, and I am eleven years old again, full of promise.

Standing on the beach, I recall the night when several dozen of us stood there transfixed, watching a dazzling exhibition of heat lightning on the horizon, a display rivaling any fireworks show I have ever seen. Here and now, in late May, the swimming and canoeing and rowing docks are not yet installed in the shallows, and the waterfront looks naked. It strikes me that this is not just a camp but a piece of lakeshore first. Over the years, it has become a spirit place, and it is this aspect of my old summer home that is truly understandable only by the folks who have spent quality time beneath the pines.

"I feel like this is my place," I tell Adam, as we watch the wind blow ripples into the lake current.

"Let's get something straight." He turns to me and grins. "This is *my* place."

We peer across the lake at a lighthouse rising from a thin strip of land jutting into the water. It used to be that our one-mile canoe test would take us toward that white tower, which seemed like such a monolithic beacon, such a *destination*. But after struggling for an hour against the wind, we would arrive to discover that it was only fifteen feet tall, powered by a single lightbulb. It was like visiting the Great Wall of China, only to discover that you could hurdle it. Looking back, maybe it was a metaphor for how the wonders of youth are made ordinary by experience.

Still pondering his last comment, Adam shakes his head and chuckles. "Do you believe I own this?"

He is only half right, of course. Everyone who passes through here feels a pride of ownership, so it is a bit like he is a CEO reporting to a board of directors many hundreds strong. As such, trying to tweak traditions here is like trying to amend the Constitution. But I understand what he is marveling about — the fact that he has managed to take a magical portion of his childhood and turn it into a profession. And this is where I take pride in what I do, too. We both decided to embark on our respective careers by letting our passions be our guide, rather than some abstract notion of adult expectations. His turned him to teaching; mine steered me toward writing. Both brought us back to this place. Here, we can revel in the setting and the myriad happy associations it triggers, and we can call it work.

For a moment, Adam and I consider grabbing some paddles and canoeing out to the lighthouse again. But then we think better of it. The view from here is fine.

XIV
rejoice! we conquer!

I peaked as an athlete in the seventh grade. Intramural flag football. Third-leading scorer. The trophy still sits on a dresser in my childhood bedroom — a miniature monument to mediocrity. Were it a true-to-life representation of me, the footballer on the tiny pedestal would have an anxious look in his eyes, as if being chased by a pack of wolves. Then the little bronze fellow would drop the pigskin and pick up a book.

You see, I forsook my sports career, such as it was, not necessarily because I lacked the talent, but because I lacked the courage. Somewhere around the age of fifteen, I found myself at a psychological tipping point in which enthusiasm for the games and an attempt at athletic achievement were replaced by a fear of failure. I became acutely aware of my athletic deficiencies. I had always been a third baseman, but then I realized I had a lousy arm. I had long played pickup basketball on my friend's backyard half-court, until I realized I couldn't shoot straight. The skills that required nerve as much as instinct — a foul shot, a long throw from the hot corner — became reminders of my lost confidence. It devolved into a vicious cycle. And once again, I failed the test of courage, deciding instead to ease athletic competition out of my life. Even now, when friends ask me to join their softball leagues or basketball intramurals, I politely decline. It has been a good twenty years since I participated in a pickup game.

The funny thing is, I always wanted to be a sportswriter, and my confidence as a writer grew while my self-belief as an athlete diminished, almost as if it were a zero-sum situation. So I began my career as an employee of the newspaper's toy department — at a daily that happened to be the *Ithaca Journal*.

Actually, the genesis of my career happened much earlier. In fact, I know the exact time and place. It was the spring of 1983 on a major-league baseball diamond. More accurately, it was May 26, and I was a fourteen-year-old sitting nervously in a corner of the Chicago White Sox dugout, sweating profusely on a rather chilly night. At a charity auction earlier that year, my parents had generously bid on a birthday present for my brother and me — a one-game stint as White Sox bat-boys. It was supposed to be a *one-person* one-game stint, but my father entered into the kind of negotiations that the team usually undertook only with duplicitous general managers and ruthless sports agents. He got his way, which meant that one of us wore a batboy uniform on that fateful evening, while the other squeezed into something likely stolen from a misshapen mannequin in the Comiskey Park gift shop.

In those uniforms — second in unattractiveness only to the team's 1976 debacle of Bermuda shorts, striped kneesocks and white nylon pullovers with navy half-collars — neither of us looked like the second coming of Nellie Fox. I was in the throes of a particularly ferocious awkward stage. My skin was like an epidermal oil slick, my glasses required lenses so thick that they couldn't fit into fashionable frames, and my hair was a wavy mess that made me look like Bozo the Clown in a baseball cap. (Every time I lament the loss of what I used to think were those gorgeous locks, Amy is quick to point out its benefits: "Trust me," she says, "you never had good hair.") Suffice it to say that if you look at the photos of this unsightly adolescent wearing a garish uniform that looked like a rejected Garanimals design, you will understand how the 1983 Chicago White Sox came up with their motto: "Winning Ugly."

That night they lost 3–1, their lone run coming on a home run by the backup catcher. A photograph exists somewhere of my brother congratulating the immortal Marc Hill as he crossed home plate, which at the time seemed like pretty much the coolest thing either one of us would ever do in our lives. However, the clubhouse was silent afterward. Our beloved team was in last place, having won only sixteen of forty games. I went home with an autographed ball and Carlton Fisk's broken bat, and I expected that to be that. Little did I know that it was the start of something big. The next day, the White Sox started a streak that would last through September. They won 83 of their final 122 games, earning a trip to the playoffs for the first time in two dozen years.

So early in my sophomore year in high school, I decided to write an account of my minor role in the majors, adding the tongue-in-cheek conclusion that, given the way the team turned its season around, it was clear that I was the spark — the MVP — of the 1983 Chicago White Sox. Some of the seniors at my high school didn't necessarily appreciate the humor, but the faculty editor of the school newspaper did. So it became my first-ever published article, and I learned two very important lessons:

1. A byline is a thrill — an introvert's version of seeing your name up in lights.
2. Given enough force from angry upperclassmen, I can fit inside a locker.

Irreverent or not, I was a diehard White Sox fan in those days — just like my father and his father before him. None of us had ever sniffed a world championship, but we believed. And let's face it, tritely but truly, sports in America is a religious experience. Although we lived north of the city, my family embraced the baseball team on the city's South Side in much the way the ancient Hellenic cities adopted patron deities. Indeed, the analogy can be broadened geographically. To pick a couple of random examples, what Artemis was to the city of Ephesus, the Packers are to Wisconsin. Ephesus had the Temple of Artemis, one of the Seven Wonders of the Ancient World. Green Bay has Lambeau Field. I'd say it's a wash.

My dad spent half of his retirement savings to attend a World Series game a couple of years back. My brother went, too. Meanwhile, I live in a section of California where they don't show many Chicago-based sporting events on TV and where there is a far mellower version of sports fandom, which is to say hardly any at all. It is as if the folks in Ephesus were to say, "Yeah, I dig Artemis, but really who has time to sacrifice oxen? I'd rather go surfing." So my sports allegiances have been diluted by the miles and the conflicting signals. Certainly, I thrilled at the first White Sox world championship in eighty-eight years. But it was a muted celebration. In some respects, I have become a man without a team, a nonbeliever. In a sporting landscape that resembles a sort of modern-day polytheism, I have inched toward atheism.

But the sportsman as so-called hero intrigues me. There is actually a source to the notion that today's athletes serve the same cultural roles as yesterday's gods and heroes. The ancient Olympic Games began in 776 b.c. and survived for more than 1,100 years before being banned by Roman emperor Theodosius I as pagan practices. According to the myths, the original Olympians were, quite literally, Olympians. The gods gathered for competitions every four years at Olympia, where Zeus was said to have wrestled Chronos in the culmination of the great and symbolic battle between father and son. Further legend has it that Hercules, son of Zeus, later founded games for mortal competitors. In the words of mythologist Hans Bellamy, the ancient winners represented "the original divine champion, able to defeat all enemies at cosmically symbolic feats."

In other words, sport arose as a sort of morality play — not an escape so much as a substitute. The heroism so often mentioned on the athletic fields was an imitation of the real thing. Now it is more of a lousy impression. Three millennia ago, the citizens of Troy and Sparta clashed on the fields of battle and feared the vengeance of Apollo. Now we cheer for USC Trojans and Michigan State Spartans, and we fear only the right hook of Apollo Creed.

·   ·   ·

I am about thirty miles east of my old summer camp in a hamlet called Ino, which is a different world altogether. Best I can tell, this blink-and-you're-past-it town consists of a few dozen residents and two business establishments. One is Ino Bar & Grill, where I find my-self surrounded by pool tables, electronic dartboards, and several dozen snapshots on the wall depicting the regulars at various birth-days and retirement parties. The other business is right next door: Marsh & Gerry's New and Used Outlet and Bar.

"This is a man's world up here," the bartender, Bill, tells me, as he takes a long drag on a Winston. "Everything is four-wheeling, ice fishing, hunting . . ." And here I am, sipping an iced tea and trying to disguise the fact that when I go fishing I get squeamish touching the worms.

Were it not the middle of the day, this place would be brimming with an everybody-knows-your-name crowd. As it is, my companions are an older chap in biker's leathers and a middle-aged blonde wait-ing for her husband. We get to talking — the kind of breezy banter between strangers that skirts the edges of anything significant — and I am told a story about a woman from Ino who was supposed to have sailed on the *Titanic*. She missed the boat somehow, unbeknownst to the folks back home. So when the ship went down, everyone thought she was lost, only to be shocked out of their snowshoes a few weeks later when she arrived by train and said, "Hi. I'm home."

I want to tell them that this reminds me of the mythological tale of Ino herself, who "was once a mortal woman speaking like our-selves, but now lives in the salt depths of the sea" as Leucothea the White Goddess. Hers is a typical narrative: Zeus fathers a child (Dionysus) and tries to hide him from his wife, Hera. He instructs Hermes to bring the child to Ino, who dresses the boy as a girl to hide his identity. But Hera finds out and drives Ino mad, leading her to boil her own son in a cauldron and then hurl herself into the sea. Yada yada yada . . .

In the *Odyssey* the sea nymph Ino has a fateful encounter with

Odysseus, who is being buffeted about miserably on the seas, clinging to the remnants of a raft that has been destroyed by a vengeful Poseidon. Ino takes pity on Odysseus, giving him a magic veil that keeps
him safe until he make it to the shore, at which point he is instructed
to throw the veil into the sea and never look back. So it is a lifesaving
encounter, albeit chance and fleeting. Odysseus doesn't trust Ino at
first and will never see her again. But theirs is a significant intersection
of lives, perhaps not unlike meeting someone in a bar.

I am itching to tell the other patrons all of this, but think better
of it. Amid slot machines and buck-hunting video games, obscure
Greek mythology is a certain conversation stopper.

Instead, Bill tells me about the Big Ball Buck Board. It is an annual contest for the hunters in the area, and the rules are simple.
Everyone puts in a dollar, then goes out and shoots a buck, after which
they bring in the testicles to be weighed. As is the case with most
things in life, the fellow with the biggest cojones takes it all. It is an
amusing image. I picture a parade of conservative Lutherans with
shotguns, stepping in from the cold and slamming the door shut
against the bitter December wind. They stomp the snow from their
boots, unwind their scarves, remove their flannel hunting cap with the
earflaps, and announce, with great satisfaction, "I'm going to go weigh
my balls."

Bill shrugs. "You have to get creative in the winter."

While such an endeavor may or may not qualify as sporting, it
is not too far off from the kind of thing I used to write about in my
early years as a freelancer — after I left the newspaper in Ithaca. I was
never going to be assigned to cover the Super Bowl or the Masters. But
I did write articles about quirky subjects like sprint football (college
football for undersized men) and the Masters of Miniature Golf (I
actually flew to Myrtle Beach to compete and finished, yes, in last
place). And for a while I carved out a bit of a niche contributing articles to *Sports Illustrated* about the achievements of overlooked sports-
men, like the first *American* to run a four-minute mile and the

Washington Senators pitcher who once struck out a record twenty-one batters in an *extra-inning* game. Ever heard of Don Bowden and Tom Cheney? That anonymity is what drew me to them.

I was always more interested in the human angle than the X's and O's. Indeed, I can't tell you what a nickel stunt defense is, or a 1-3-1 zone, or the difference between a sinker and a slider. Which is probably why my stint as a newspaper sports reporter lasted only eighteen months. My problem — and the reason I now prefer nothing more strenuous than a round of eighteen holes — is that I have trouble taking sports too seriously. I can no longer muster the intensity needed for competition, nor the patience to listen to the incessant wailing of talking heads dissecting the mind-numbing minutiae of last week's Steelers-Browns game, nor the adulation expected of a diehard fan. I cannot seem to root with abandon. I feel self-conscious and, frankly, a little reduced in stature, as if to excessively glorify others is to diminish myself. I tend to prefer to watch and play the kinds of things that seem less adversarial, less an approximation of battle. Hence, golf.

Of course, that doesn't preclude humiliation. My most embarrassing moment — probably even more so than the time I fell down the stairs at a college bar in Ithaca — came on the first tee at the famed Pebble Beach golf links. Here I was, readying my opening drive on one of the world's classic courses. The gallery surrounding the first hole surely included a couple of titans of industry, not to mention a gaggle of cynical caddies. I took a deep breath, tightened the glove on my left hand, visualized my swing, told myself to keep my head down . . . and promptly whiffed. I grinned sheepishly, hurried through the routine again . . . and whiffed again. Sweating now, hearing freight trains in my head, trying to conjure up any feasible excuse, I took another quick swing — another whiff. The fourth time was a charm, right down the middle. But here was my childhood fear of failure on a grand scale — for adult public consumption. So while I may not prefer warlike competition, the battle still rages in my mind.

It used to be that sport was, indeed, a substitute for war. It is said that a truce was called during the ancient Olympic Games, that military actions and public executions were suspended. But the games themselves were a surreal jumble of religion and sex and horrific violence. The athletes made animal sacrifices. They visited brothels in between events. If they broke any rules during competition, they suffered lashings from sadistic judges. When they competed, it was often to the death. These days, Mike Tyson is vilified for chomping off a chunk of his opponent's ear. Back then, a pugilist named Demoxenos was disqualified for splitting open an opponent's torso and yanking out his intestines. And you want Olympic sacrifice? In A.D. 165, the Greek philosopher Peregrinus Proteus committed suicide by cremating himself on the Olympic flame.

Over the ensuing centuries, the battlefields and the athletic fields remained culturally intertwined. Lacrosse? Early Native Americans used it as a means of training young warriors for battle. The Iroquois called it *tewaarathon*, which means "little brother of war." Soccer? It derives in part from an eleventh-century British game called melee, in which athletes would occasionally kick around the head of an enemy soldier. The cultural connections to war have lessened over time. Today, a soccer ball is just a soccer ball. But linguistic associations remain. Bombs and blitzes have become so natural on Sundays that we forget they are not intrinsic to football.

For a while, after the horror of September 11, sportswriters noted the distance between silly games and profound reality. They admitted that military metaphors might be inappropriate, even disrespectful, and vowed to tone down the war rhetoric. That lasted, oh, about three weeks. Now we once again marvel at aerial attacks and battles in the trenches and field generals. We still talk in hushed tones in losers' locker rooms, as if someone did actually die. And we still venerate our sports heroes.

Certainly, there are some who qualify. The occasional athletic pioneer — Joe Louis, Jackie Robinson, Arthur Ashe, Billie Jean King — makes society take a close look at itself, as sport occasionally outpaces the moral curve. Once in a great while, an athlete transcends the games. Muhammad Ali took a heroic stance against the Vietnam

War. Roberto Clemente died bringing supplies to earthquake-ravaged Nicaragua. Ted Williams risked his life flying combat missions in two wars. The late Pat Tillman was a hero exactly because he shook some sense into our understanding of priorities. But that is a short list, and it has very little to do with athleticism.

Yet visit our cathedrals of modern sports, and you'll find athletes quite literally placed on a pedestal—sculpted in marble or bronze so as to make them immortal. Like the Statue of Zeus at Olympia, there is Stan Musial stepping into a pitch in front of the ballpark in St. Louis and Michael Jordan in mid-flight at the United Center in Chicago and Johnny Unitas in throwing pose on the north side of Baltimore's football stadium. But while the old quarterback possessed remarkable skills and poise, without fawning sportswriters he doesn't necessarily graduate into immortality. If it weren't for the people who knew how to turn a life history into a riveting narrative and how to transform a routine event into a three-act drama, maybe Johnny U just would have been merely John Unitas, a guy in a crew-cut who could toss an inflated bladder covered in pigskin.

There is an interpretation of the sea nymph Ino that seems relevant here. She was said to be the daughter of Cadmus, a Phoenician who brought writing to Greece, and so there are those who contend that her presence in the *Odyssey* is really an homage to the power of the written word, that she graduated into immortality the way an epic story can last through the ages. And she saves the hero. Without Ino, there is no more Odysseus. As a writer, this appeals to my vanity.

I am not asking people to start carving statues in my honor (though if they do, I would like to be a bit taller). Certainly, if athletes are overrated as heroic protagonists, so are the frumpy, envious scribes who glorify them. But if anything, there should be a larger-than-life effigy of a fellow named Gilbert Patten. In the early twentieth century, under the pseudonym Burt L. Standish and in the pages of *Tip Top Weekly*, he almost single-handedly created the modern notion of the heroic athletic ideal. Before Jordan and Unitas and Musial, before DiMaggio and Dempsey and Grange, some 300,000 children each week read the exploits of Frank Merriwell, a fictional student-athlete who excelled in every pursuit and was damn near close to a perfect human being. As former *Sports Illustrated* writer Robert Boyle once put it, Merriwell simply stood for "truth, faith, justice, the triumph of right, mother, home, friendship, loyalty, patriotism, the love of alma mater, duty, sacrifice, retribution, and strength of soul as well as body." He was the blueprint for the great American sports hero. So what Homer was to Odysseus, Patten was to Merriwell. Every so-called hero since is judged against their standards.

But alas, they don't devote many statues to great American writers. Instead, we tend to honor our poets and dreamers with stretches of pavement. There is a Walt Whitman Bridge spanning the Delaware River. There is a William Faulkner Memorial Highway in Mississippi. In Missouri, Interstate 70 is known as the Mark Twain Expressway. But here's the thing: A portion of that interstate was renamed in 1999. It became the Mark McGwire Highway.

So there you have it.

I am headed toward a town called Marathon. Having cruised along the southern shore of Lake Superior, I turn south on Highway 51 (the Korean War Veterans Memorial Highway), pass through a town called Hurley (where a Vietnam Veterans memorial consists of a tank and a disturbing sculpture of what appears to be a crashing helicopter), and finally, a couple of hours later, go west on Highway 29 (the World War I Veterans Memorial Highway). So the road has me pondering the difference between soldier and sportsman. It is late afternoon by the time I arrive in Marathon, a word that harkens back to perhaps the first athlete ever mythologized beyond his due.

The traditional story goes something like this: In 490 B.C., following the remarkable battle of Marathon, in which it is recorded that some 6,400 Persians died against the loss of only 192 Athenians, a herald named Pheidippides was sent to Athens to announce the great Greek victory. Other versions have him racing to Sparta and back in an attempt to enlist aid, but the salient fact is the guy was running, and it was a long way. He raced there on foot — some forty-two kilometers (twenty-six miles)—and arrived to proclaim, "Rejoice! We conquer!" Then he died on the spot.

From this ancient tale, we have the creation of the modern marathon, a sort of athletic homage to a heroic feat that has been celebrated for 2,500 years. The only problem is this: it didn't happen. Half a century after the battle, the Greek historian Herodotus wrote the definitive history of the Persian Wars. He makes no mention of Pheidippides. But as occurs so frequently with ancient icons (see: Homer, blind), the story was invented and then exaggerated and then muddled over time, and myth evolved into misattributed fact.

Robert Browning wrote a poem about Pheidippides in 1879 in which he recounted the wholly concocted tale ("Run, Pheidippides, one race more!"). Seventeen years later, this poem inspired Baron Pierre de Coubertin, founder of the modern Olympics, who set the inaugural games in Athens and created a running race called a marathon that covered those famous twenty-six miles. This was the accepted distance until 1908, when the British Olympic Committee wanted the race to go from Windsor Castle to the Royal Box in London Stadium — which added 385 yards. So the 26.2-mile marathon exists today because, in chronological order, man invented gods to explain the inexplicable, man invented games to honor the gods, man invented stories to bolster the narrative of seminal historical events, a British poet embellished a Greek anecdote, a French baron liked Greek history and British poetry, and the king of England wouldn't move his fat ass.

Technically, the name of this city of some 1,100 in the center of Wisconsin is Marathon City, which distinguishes it from Marathon County. But most folks drop the second word, so it is Marathon for short. Yes, there have been marathons in Marathon — specifically, a footrace that starts in the city, weaves through the hills of central Wisconsin, and ends 26.2 miles later in the hamlet of — you guessed it!—Athens. They call it the American Odyssey Marathon, and on occasion participants have been known to compete while wearing togas and olive wreaths. Of course, Pheidippides had nothing to do with the *Odyssey*, and wreaths were usually reserved for the winners in the ancient games. But that's just nitpicking from someone who gets tired *driving* twenty-six miles.

Actually, there is a more impressive factoid about Athens, Wisconsin: its coordinates are 90 degrees west and 45 degrees north, meaning it is halfway between the North Pole and the equator and halfway between Greenwich and the international date line. So a tiny farming community named after the cradle of western civilization happens to be the center of the Northwestern Hemisphere. Which is pretty cool.

I arrive in Marathon to find three taverns surrounding the Marathon State Bank. As I am admiring the bank's logo, which depicts an ancient Greek runner in full stride, I notice a parade of school buses, all of them heading in the same direction, which is odd since it is the cusp of evening. So I follow them to Marathon High School, right next to the Marathon Cheese Corporation. And here is where I come upon an Ino-and-Odysseus kind of chance encounter. Tonight, Marathon is hosting a regional track meet.

Fleet-footed Hermes was said to be the god of the unexpected, of coincidence, of synchronicity. He also guided lost travelers, and he seems to have made mine an excursion through recurring happen-stance. What are the chances that I would be strolling the neighbor-hoods of Seattle and come upon the Cyclops Café? Or that the train that crashed decades earlier in Calypso, Montana, would be called the Olympian? I am well aware that this particular journey of mine makes me more attuned to certain words and images. But these coincidences keep happening to me.

There was that fellow in Troy whose father was from the Aeolian Islands that figure so prominently in the *Odyssey*. And the time I pulled into my camping spot at a KOA in South Dakota right next to a tiny trailer with "Odyssey" stenciled on its side. And Dawn, my waitress in Siren, who had just finished reading the *Iliad*. And of course, that nagging injury to my Achilles' heel.

Given all that, I am not entirely surprised to find a horde of run-ners in Marathon. Thirty-six high school track teams have gathered here, and people are roaming in packs of colors, like nimble gangs. In the ancient Olympics, athletes slathered their naked bodies in olive oil and dusted themselves with colored powders. Here, it is sweat-shirts and sweatpants — the green and yellow of the Colby Hornets, the purple and white of the Chetek Bulldogs, the black and orange of the Clintonville Truckers.

High school runners in Marathon, Wisconsin

I stroll past a handful of teenage couples pressing against each other in showy displays of affection, and I make my way to the grand-stand, where several hundred friends, family members, and teammates sit in scattered groups. Coaches drape their arms over a chain-link fence, holding clipboards and stopwatches. A dozen girls dash around the track, and each time one of them sprints past the grandstand, her ponytail bouncing with every stride, she receives a show of support from her modest posse.

"C'mon, Natalie! Way to go, Amanda! Keep it up, Christine!"

The late sun is peeking through a hole in the clouds, as if shining a spotlight on the track surrounding the Marathon football field, and I am overcome by the feeling that maybe this is sport as it should be — a diversion instead of a confrontation, a personal challenge and not a regional war. There are no heroes here, only some ambitious teens testing their limits, sprinting to the finish line amid a crescendo of cheers, and gasping for breath with their hands clasped atop their heads. And perhaps there is a lesson — that it is possible in the realm of competition to rejoice without having to conquer.

XV

sparta's warriors

After a brief tour of Athens, I head toward Sparta, a route that neatly encompasses the yin and yang of ancient Hellenic city-states. In Plato's *Republic*, the author (through the character of Socrates) describes Sparta as a culture in which honor is the goal and courage is its special virtue — in contrast, he says, to one in which wisdom is the virtue and justice is the goal. History has conveniently generalized the latter as a society of philosopher-statesmen and the former as a warrior culture, so I find it appropriate that the only U.S. Army installation in Wisconsin is located on the outskirts of Sparta.

This midsize hamlet of about eight thousand Wisconsinites, roughly seventy miles northeast of Madison, actually declares itself the "Bicycling Capital of the World." Indeed, the World's Largest Bicycle can be found in a city park on the edge of town — an enormous sculpture of a nineteenth-century cyclist straddling a high-wheeler. But Sparta really rides tandem instead with the cultural and economic influence of the nearby army base. Fort McCoy is named for Robert Bruce McCoy, who was the son of a Civil War captain and who himself reached the rank of major general and became mayor of Sparta. The base's Total Force Training Center has been the jumping-off point for tens of thousands of reserve and active soldiers.

Meandering through town, I drive past the high school, where a colorful Spartan warrior stands with one foot atop a marquee; past a healthy business district of several square blocks, spangled with crisp stars and stripes every fifty feet or so; past the tiny offices of a local radio station, WCOW. Veering onto Highway 21 east toward Fort McCoy, I pass the Sparta American Legion Post, a banner announcing, "We support our troops," a billboard for the Army National Guard, a tavern called the Foxhole Pub, and then signs for AMMO CONVOY ROUTE and TANK XING. And I feel increasingly uncomfortable, as if I am trespassing, as if I don't belong.

A warrior guards the high school in Sparta, Wisconsin

The military is not and never has been a significant part of my life. This is a product of where I come from — a generation slotted blissfully between the death tolls of Vietnam and Iraq and a middle-class suburban bubble in which personal achievement was celebrated, getting into a good college was paramount, and joining the military just wasn't *necessary*. In fact, it was tantamount to running away with the circus.

But for me at least, it isn't only that military service wasn't a realistic option; it is simply not in my genetic makeup. I don't know if it stems from my lack of competitiveness, my cynicism, my physical laziness, my global perspective, or my potent fear of death. I just know that I could not handle the trauma, the pressure, the moral anguish of combat. Hell, I've never even been in a fistfight.

I suppose there actually are some soldierly strands in my ancestral DNA. I have a first cousin who graduated from West Point. My maternal grandfather fought in the first World War. Even my father, a retired insurance broker known more for his comedy than his combat-readiness, joined the army reserves in the early 1960s, although he seems to have been most useful as the French horn player in the army band. But at least he made it through basic training. Nine weeks? I wouldn't last nine minutes. I am antiauthoritarian, high-maintenance, and terribly nearsighted. I get winded by running a quarter-mile. I like to sleep through the morning. Oh, and as Amy often reminds me, green clothing makes me look sickly. One sight of me in uniform would be enough to embolden the enemy.

I have a good friend, Doug, who was a Navy SEAL and is now a professor at the Naval Postgraduate School in Monterey, California. During Operation Desert Fox in 1999, he made night jumps out of helicopters onto hostile ships in exotic seas. Me? I have to wear anti-nausea wristbands on cruises. Doug and I saw a movie together not long ago, *Letters from Iwo Jima*, and I walked out mumbling that I could not conceive of myself in such a kill-or-be-killed confrontation.

"Obviously," he said quietly, "I can."

And we left it at that, each perhaps trying to grasp at the other's mind-set, as I wondered which one represented a higher plane of perspective.

I suppose I have blind faith in nothing — neither a spiritual power nor a superpower. Were I two generations older, I am pretty certain I would have accepted the call to arms in World War II — grudgingly, fearfully, possibly even usefully. However, were I only a generation older, I might have burned my draft card and made straight for Vancouver instead of Vietnam. And, frankly, I see some courage in that, too.

Often forgotten is this: Achilles and Odysseus were erstwhile draft dodgers. When King Agamemnon's envoy, Palamedes, came to recruit Odysseus for the fight against Troy, Odysseus feigned madness, yoking an ox and horse to his plow and sowing his field with salt. When a circumspect Palamades placed the infant Telemachus in the path of the plow, however, Odysseus swerved to avoid his son and the jig was up.

The fact that Odysseus later manufactured evidence to frame Palamedes as a traitor suggests he never quite got over the deception that revealed his ruse, yet he soon pulled much the same trick on another Achaean superstar. The sea nymph Thetis tried to hide Achilles, her son, knowing that his fate was to perish in Troy if he went to battle. She dispatched him to the court of King Lycomedes, where he disguised himself as a maiden and joined the king's daughters. So here we have the greatest of Greek warriors dressing in drag to avoid combat — mighty Achilles as Max Klinger. Odysseus came to find him, apparently figuring, If I'm going, you're going. He appeared before the women as a peddler, offering trinkets and jewelry — and weapons — for sale. While the daughters naturally gravitated toward the so-called feminine objects, Achilles couldn't resist the swords and daggers, thus revealing himself. Which means he wasn't only a draft dodger, he was a none-too-bright, cross-dressing draft dodger. Odysseus and Achilles proved to be superior soldiers, of course, but they were certainly reluctant ones.

First Sergeant Scott Frey is not.

I meet him soon after I park the Aspect at the Pine View Recreation Area, on the fringes of the army base, alongside a trailer festooned with decorations and surrounded by tents, chairs, little plastic riding toys, and what are clearly three generations of a clan gathered for Memorial Day weekend. Memorial Day is supposed to be a time for remembrance of those who died in our nation's service. I have to admit, though, I have always primarily viewed it as merely a long weekend signaling the arrival of summer. A holiday meant as a tribute to soldiers has evolved into a celebration of family. As I learn the story of Scott and Kim Frey, however, I realize there is honor in both.

"When I first started out, I wasn't exactly sure what I wanted to do with my life. But when I do things, I jump in with both feet," says Scott, sitting across from me at a picnic table with his wife by his side. Kim wears an oversize sweatshirt and sits close, as if warmed by his presence. Her husband has the broad shoulders of a former athlete, and beneath a camouflage cap, he speaks with his mouth drawn tight, as if he is afraid he might swallow a mosquito.

"I was working construction — insulating low-income houses for the state. Just a messy job, you know. I was young — eighteen, nineteen. I just figured there's no retirement in this, no end in sight. I was coming home with caulk and insulation all over me. My grandpa had been in the army. He was in World War II. Every Veterans Day or Memorial Day, my dad would go out to his gravesite and put some flowers out. My dad, he was pretty strict in the household, but he brought us up with a level head, and he said, 'There's always the military if you don't know what to do with your life.' So one day I just went up there to the recruiter's office and checked it out to see what they had to offer. I'm reading the occupational skills and job descriptions. Nothing was appealing to me. But I did read about one job, which was EOD — explosive ordnance disposal, kind of like the military bomb squad. And basically I said I'd like to do that."

And I'm thinking, insulating houses must *really* be a messy job.

"He's done awesome," says Kim, her vowels as flat as a Wisconsin prairie. She hooks her arm around his and pats his shoulder. "Fourteen years, and he's a first sergeant. I'm very proud of him."

Scott is second in command of his company at age thirty-one, one step below sergeant major, which is the highest he can go as an enlisted man. His odyssey has taken him to army training centers in South Carolina, Alabama, Florida, and Maryland, to Fort McCoy, to Kuwait for the cease-fire campaign of Desert Storm, and to Egypt as part of a peacekeeping mission. He finally returned to Fort McCoy, but his first marriage, which produced a daughter, didn't survive the constant upheaval. Soon after, he met Kim, a fellow divorcée, at the local fitness center. They were married in February 2001, and Scott deployed to Iraq two years later, just before the bombing of Baghdad and a couple of months after the birth of a daughter.

Kim fiddles with her wedding band. "When we decided we were going to get married, Scott said to me, 'I *will* deploy. I *will* go to war sometime.' I knew. I mean, I didn't want to know, but . . ."

"Even while we were dating, because my field was so active, sometimes I would call and say, 'I'll be gone a week. See you later.' Sometimes it was real, and sometimes it was to see how she would react," Scott admits.

It is a sobering image — a soldier essentially putting his wife through basic training, priming her for absence and anxiety and self-sufficiency. The image has its iconic model in Penelope of Ithaka, waiting for two decades for word of Odysseus, and I suspect she may have been a lot like Kim of Sparta — young, attractive, newlywed, holding an infant in her arms and bidding her beloved farewell as he traveled across the sea toward a war in Asia with a dubious genesis and no discernable end.

"With all the things going on in the world right now, and with the way the army is involved in the missions, the operational tempo is picking up, and it's very hard on the soldiers," says Scott, solemnly, and then he tilts his head toward his wife. "But it's *a lot* harder on the spouses. The worst we have to worry about is our wife at home burning herself on the oven or hurting herself at work or a car accident. The spouse has to worry about whatever she sees on the news and then whatever her imagination can think up in the time when you talk with her from one week to the next."

The tale of the original soldier's spouse, Penelope, is a chronicle of faith (that her husband will return, that sacrifices will someday be rewarded, and that theirs is a destiny marked with good fortune in

the course of a conflict defined by random tragedy). It is also a proverbial example of faithfulness, as 108 suitors invade Penelope's house
and ask — then demand — her hand in marriage. Forced to protect
herself, Penelope cunningly misleads the suitors for years, offering
hints but no promises. On a great loom, she weaves a shroud for the
eventual funeral of her father-in-law, claiming she will decide on a
husband as soon as it is finished, and then secretly unravels her work
at night. It is a metaphor for biding time, which I suppose is the primary challenge of a soldier's wife.

Most military spouses don't have to fend off scores of suitors,
but theirs is a call to devotion — to a life partner, to a lifestyle, to a
cause — and their mission is heroic in its maintenance of hope and
dignity. Like Penelope, a soldier's wife becomes a de facto single
mother, her husband essentially missing in action until she hears from
him next. Beset with the challenges of maintaining her castle, not to
mention her sense of well-being, she recognizes the futility of worry.
The soldier thinks of his beloved and draws comfort; the spouse has
no such psychological crutch.

Kim chose to address the problem by not watching the news. "I
know he's over there," she says stoically. "When I hear from Scott, I
know he's fine."

Hearing this, I feel silly, knowing that I have been instructed by
my wife to check in nightly, as if mine was some perilous expedition,
as if the North Dakota prairie were the cracked desert of Iraq and a
paddle on the Missouri River were a voyage into the heart of darkness. I have two healthy sons at home whom I can talk to at the push
of a button, two boys who always seem younger and more fragile over
the phone, but who are thriving while Daddy gallivants across the
country. I have a saintly wife who is occasionally overwhelmed by this
willful pair, but who does her best to bear it without undue com-
plaint, figuring the minutiae of home will somehow detract from the
presumed profundity of my journey. Yet I have still managed to whine
to her about the long miles I have driven and the speeding ticket I
earned (on the way to Siren, ironically) and the sore Achilles' heel,

somehow managing to convince myself that I deserve any sympathy at all. I am a wanderer but no warrior — no Achilles, no Odysseus, no Scott Frey.

Then again, Scott, too, is neither Achilles nor Odysseus — in the sense that he eagerly accepted the call to arms. "Oh, he couldn't wait to go the first time," Kim says with a wide smile.

Scott shrugs. "I was excited. I was scared. You have so many emotions running through your body when you get on a bird and you're going somewhere. You've trained all this time. Are you going to do your job right? Are you going to get killed? I wanted to go over there and do what I knew I could do."

Which consists primarily of either defusing or disposing of unexploded ordnance and improvised explosive devices. The EOD crew is the first to have hands on the actual threat — be it a suspicious vehicle parked on the side of the road, a convoy that was hit, or a suicide bomber who has already detonated but whose smoldering corpse might be rigged with booby traps. Most army tours of duty last ten to twelve months. Largely because of the danger and high stress level, EOD soldiers have six-month deployments. Scott estimated that in his first six-month tour, his guys handled at least three hundred devices of one kind or another.

"If you ask anybody in the military who knows anything about EOD, they would tell you we're crazy. 'You guys are the ones who play with bombs!' But the bottom line is, if we're not out there doing it, how many soldiers could die?"

I wonder if it must be a comfort to know that saving lives, rather than the taking of lives, is the mission. But this is a pacifist's perspective, and it assumes a warrior has the need for a heap of rationalization with his rations.

Here was Joseph Campbell's view of combat and humanity: "The battlefield is symbolic of life, where every creature lives on the death of another. A realization of the inevitable guilt of life may so sicken the heart that . . . one may refuse to go on with it. On the other hand, like most of the rest of us, one may invent a false, finally unjustified, image of oneself as an exceptional phenomenon in the world, not guilty as others are, but justified in one's inevitable sinning because one represents the good."

And here is Scott Frey's perspective: "It don't really matter what I think."

His job is to complete the mission, he says, to make sure his soldiers are prepared to complete it, to make sure they have all the right tools and equipment to do so. He says that while he doesn't hear much criticism of the war in military circles, he is aware of it and considers it any American's right. But his prelude to war did not include soul-searching and hand-wringing.

"When I was younger, I always wanted to serve my country. Even now, I still want to serve my country. In most countries, it's a mandatory thing," says Scott. "My grandpa served, my dad tried to join, and I always wanted to do it. Then when I joined, I didn't know how I'd take it. Will I be able to handle the army? But once you adapt to the structure, it's a job. It's a very good job. I wouldn't want to do anything else." He pauses, then grins. "Except win the Lotto."

There is a difference, of course, between serving your country and risking your life for it. A teacher in a one-room schoolhouse in Troy and a civil servant in Athena serve their country as well, but they don't have to defuse bombs.

"A lot of soldiers out there, they like the duty, honor, country, and all that, and the loyalty and values of the army. But when it comes down to it, you're going to lose that soldier if he has a family and he's gotta put food on the table for four people. We have a heck of a time keeping soldiers in, especially *our* soldiers, because they can leave the military and get a civilian EOD contracting job and make two hundred twenty thousand a year — doing what my soldiers are doing for two thousand a month."

So, in its finest incarnation, this is sacrifice and fortitude and purposefulness and all the other attributes we all like to imagine we have. But a relative few have tested them to the extreme. In my quest for insight into the heroic, here would seem to be the paragon. And yet . . . the proverbial war hero has evolved into a figure of ambivalence, subject to judgments about politics and motivations.

About the only thing most everyone agrees about is the notion that you can hate the war but not the warrior. However, there is a difference between supporting troops and glorifying them. About a year before my visit, when Fort McCoy opened its gates to the public to commemorate Armed Forces Day, the theme of the celebration was "A Tradition of Heroes." But increasingly, observers are wondering where all the war heroes have gone. As one *Chicago Tribune* essay opined, after noting the heroic tales of gritty war deeds that fill history books, "in our current war, such heroism seems elusive." The essay suggested that the absence is not in the valor of the soldiers but in the perception of the beholders. It blamed American culture for overusing the term. As one political science professor put it, "The whole hero phrase has been cheapened." The essayist blamed the Vietnam War for transforming a nation's perception of heroism — an unpopular cause muting a nation's will for unbridled idolatry. He blamed the media for focusing on the negative, for perhaps fearing to glorify violence. He blamed the military, too, for often being slow to publicize feats of bravery and even slower to award medals.

On the other hand, the consensus among my Greek chorus — a group of coffee-shop philosophers in blue-state Washington, you'll remember — was that war heroes seem to be a dime a dozen. Their attitudes reflected their frustration with the Iraq debacle. They condemned what they considered to be the manipulation of the word by those who wished to propagandize the war. One philosopher spoke of a news story about a soldier killed overseas, described as a hero: "It turns out he died in an automobile accident in Iraq. For this, he's called a hero? You know why? It's to inoculate against criticism of the war — to say that this isn't a terrible waste of humanity when there are heroes dying every day."

"But can't soldiers be heroic," I wondered, "without it being manipulative to call them that?"

The chorus responded by veering into a discussion of motivations, of reasons for wearing the uniform, of actions. Campbell's thumbnail sketch of a hero is someone who has given his or her life to something bigger than oneself. That is never more obvious than in war. But the U.S. military itself sets the bar high for heroism and only bestows its highest award, the Medal of Honor, to a GI who "distinguishes himself conspicuously by gallantry and intrepidity at the risk of his life above and beyond the call of duty."

So where does that leave Scott Frey, a man who chose a career in the military as a better career option, but who was also spurred by patriotic impulse; a man who has devoted himself to a cause but who leaves the moralizing to those outside the fray; a man who admits he is just doing his duty, albeit a duty far beyond the courageous norm? He surprises me and echoes the sentiment that not all soldiers are created equal.

"I think it's all in your heart. You have to ask: Does this person signing up for the military actually believe that they may *not* have to go to war? And if they do, then they signed up for the wrong reason. You go into the military to train to be proficient in your duties — to perform in a wartime situation. Of course, the mission of the army is to deter war. But if a war occurs, the mission is to win."

When Scott's nine-year-old daughter was asked in school to write about her hero, she chose her father, the soldier. "Even though I don't think she likes it, because I'm gone all the time, I think she kind of understands it. But I don't think of myself as a hero." He shifts in his seat and leans forward. "I think soldiers in our field, if they look at themselves as heroes, then they're pretty much in it for the glory. Then they're also in it for the wrong reason."

His comments somewhat echoed those of my chorus, surprisingly. The trained philosopher among the group discussed ethical egoism and the idea that there's no such thing as an unselfish act. And the storyteller among them mentioned a tale about a boy scout trying to decide if he should help a little old lady across the street. "He knew, as a boy scout, he should do this. It was his duty. But he knew as soon as he took the lady's arm that everyone would think what a fine young man this is, a boy scout doing his good deed. And to him, this knowledge would taint the purity of his motives. He could not be a selfless helper of little old ladies crossing street if he had the least bit of imagination."

I respectfully disagree with everyone — the Greek chorus that despises the manipulation of soldiers, as well as the soldier who suggests a lesser valor in those who are in it to manipulate the system. Aside from the handful of criminals who take advantage of their wartime powers and the chaos of the conflict, I say give them all medals. To me, a war hero is someone who is asked — by a nation that they firmly believe represents the Greater Good — to confront danger and endure hardship and ponder the ultimate sacrifice, and who does so. So often we evaluate soldiers by their actions on the battlefield, forgetting the courage evident in their very presence there.

Just as remarkable to me as their willingness to go there — to duck into a rat-infested trench in Ypres, or pile out of an LCVP landing craft at Omaha Beach, or defend an air base in Da Nang, or ride a convoy into Mosul — is their ability, when the time comes, to come home.

Here is the dichotomy of the the *Iliad* and the *Odyssey*. The former is a tale of battle-tested heroism, of fearlessness and loyalty and glory and violence and death. The latter is about returning from war — a return to life. It is a story of reentry into humanity and recognition of what it means to be gallant far from the battlefields. Odysseus's journey is a reminder that the toughest battles may exist when the war is left behind.

Less than a month after Scott Frey left on his second tour in Iraq, his first son, Terek, was born at Fort Leonard Wood in Missouri. Two days later, as Kim and the baby were readying to leave the hospital, the pediatrician noticed signs that something was wrong. Terek was panting. He didn't have any pulse in his upper legs. And soon, there was this bit of news, whispered to a young woman with a toddler at home and a husband six thousand miles away: the left side of Terek's heart was half the size of his right side. Her newborn would need open-heart surgery.

"His kidneys shut down. He was on dialysis. His chest was left open for a week," says Kim, her voice matter-of-fact, as if reciting a grocery list, but her eyes telling a different story. "But before I left for St. Louis, I did get a Red Cross message sent to Scott, telling him what happened and saying, 'I don't know if you can get home.' And he did get home. It took him about two days to travel. But he did get home."

Scott arrived a day after the surgery, and he and Kim would live for the next three months at a Ronald McDonald House while Terek was at St. Louis Children's Hospital.

"It was five weeks until we thought everything was fine," Kim continues, "and then the doctor said to us, 'Something still isn't right. We need to go back in.' They opened him up again, right down the

The Frey family

middle. At six weeks old, they did his second open-heart surgery —
to patch a hole in the upper chamber of his heart. Then they kept his
chest open for another week, and during this time he was pretty much
paralyzed. They had him on paralysis medicine, so he wouldn't move.
He was breathing through a ventilator." She shakes her head. "It was
something I would never want my worst enemy to go through. I never
thought it would happen to us."

Kim and Scott handled it differently. She didn't want to leave his
bedside. He hated seeing his son like that.

"In the hospital, there ain't nothing you can do. The child doesn't
move or open his eyes. I just wanted to get into a routine. Go see him.
Go eat lunch. Cuz there was nothing we could do at all except sit
there. It drives you crazy," he says. "Not to mention that I had soldiers
back in Iraq. So not only am I worrying about my son, but I'm worried about my guys, too, because I'm in a leadership position."

So here was a man of action, torn between two potential tragedies
and suffering through the realization that he had no control over the
outcome of either one. He was a guardian — first sergeant and father
— unable to protect his charges from the vagaries of fate; he was help-
less and temporarily paralyzed, just like his son.

A year later, when I arrive on the scene, Scott has yet to return
to Iraq, but he knows he will. "Yeah, EOD will be over there for a
while." And Terek has just celebrated his first birthday. He is still fighting to overcome developmental delays, still learning to eat and drink
without a feeding tube, still taking lots of meds. But he is generally
happy and social. "All smiles," says Kim, and they are, too, as they return to their weekend home and their Memorial Day gathering and
their parents and their children.

And I pick up my cell phone and call mine.

XVI

mementos

What is reality anymore?

I am surrounded by Zeus and Poseidon, Medusa and Polyphemus. Standing above all is a sixty-foot-tall Trojan horse, surveying the scene with strobe-light eyes. I suspect he would roll them if he could. My journey is taking me through my childhood home north of Chicago, but en route I have decided to stop for the night at Wisconsin Dells, a vacation destination that is to kitsch what the Catskills are to borscht. Here is Robot World. There is Monster Truck World. Over there, a building constructed to look like an upside-down White House. It is Wisconsin, and this place is cheesy.

Mount Olympus Water and Theme Park is closed for the evening. But the ticket booths are unmanned and the security chains are down, so I walk right in. And here is what I learn: strolling around an empty theme park, accompanied only by silent thrill rides and cardboard cutouts of ogres and immortals, is a tremendously creepy experience.

But I am lost in a loop of thought — about war and weary return and their potential to be trivialized in the long run. I explained earlier that a story like Odysseus's reveals my psyche — all of our psyches — manifest on a societal level. His heroism is a sort of ethereal aspiration, evolved and embellished from what was perhaps originally an actual and ancient adventure. But Sergeant Scott Frey seemed to me to be a contemporary version, a tangible Odysseus — off to battle as a matter of responsibility, back home to an anxious wife and an endangered son, wondering what the gods will throw at him next.

Looking for bombs in the desert — that's real. Everything else is an inadequate approximation — including, I begin to think, my so-called hero's journey. Is it merely a traveling version of this theme park? I am suddenly aware that the road I have taken may be no more real than a two-dimensional cutout of a one-eyed Cyclops.

I guess what I'm wondering is this: When your directions home call for you to turn at the Trojan Horse, have you lost your bearings? Or are you simply making a left turn toward understanding?

A Trojan Horse at Mt. Olympus Water and Theme Park

An Olympus-themed amusement park nearly three thousand years after Homer's existence is the end result of a series of derivatives that accelerated exponentially in the past century, fed by the churning wheels of commercialization and mass communication. Once upon a time, the gates of Troy saw severed limbs and crushed skulls and death throes and widowed wives and conquer and capture. But what is a Trojan today? A top-selling condom. Do time and psychological dis-

tance inevitably turn profound moments into caricatures? History becomes myth, which is reimagined as the stuff of literature and legend,
which alters and embellishes it for mainstream commercialization,
which completes the transformation from profound reality to pop-
culture fluff. So we eat Caesar salads and play with Lincoln Logs and
film *Titanic* love stories. And we roll blissfully on.

Southeast through the lakeside resort communities of the Wisconsin-
Illinois border, and I find myself in familiar territory, suddenly switching gears from cartographic to instinctual navigation. I have lived in
California for close to a decade, but I still find myself slipping and
saying that I'm going "home to Chicago" for a week.

I was one of those rarities in an increasingly nomadic nation —
from the age of six months until I set off for college, I knew one
address. As American society becomes more and more defined by
reinvention and relocation — what Steinbeck once described as "the
hunger to be somewhere else"—the notion of "home" has veered toward a conceptual connotation. The house itself is only a physical
manifestation of an idea; it is almost incidental. But when symbolism
and structure are one and the same over almost two decades, when
home is inseparable from house, it is a powerful merger. For most of
my peers, that kind of attachment to place was motivation to remain
attached, to fashion a future for their children from a blueprint of
fond memories. It is an if-it-ain't-broke-don't-fix-it perspective, and an
understandable one.

I had the opposite reaction. For a long while, familiarity bred
contempt in me. I would focus on the negatives of my hometown,
which I perceived as fostering an insular sense of entitlement, and tell
anyone who would listen, "I don't want to have a comfortable life. I
want to have a special life." It isn't always entirely comfortable to be
two thousand miles away from the ones you love. And, admittedly, it
may not be all that special. But, aside from the fact that Californians
use some odd phrases ("We're going to the snow next weekend!"),
Amy and I are undeniably satisfied.

Really, it's that whole white buffalo thing again, and I understand now that my attitude to my hometown was unfair. It took me several years to realize that comfort isn't necessarily complacence, and that my hunger to be somewhere else was really just a desire to explore, not an indictment of the place I was leaving. And it took me even longer to realize the obvious: the formative elements I was railing against as somehow limiting perspective and stunting inspiration were the very forces that created me.

My parents still live there, at the same suburban address, with the same redbrick foundation and white aluminum siding and black shutters, the same bush-lined front yard that seemed much larger to a ten-year-old. There is also a gray metal box alongside the front door where the milkman used to deliver his wares back in the day. It remains there as a sort of anachronistic icon, a revelation that a family that once seemed like the new kids on the block now represents the neighborhood elders.

I always seem to approach my childhood home with a sense of surprise. Steering into the quiet of the neighborhood, I am consistently astonished by the lushness of the surroundings. My memory of the place seems to be entrenched in a previous generation. I expect it to look as it did in overbright photographs from 1979, the ones in which my glasses seem to have been swiped from Buddy Holly and my pants match the living room drapes. Back then, the trees of the young housing development dreamed of leafy gravitas. A quarter-century later, I find myself driving beneath a canopy of overhanging branches, past houses half hidden by great maples and sycamores.

And my dead-end street is now merely a means to an end. Once, there were but five houses on Crestview Drive, which was enclosed on one side by a chain-link fence standing as a barrier to the mysterious and wild beyond. There were horses behind the fence and strange undulations of undeveloped land. We would play touch football in the street without worrying about traffic. Now, where the wilds used to be, there is an upscale extension to the neighborhood — a dozen houses with three-car garages and vaulted ceilings. The neighbors rush past without waving, piloting their Lexus SUVs toward their wannabe mansions, like first-class passengers forced to walk through the coach section.

I spend much of the weekend eating meals with my parents, seeing old friends, and sleeping in the same room I used to share with my brother. The garish 1970s wallpaper is gone, but the view out the window is roughly the same. I moved into another room when I reached high school, the one above the garage. It is a warm place now, having been converted into my parents' office, but I remember it as cold and dim, particularly during the dead of winter. I would lie on the floor next to a bulky space heater and struggle through ninth-grade geometry proofs. That seems to be the dominant memory — manufactured warmth and a series of givens and conditionals and postulates and theorems. I was a freshman, suddenly overwhelmed by the complexity and occasional chilliness of the world. Heat and logical deduction were medicinal.

The Herzog family home, circa 1995

As I mentioned earlier, my memories of childhood are somewhat sparse — nothing particularly repressed, just an incompetent recall chip in my brain. It could be the result of a childhood largely free of crisis. Tragedy is burned into memory, but normalcy slips into the back of the mind. At least, that was my theory until I realized that my younger sister remembers every toddler-to-teenager event. She is the family's fount of oral history, perhaps only some of it mythology. Three thousand years ago, she might have been a wandering minstrel, committing whole epics to memory. I would have been abandoned by the muses, relegated to recounting heroic tales the way Woody Allen summed up his speed-reading critique of *War and Peace*: "It involves Russia."

As a father now, it is frustrating to think that the memories being forged with my sons may someday be lost in the haze of time. *They're not going to remember my bedtime stories? Our cross-country RV excursions? What about that trip to the Magic Kingdom?* Instead, someday they'll come across old photographs or a postcard from Carlsbad Caverns or fading Mickey Mouse ears. That is what most of us are left with — mementos in place of memories.

I find mine in an overstuffed box in a bedroom closet, and I spend an evening sifting through the collected accoutrements of childhood:

An autograph book containing names that I don't particularly recall collecting — Rod Carew, Steve Martin, Laverne & Shirley. Several pairs of old eyeglasses (I got my first when I was four), saved for Zeus knows what reason, perhaps as an acknowledgment of the love/hate relationship between a bespectacled child and his means of seeing the world. A Swiss army knife rusted shut. A script from a fourth-grade production of *The Music Man*. I played Newspaperman No. 3 and had one line: "Hill?" Which was a step up from my sixth-grade part as one bank of a river (my twin brother was the other) in *The King and I*. Such was my last foray into theater — shaking one end of a blue bedsheet.

An invitation to Brian and Brad's b'nai mitzvah — September 19, 1981, which battled for entertainment headlines that day with Simon & Garfunkel's famous concert in Central Park. A party favor consisting of a switchblade comb with BRAD stenciled on the handle. Photographs from an eighth-grade trip to Washington, D.C. A collection of Dungeons and Dragons booklets, which my brother, my friends, and I never quite figured out how to use correctly. I was the dungeon master, and I winged it. It was impulse adventure, whole worlds at the

mercy of whim, not unlike Odysseus's confrontations with the gods.
That was in the days when I would lock myself in my room and create universes populated by elves and wizards and arcane languages and
magic swords and quests, all of it obviously imitative but exhilarating.
I wonder if it was an outlet for creativity or merely an almost medi-
tative need to dive into a realm of which I was master and creator. I
can see this type of behavior in my oldest son, too — anxious and inventive and obsessive, wary of the world and able to ingeniously construct his own.

A book report about various courageous acts in *To Kill a Mock-
ingbird*. Could it be that I already was interested in the gradations of
heroism? Two decades later, had Amy and I spawned a girl, we were
prepared to choose Scout as her middle name. I wonder why we didn't
focus on Atticus or Jem for our two boys. Why the narrator, the observer of valor? Did I identify less with ethical acts and more with
ethical awareness?

My high school graduation cap. An acceptance letter ("We are
delighted to inform you . . .") to the university on the hill in Ithaca.
My Greek fraternity pledge paddle, designed to look like an Olympic
torch and never once used, thank goodness. A rather bogus senior
honors thesis in psychology examining the relationship between am-
bient heat and aggression in sports, as if all the world's ills could be
cured with an understanding of penalty yards and batters hit by
pitches.

Is this all of me?

A collection of personal mementos is essentially the anti–Greek
epic. It is much the opposite of the mythologizing process. Myths
embellish encounters with deep-seated emotions — fear, passion, jealousy — quite possibly turning the historically mundane into the stuff
of legend. Conversely, a box of mementos — or at least *my* box of
mementos — feels like self-edited history.

Joseph Campbell pondered the curious fact that "our conscious
views of what life ought to be seldom correspond to what life really
is." Self-delusion, he suggested, is a staple of the human condition:

"We tend to perfume, whitewash, and reinterpret," he wrote, "meanwhile imagining that all the flies in the ointment, all the hairs in the
soup, are the faults of some unpleasant someone else."

When one's keepsakes are all trophies and certificates and posed
photographs, where is the angst? Where is the failure? It is a box of
selective recall. This isn't to say that the satisfying moments of one's
life — the rites of passage and achievements and hobbies — aren't full
of sentiment and influence. But some of our most pivotal moments
are random and spontaneous and discouraging. They are the events
that don't leave a trail of souvenirs. So in a box of mementos, the real
emotion is in the omissions.

If I truly wanted to accumulate memories that shaped me, then
I also would have left a Box B filled with college rejection letters, my
cummerbund from the junior prom tux I rented a couple of weeks before I got dumped by my girlfriend, the left shoe of mine that the
eighth-grade bully tossed into the junior high parking lot, maybe some
broken branches from the time I got lost in the woods on the fringe
of my neighborhood, a candid photo revealing the horror on my face
when the babysitter walked in while I was sitting on the john . . .
Those recollections are much more vivid.

So again I come back to the question: In the face of so many
derivatives, what is reality? Is it the truth of one's whole personal
history? Or is it merely the history we choose to remember? The
former produced the current me. The latter creates the future me. It
is perception and reality in an endless loop.

And maybe that is the genesis of mythology. The so-called king
of Ithaka may have been merely a philandering pirate who got lost
on the way home. But his biographer-minstrels remembered him
heroically, and that historical perception has fossilized into legend. It
is spin on an epic scale.

One memento, in particular, is cause for extended reflection. It is
a framed collage — consisting of a photo, matchbook covers, and a
moldy corsage — put together with care by my then-girlfriend Amy,
commemorating our senior prom. She looks perfect in a white dress.

I wear a white tuxedo and tails, pink shirt and red bow tie, looking very much like a suburban adolescent pimp. In the photo, we're staring at each other, hands clasped, and I imagine that we see the future in each other's eyes. Proms have an air of finality, but this was a beginning, a launching point toward life partnership. *God, that was half a life ago.* I walk to my parents' backyard and stand in the exact spot where the picture was taken, but I am struck by the notion that I am very much alone, having been prodded by that same woman in the white dress to light out in search of . . . something missing.

I have ten days until our scheduled rendezvous in Ithaca. My perception is that I seek an understanding of a heroic life that seems to have eluded me. But maybe the reality is that she just wants her old hero back.

XVII
the allegory of the cave

I am on the eastern fringe of the third-largest Amish community in the United States and en route to a community called Plato. There could hardly be a more incongruous name for an Amish-populated place.

Plato was an experienced soldier and a well-traveled man of the world. The Amish reject warfare and violence, the bearded men even forgoing mustaches because of the long association of mustaches with the military. They believe in remaining separate from the rest of the world, which is partly a reaction to ancestral persecution and partly proactive against the perceived polluting influence of "the English." Their homes don't draw power from the electrical grid. They don't collect social security or vote. They avoid many of the features of modern society, developing practices — no driving, no home phones, no televisions — that isolate them from American culture.

Plato founded his famed academy in 387 B.C. (on land belonging to a fellow named Academos). As the first university and, with a lifespan of more than nine hundred years, the longest-surviving university known, it was devoted to research and instruction in philosophy and the sciences. Over the door of the academy was written, "Let no one unversed in geometry enter here." However, the Amish put a halt to formal education after the eighth grade, just before geometry arrives.

While Plato's *Republic* was his vision for a paradise on earth, the Amish live their lives with much the opposite point of view. They don't believe that anyone is guaranteed salvation through baptism or a conversion experience or joining the church but rather that God weighs one's lifetime journey and then decides which afterlife off-ramp is appropriate. You live a life of hardship and obedience to church, and you die not knowing if you may still be headed for an eternity in hell.

The foundation of many of Plato's beliefs was the notion of a duality of existence — an imperfect physical world along with a perfect world of ideas. In this universe, only an enlightened philosopher caste could truly understand life's esoteric truths, but it was in the best interest of society to keep those truths under wraps, telling "noble lies" to the masses in order to benefit the public good. Sort of a politician's dream rationalization, don't you think? It's the kind of thing that leads statesmen to declare that the reasons for war are incidental to the righteousness of the war itself. According to Plato, flawed behavior like deception could have heroic intent — a very Odysseus-like heroism. Once again, this harkens back to the perception–reality disconnect.

So here I am in Amish country, and so far I am finding it difficult to pinpoint reality. More accurately, I am struggling to reconcile what I see with what I expected. Indeed, as I stop for a spell about fifteen miles west of Plato in the quaint Indiana crossroads of Shipshewana, I find myself surrounded by an unanticipated element of Amish culture — brazen entrepreneurship.

Here, the residents are real enough, piloting their horse-drawn carriages along a manure-strewn buggy lane. But the names of the business establishments — using words like Olde and Tyme and Shoppe — make me uneasy. They suggest unadorned simplicity, but they feel like artificiality. At the center of town sits a massive barn structure, a Mennonite Anabaptist Interpretive Center. Among the various well-planned historical displays are a replica of a sixteenth-century dungeon where Anabaptists were imprisoned and a Tornado Theater where one can experience a simulated twister. I am not quite sure what I expected, but I didn't expect special effects.

Across the street is the Trading Place Flea Market, which began in 1922 when six pigs, seven cows, and several head of cattle were sold at the very first auction. It is now a twice-weekly event in which 860 vendors descend on this small community of 536 residents. The variety of bargain hunters — a tall African American fellow in a long blond wig, a wild-eyed lady wearing a purple boa, an overweight woman pulling a wagon with a Chihuahua in it — is surpassed only by the assortment of items for sale. I wander through row after row of not one damn thing I need — miniature windmills and five-story birdhouses, pan flutes and whirligigs, steering wheel covers, flagstones engraved with inanities like "If I'm not at home, try Wal-Mart," Russian *matryoshka* dolls of Dale Earnhardt and Robert E. Lee and Obi-Wan Kenobi.

Apparently, greater urbanization and a dearth of affordable farming opportunities have led this traditionally agrarian society to embrace the possibilities of the tourist trap. Certainly, I don't begrudge them — no more than I begrudge Native Americans turning sacred lands into casino cash cows. Obviously they don't find capitalistic enterprise to be antithetical to their belief system. But still, I can't help but think it *should* be. Perhaps this is just an atheist's skewed expectations of piety, but there is something disconcerting to me about a man wearing a straw hat and speaking Pennsylvania Dutch — emphasizing his separation from the world — while holding a frozen drumstick for sale in one hand and a wad of cash in the other. Or, for that matter, a young woman wearing a prayer covering while working a credit card machine.

Later that afternoon, after a lengthy inner debate, I decide to embark on a horse-and-buggy ride to an honest-to-goodness Amish home. The debate stemmed from my aversion to treating an exploration of a subculture like a trip to the zoo to observe the polar bears. The difference — and I suppose the reason I decide to try it — is that here the polar bears get a cut of the profits. So I fork over thirty-three bucks and set off (along with a couple of middle-aged women on vacation from Kentucky, a driver named Bill, and a horse named Daisy) for a short ride into the countryside.

Backed by the clippety-clop of hooves on pavement, Bill tells us about our hosts for the evening, Betty and Joe Winger — how they live in a modern house with running water and amenities run via air pressure instead of electricity, how there is an off-site phone a quarter-mile away, how we won't see any buttons or zippers on the women's dresses because anything other than straight pins is considered too elaborate. "The Amish want to live a life of simplicity and humility because this is the life that Christ lived," he explains. "This is their way of living in the world without being part of the world."

We arrive to find a couple of barefoot and blond boys in suspenders waving to us from beneath a basketball net next to an immaculate white farmhouse. Their grandparents, Betty and Joe, he in a beard, she in a prayer covering, are fifth-generation farmers and somewhat unique in LaGrange County in that their surname isn't Miller, Yoder, Bontrager, Hochstetler, or Mast. Some 55 percent of the county's Amish residents share one of those five names. Not so unique, apparently, is the intrusion of tourists into their simple home. Betty tells us that last night they had thirty guests.

The meal, particularly given my assault on nutrition over the past few weeks, is a heaping helping of comfort — homemade bread and peanut butter, homegrown green beans, Salisbury steak, mashed potatoes, breaded chicken breast and pasta, punctuated by a choice of strawberry or pecan pie. The conversation, however, is somewhat less satisfying. Betty doesn't sit with us, busying herself in the kitchen instead. And Joe takes his leave halfway through the meal, saying he's sorry but he has to hay the field. They are welcoming and friendly, but clearly less interested in us than we are in them.

While Joe is sitting and Betty is listening, the Kentucky tourists are asking about recipes and crops and such. But I want to know about their worldview. So I switch gears and ask Joe, somewhat out of the blue, how he would define a life well lived. He thinks for a moment and wipes the corner of his mouth with a napkin, as his ten-year-old grandson speeds by the window, driving a team of Belgians toward the hay field.

"I suppose it's about honesty," he says. "Doing well unto others." And with that, it's off to work.

The Winger family

Minutes later, as we trudge outside and watch with absurd delight while Joe and his family stack bales of hay on the wagon, two unexpected words crowd my thoughts — reality television. There is, of course, no such thing. Telling a group of reality show participants — especially, as it is nowadays, a group of narcissistic, emotionally unstable wannabe actors — to act normal while a TV camera follows them around is to ask for the impossible. It is why reality television has devolved into a stage for dysfunction. If you're self-important, self-destructive, and shameless enough — and if you're *just* famous enough — well then, congratulations, you get your own show on basic cable. And you get to pretend to be real in an entirely contrived universe. In the world of psychological experimentation they call this the observer effect, a confounding variable in which the participant's behavior may change as a result of the observer's presence. I am not suggesting my hosts acted any differently as a result of our visit, and certainly their lives — humble, respectful, functional — are just about everything that Paris Hilton, Ozzy Osbourne, and Flavor Flav are not. Still, the notion percolates.

About thirty miles southwest of Shipshewana, in the town of Nappanee, curious tourists can visit Amish Acres, a re-creation of an actual Amish farm — only this one has electricity and a Round Barn Theatre, where you can watch a re-creation of *Fame*. My visit with the Wingers is a heck of a lot more authentic than that. But when a culture devoted to separating itself from the world decides to invite the world into the kitchen for some pecan pie, there has been a revision of reality. Here I am, searching for some profound truth, but I still feel as if it is hidden behind derivative layers, like those Russian nesting dolls for sale at the flea market.

The first thing I notice upon my arrival in Plato is an Amish buggy moving in the opposite direction. The second is basically the only commercial establishment in town — a business that sells tombstones. There is a NO PASSING ZONE sign standing right in front of it. Can I possibly be the first person to get a chuckle out of this juxtaposition?

I step into LaGrange Monument Works, prepared to offer up that very query. Instead, I stumble into the least friendly encounter of my journey. While I was parking, I noticed an older gentleman inside pulling off his cap and patting down his hair, prepared to charm the life out of me. But, much to his chagrin, I am not in the market for a grave marker, and he quickly interprets my attempts at conversation — How ya doin? What's your name? Do you live around here?—as an interrogation.

"Okay, why all the questions?" he asks with undisguised irritation.

"Actually, I'm traveling cross-country. I'm planning to write a book about —"

"I don't care. I don't want to be in your book."

This is a first. Most of the people I have encountered in my travels are cordial, receptive, at the very least somewhat curious. "Um, okay. Well, are there any other businesses in Plato?"

"This is Plato," he says, and he walks away.

And this is irony, too, because it was Plato who believed that knowledge came not from teaching, but from . . . that's right . . . questioning. Just my luck to run into a grumpy rhetorician.

Plato turns out to be one of those quiet country hamlets that failed to snag county seat status, missed out on the railroad, and never amounted to much. First platted in 1836, it was originally called Bloomfield. And then Hill's Corners. The reasons for its conversion to Plato appear to be lost to time. Mostly fields and farmhouses, it is an amorphous settlement with no center and, best I can tell, no real personality. I wander the back roads for a while until I have lost a sense of exactly where I am. Finally, I pull to the side of the road in front of a farmhouse and a barn surrounded by an ark's worth of animals — horses, a miniature pony, dogs, chickens, turkeys, pheasants, peacocks. As I struggle to unfold a map, a young Amish fellow walks up from behind a buggy. He wears a straw hat, tinted glasses, a blood-flecked shirt, and filthy boots. I roll down the window.

"Hi . . . can you tell me . . . am I still in Plato?"

"I guess so," he says, apparently as uncertain as I. And so I meet Howard Mullett. It is the kind of encounter I had been hoping for in Amish country — no buggy tour package, no flea market business transaction, no museum display, just a comparatively random intersection of subcultures. I am sure we will come away with divergent views on the meeting. He will likely remember it as an inquisitive guy in an RV trying to find his way. I will too, only figuratively.

We talk about his family (he had seven brothers and seven sisters until four years ago, when his mother and his youngest brother died in a house fire), his future (he is unmarried — thus beardless — and looking for a mate if he can find "the right one at the right time"), and the fact that outsiders like myself come around and poke into the lives of people who have made a mission out of being left alone ("I'm used to it," he says. "Doesn't bother me").

But I am most curious about the resilience of his faith. I approach the metaphysical question somewhat cautiously, as if somehow I would be planting a seed of discontent, and ask about his temptations instead. Has he ever yearned for a beer? An NFL Sunday? A few minutes behind the wheel? He answers literally, but I hear a metaphor.

"We just learn it from a baby up," he says, and he points toward my house on wheels. "You're used to that." He then tilts his head toward a couple of horse-drawn buggies in the driveway. "I'm used to this. For me, I wouldn't even want to drive a vee-hickle. I ain't supposed to, so I'd rather not even get in and drive it."

The Mullett homestead in Plato, Indiana

It is all he has known in his twenty-two years. It is his reality, and he embraces it. I have come to realize, along this stretch of Indiana, that one can't begin to ascertain how to fashion a heroic existence without a true understanding of the *parameters* of one's existence. In other words, when trying to ascertain the meaning of life, perhaps it all depends on whose particular life we are examining.

The duality that I mentioned earlier — physical existence versus the world of ideas — was the focus of Plato's "Allegory of the Cave" in *The Republic*. In the allegory, which was supposedly an inspiration for the film *The Matrix*, Plato (through the character of Socrates) imagines prisoners in a cave who are unable to turn their heads and can see only the wall of the cave. There is a large fire burning behind the prisoners, and puppeteers stand in front of the fire, carrying various animals and plants and objects that cast shadows on the cave wall. All the prisoners have ever known is those shadows. It is their only reality.

When the prisoners are released, they can turn their heads and realize (eventually and reluctantly) that they have been misinterpreting appearance as reality. If they leave the cave — a journey upward that Plato likens to the "ascent of the soul into the intellectual world" — the enlightenment will be that much greater and that much more difficult to grasp. And if they try to free their "fellow bondsmen," they will meet with doubt and resistance.

It is Plato's view that the bulk of humanity is trapped in the depths of unawareness, is not even aware of its own restricted perspective, and is comfortable with that ignorance because it seems to be the only reality. It is an ignorance-is-bliss perspective. But there are, says Plato, invisible truths — a sort of absolute reality — that, for one reason or another, all but the most enlightened folks fall short of understanding. And those who are able to make that cerebral journey are often misunderstood by the many who don't. It is essentially Intellectual Elitism 101.

There is, in some respects, an Amish analogy to Plato's analogy. It is *rumspringa*, which loosely translates as "running wild," a tradition practiced by some Amish groups in which older teens are allowed to embrace the outside world to a certain extent. They may date, go to parties, experiment with alcohol, dress in contemporary styles. The intent is that they will be well informed before choosing adult baptism. Most decide to return to the faith, but as many as 10 percent, according to some estimates, do not. Practically speaking, it makes sense to allow a sort of adolescent rebellion, which seems to be an instinctual part of the life course. I mean, even Gandhi supposedly went through a phase when he smoked cigarettes and ate meat and questioned his faith — although I'm pretty sure Gandhi wasn't Amish.

Not surprisingly, given the depths to which popular culture is plunging, there was a short-lived fish-out-of-water reality TV show, *Amish in the City*, that briefly drew some attention not too long ago. The program was constructed around the *rumspringa* experience — five Amish young adults cohabitating with six worldly "English" roommates at a house in the Hollywood Hills. It represented, of course, a contrived assault on Amish reality, particularly because the Amish view complete humility as perfection. It is why they don't pose for photographs and why they conduct funerals without eulogies or flowers or adorned caskets. It is why an anecdote tells of an Amish father happily remarking to his wife and children, "I believe we were the plainest family in church this morning."

The temptation is to interpret *rumspringa* as some sort of escape from the limitations of the cave. But who is to say that a more complicated existence is the route to revelation of invisible truths? Whose life path better represents an understanding of absolute reality? Is it the hardworking carpenter who constructs tangible things, questions nothing, and believes with all the power of his faith that there is an eventual purpose to his existence? Or is it the pink-palmed intellectual who constructs sentences, questions everything, and steadfastly believes that faith is a mirage?

If revelation of the so-called big picture accepts a worldview that makes room for materialism and envy and vanity and superiority and all sorts of superficial tabloid titillations, is it possible that this is actually a limited perspective that spawns a skewed concept of reality? Amy and I have a rustic-looking sign hanging in our kitchen at home, a piece of folk art really, but also a reminder. It says only SIMPLIFY, and we try hard to keep our lives free of frenzy and convolution. However, everything is relative. And maybe, despite our efforts, we're actually the ones in the cave.

Chatting with a twenty-two-year-old with an unequivocal acceptance of his purpose and his potential, I feel pangs of self-absorption and conspicuous consumption, along with a sense that maybe the layers I believed were obscuring reality have been layers of my own making. Look too hard at something, and your eyes get tired. You lose focus. You blink. I have spent the past several weeks trying to make some sort of determination about what I am and what I am not. Howard just *is*.

I decide to ask him the same question I posed to Joe Winger amid second helpings of Salisbury steak. What, in his opinion, constitutes a life well lived? "Just keep praying to God and do what you can. That's the only way I know how to say it." He shrugs and walks off, leading a pony into the barn.

XVIII

pandora

A couple of words are the most memorable part of my journey toward the Ohio hamlet of Pandora. I head east in the late afternoon, and about eight miles from the Indiana-Ohio border, I pass a barn that used to have the iconic advertisement of the Heartland — CHEW MAIL POUCH TOBACCO — painted on its side. But time and the elements have faded the lettering, so that all that stands out is AIL.

Soon a sudden rain shower arrives, and I pull over for the night in a Wal-Mart parking lot in Bryan, Ohio. About half an hour into my drive the next morning, I am musing about the story of Pandora, who is of course blamed in Greek mythology for opening up a vessel and releasing misery into the once-perfect world of man. As I contemplate the virtual impossibility of leading a life free of vice and sin and trouble, I reach the crossroads of Kieferville and another sign — an ancient-looking billboard for the Pure Oil Company. Rusted, flaking, weather-stained, it says, in sickly letters, PURE.

In his preface to his translation of the *Iliad*, W. H. D. Rouse discusses how the tale is essentially the tragic story of one man, Achilles, and his journey toward self-mastery and inward peace. He describes it as "Homer's reading of the riddle of life — purification through suffering." So, since I have that sore Achilles' heel and all, I attempt much the same thing — by taking a deep breath and diving into the murky realm of talk radio.

Immediately, the suffering begins. I cannot escape Rush Limbaugh on my dial — at AM 1280, AM 1330, and AM 1370, each slightly unsynchronized, a constant stream of blither and blather. I feel like Prometheus, who suffered the retribution of Zeus after stealing from Mount Olympus. The poor sap was chained to a rock on Mount Caucasus, where an eagle pecked at his liver, which was renewed as fast as it was devoured. Only the heroics of Zeus's mortal son saved him. As Limbaugh bloviates — on three separate stations — about what he insists were ethical lapses by Bob Woodward and Carl Bernstein, I'm thinking, Where is Hercules when I need him?

Eventually I manage to avoid the Rush, pausing instead on the voice of an evangelist, who is working himself into a frenzy while discussing the notion of predestination: "Now, I'm not a prophet, but I can tell you the will of God right now — and I don't even have to go and lay hands on you one by one. I'll give you a blanket prophecy… You ready? Here's God's purpose for you: That you be conformed into the image of his son! That's what God has predestined for you! He has predestined that all who choose him will be conformed into the image of his son!" But then I hit the scan button, and I land on the gospel according to Doris Day. "Que sera sera . . . Whatever will be will be . . . The future's not ours to see . . ."

Yet when I arrive in Pandora, it all feels pleasantly predictable, as if I have already seen it on the cover of the *Saturday Evening Post*. Tractors trail clouds of dust alongside neatly plowed fields. A creek meanders through town. Children frolic in a sprinkler. A man rides a mower, perfectly trimming his lawn in diagonal stripes. Stiff U.S. flags protrude from front porches. A marquee on a missionary church shouts, GOD BLESS AMERICA.

The town used to be called Pendleton. But what fun would that be? Then you would have businesses with names like Pendleton Excavating and the First National Bank of Pendleton. But add "Pandora" instead, and it opens a whole new can of worms. On a trailer on the outskirts of town, I spot an advertisement for Pandora Self-Storage, which I find hilariously ironic. And in the center of town, moments later, I find myself ordering a grilled cheese sandwich at an eatery called Pandora's Lunch Box.

First things first: by most accounts, it wasn't a box. It was a jar —
Pandora's jar, which was supposed to remain unopened. But that was
only part of the trap set by Zeus to punish mankind for daring to
deem itself worthy of stolen Olympian wonders. The other was Pandora herself. Zeus commissioned the creation of "an evil thing in
which men will all delight while they embrace their own destruction."
She was molded by Hephaestus out of a lump of clay and imbued
with the attributes of several gods and goddesses. Aphrodite gave her
grace and charm. Athena taught her embroidery and weaving. Hermes
provided her with the powers of persuasion. Pandora was also given
one more personality trait — curiosity — before she was delivered to
Epimetheus, brother of Prometheus.

Before Pandora, there is no mention of women in the Greek histories. Men lived in a paradise "free from evils, harsh labor and con-
suming diseases." Then Pandora opened the lid of the jar. Out came
a multitude of plagues — sorrow and mischief, spite and envy, everything from revenge to rheumatism. The Greek historian Hesiod, who
told Pandora's tale, ends his story thusly: "This was the origin of
damnable womankind, a plague with which men must live."

There is an obvious similarity to the story of Eve and the apple,
including the notion of women as divine afterthought, but it is unclear whether these were two strains of the same primeval story or
simply two creations stemming from a misogynistic strain in ancient

storytellers. Certainly Hesiod was in need of a bit of therapy. In his writings, he rattles on and on about the evils of the fairer sex, going so far as to say, "Any man who trusts a woman trusts a deceiver." Then again, Homer may have influenced him. "No woman merits trust," Agamemnon tells Odysseus when they meet in Hades. So there are times when the ancient Greek texts read like the pages of *Maxim* magazine.

I am surrounded only by men in Pandora's Lunch Box, which has low ceilings, fluorescent lights, and an incongruous nautical theme, although I suppose seasickness was Pandora's fault, too. Despite the loud buzzing of an air conditioner, I try to eavesdrop on the banter between the older gentlemen who seem to have gathered for a weekly summit at Table No. 1. Every time someone wanders into the restaurant, he pulls up a chair at the table, no invitation necessary. One of the men, apparently a retired police officer, is regaling the others with stories of bank robberies and murder suspects. The talk then turns to mowing lawns, trading in cars, rupturing discs, and finally to a fire that galvanized the residents of Pandora three weeks before my arrival.

Across the street from the eatery, there is a hole in the center of the block where a building used to be, and the three-story edifice next to it is significantly damaged, its roof caving, its windows smashed, its side blackened. As I stand and stare at the scene, which looks like a rotted tooth next to a missing one, a volunteer firefighter named Gary notices me and regales me with his own tale of courage and solidarity. Twelve area fire departments responded and worked for thirty-six hours to battle Pandora's biggest fire in more than a century. Everyone pitched in to help. A group of locals formed a line to move furniture out of an endangered ground-level store. The Ladies Auxiliary brought out cold towels and water. Nearby communities offered free meals from Wendy's and Burger King. The pharmacy gave out candy bars. In the end, the building was lost, and the one fellow who had been inside managed to escape. Two firefighters were slightly injured, but not before the crew managed to save a bird, several fish, and an Elmo doll.

Gary, the volunteer firefighter, in Pandora, Ohio

The irony is that, according to mythology, fire is what spawned Pandora. It was a flame from Mount Olympus that Prometheus stole for mankind. That is what Zeus was so enraged about — why he sent Prometheus to be eaten alive and why he sent Pandora to spoil man's paradise. The story goes that when Pandora saw the ills she had released into the world, she hastened to replace the lid on her jar. But all the contents had escaped except one thing, which lay at the bottom. It was mankind's sole comfort — hope. Which is why I read the story of Pandora not as a tale about the introduction of vice and sin into the world, but rather as the genesis of unpredictability.

Fire is volatile and erratic. Pandora's curiosity reflects undependability and impulsiveness. The misery she releases is fickle and capricious. The fact that the sustaining virtue of hope is all that remains suggests a changeable future, an unknowable path. The town of Pandora, which seemed so predictable and perfect upon first glance, has a charred hole in its heart as the result of a random twist of fate.

But if you ask me, Pandora didn't screw up paradise; she just made it more interesting.

I decide that I need a haircut. Mind you, I long ago lost my hair — indeed, the farewell tour began when I was still in Ithaca. There are few fates more predictable than the onset of male pattern baldness. It is the very notion of inevitability that evokes such angst. It is a *receding* hairline, an ongoing phenomenon. The catch-22 of it all is that stress is reportedly a major cause of baldness, which is a bit like being told that worrying about chest pain causes heart attacks. So instead of worrying, I try to rationalize by considering the heroic men in history with hairlines similar to mine — William Shakespeare, Ben Franklin, Homer Simpson. My friends often add to the rationalization by offering hollow compliments. If I only had a nickel — or better yet, a follicle — for every time I heard, "It's okay. You have the face for it." Which always reminds me of that scene from *Caddyshack* in which Rodney Dangerfield's character remarks that a hat on sale is the ugliest thing he has ever seen. Then he turns to see Judge Smails wearing that exact hat. "Oh," he says, rolling his eyes. "It looks good on you, though."

I tried using Rogaine for a while, which at the time was only the latest in a long line of hair loss antidotes. In ancient Greece, for instance, Hippocrates concocted a potion consisting of beetroot, horseradish, spices, opium, and pigeon droppings. Don't think I wasn't tempted to try it. But the spray-on treatment didn't grow hair as much as make a sticky mess of what hair was left. So I abandoned the cause and let nature take its course. Considering the growing acceptance of hair transplantation, the recent "miracle" hair-loss medications, the ever-increasing number of young men who use them, and the fact that there is a point in one's chromedomeness when one has — physically, socially, and psychologically — missed the prevention boat entirely, I can only conclude that I may indeed wind up as the last bald man on earth. So I have that going for me.

Nowadays, some courtesy stubble rings my scalp like an olive wreath. I keep it as short as possible, mostly to minimize the contrast between head and hair. Amy is my stylist, a responsibility that requires some shears and about five minutes of free time. On the road, I leave it to fate — which, thanks to Pandora, can be fickle. It turns out that Pandora's barbershop was located in the building destroyed by the fire. So the barber moved his business to Sara Beth's Beauty Shoppe next door to Pandora's Lunch Box. But the barber isn't around when I arrive. I start chatting with Sara Beth, who tells me about her elderly father, and I forget about the haircut entirely. I want to meet her dad, who has been recording Pandora's unpredictability for more than half a century.

Ray Burkholder lives in a modest redbrick house on Jefferson Street, and like Thomas Jefferson, he is a farmer, a scholar, and a climatologist. As Elvina, his wife of sixty-six years, busies herself pulling weeds in the front yard, Ray motions for me to sit next to him in his living room. Dressed in a plain white undershirt, green cotton pants, and moccasins, Ray looks every bit of his eighty-seven years. Gravity and cavities have taken their toll. But he has a preference for exactness, as evidenced by the digital clock on the wall. And he has a yen for lists, like the replica of the Ten Commandments resting on the floor a few feet away.

Since December 1, 1949, Ray has been recording the weather. Each day for two generations, with the exception of the rare illness or injury, he has reported to the National Weather Service, announcing Pandora's high temperature of the day, low temperature, current temperature, and precipitation. He has spent much of his life simply waiting to see what the gods throw down.

Ray pulls out a notebook filled with dates and numbers and notations, reflecting a lifetime's worth of watching the skies. But much of the data is stored in his memory. Impulsively, perhaps impolitely, I quiz him.

"What's the highest temperature you ever recorded?"

"The answer's 103. It was during the real dry summer of 1988 — June 25, 1988."

"And the low?"

"Twenty-three below zero. February 26, 1963.

"The biggest rainfall?"

"June of 1981. We had 3.69 inches of rain in twenty-four hours."

At the very least, Ray disproves the notion that everybody talks about the weather, but nobody ever does anything about it. His philosophy is simple: You have a job to do? You do it. He was born about five miles northeast of Pandora and has lived in the area his whole life. His father, who ran the family farm, said he could go to college if he was valedictorian of his high school class. So he worked hard and achieved it. Three days into college, his father begged him to quit school and help him on the farm. So he did that. He applies the same dependability to recording the weather.

Since 1963, Ray has been taking his measurements at midnight. At that time, he worked the third shift at a factory, clocking out around then, so he figured it was a good time to record the day's readings. Nowadays, he is asleep by 7:00 or 8:00 p.m., but he naturally wakes up at midnight, collects the data, reports to a weather station in Indiana, then returns to bed. On the rare occasions when he has missed a day for health reasons — a heart attack in 1989, quintuple-bypass surgery in 1991, a stroke in 1994 — some of his nine children have been known to pinch-hit (he and Elvina also have twenty-seven grandchildren, thirty great-grandchildren, and three great-great-grandchildren).

Is there not a heroic element to being the Cal Ripken of climatology? Are not commitment and endurance as much beyond the norm as courage and daring? Maybe Thomas Wolfe was on the mark when he wrote that "it is the union of the ordinary and the miraculous that makes wonder." Day-to-day dedication made Ripken a Hall of Famer; why not Ray? Maybe the problem is that our heroic archetype was developed in an era when life was short, and thus brilliance was more honored than resilience. Here is what Emerson had to say on the matter: "The characteristic of heroism is its persistency. All men have wandering impulses, fits and starts of generosity. But when you have chosen your part, abide by it."

Ray grabs his walker-on-wheels and shuffles to his backyard to show me his rain gauge and his electronic temperature sensor. Then he leads me to a small office in the back of the house that serves as a trophy room of sorts. For his years of service, he has been honored by the National Oceanic and Atmospheric Association, the Pandora community, and the Ohio General Assembly. Along with the plaques and certificates, there are barometers and thermometers on the wall, and there is a digital weather computer in the room, a gift from his kids. But it isn't functioning anymore — not since it was struck by lightning. Again, here is the work of Zeus, a thug with a sense of humor.

I ask Ray to try to explain his devotion to the cause, but all he can offer is an it's-just-what-I-do shrug. "I always liked figures," he says, "ever since I was a little guy."

As I chat with him, I find myself musing on my childhood days, many of which were filled the way his have been — by fixating on a task and reveling in the details, by studying series of numbers and trying to uncover discernable patterns.

In junior high school, I used to join my brother and a friend in games of Statis Pro Baseball, which uses charts and pitcher and batter cards that accurately represent statistics for real-life players. We drafted teams, played a full 162-game schedule, and then generated *next year's* cards based on *this year's* statistics. So over the course of a few years, we devoted countless hours to creating our own derivative, stat-loaded world of baseball. It was our irrational pastime. A couple of years later, after taking a high school class in computer programming, I created a hypothetical baseball season in which an individual player would have four at-bats per game over 162 games. Once again, I sat for hours, playing and replaying the program, recording the random highs (54 homers!) and lows (a .238 average!) in a looseleaf note-book just like Ray Burkholder's. It is a wonder I ever went on a date.

I wish I could say the behavior stopped with the onset of adult-hood, but alas, it may have gotten worse. In my twenties, I read the three-thousand-page *Baseball Encyclopedia* cover to cover, collecting sta-tistical quirks that I was pretty sure nobody had ever noticed. *Hank Bauer and Hank Sauer each batted .259 for New York teams in 1957. . . . The 1971 Oakland A's featured players named Larry Brown, Dick Green, and Vida Blue. . . .* That sort of thing. I organized my discoveries — hundreds of them, filling dozens and dozens of pages — into a book that I called *Everything You Didn't Need to Know About Baseball.* It hides still in a file in my home office; I have never shown it to a single person.

My first published book, *The Sports 100,* a four-hundred-page ranking of the one hundred most important people in American sports history, was the upshot of being an inveterate list maker. In-deed, such lists are like pop culture sugar to me — the ten best movies of the season, the top fifty songs of the 1970s, the one hundred great-est novels of all time. Someone could develop a show dedicated to the Twenty Most Misunderstood Salad Dressings, and I would spend an hour riveted to VH-I.

Oh, and as far as U.S. geography is concerned, let's just say that I have it covered. As a result of my travels and my fanatical forays into the squiggles and dots of the Rand McNally, I have lists upon lists of every quirky town name in the fifty states. I have reams of mostly useless information, all of it solemnly recorded. Would you like a list of towns named after Shakespeare characters? Planets? Numerals? Shapes? Adjectives? I have them all. I can tell you that there are Cali-fornia towns named Hawaiian Gardens, Michigan Bluff, Virginia Colony, Nevada City, and Oregon House; and that Indiana has five communities named Mount Pleasant; and that there is an Arizona hamlet named Why and a Mississippi town named Whynot. See what I'm doing? While pretending to discuss my problem, I am just feed-ing the habit.

Given such revelations, it surely comes as no surprise that Amy chides me about my obsessive-compulsive streak. Actually, she pretends to laugh it off, but it really bugs the hell out of her. It isn't only that I tend to straighten picture frames that don't need straightening. There is a bigger philosophical conflict. She is a world-class multitasker, able to manage myriad responsibilities with the aplomb of someone juggling bowling pins while pedaling a unicycle. I am a linear thinker — one thing at a time. I can barely write and breathe simultaneously. My mind does not handle clutter well.

So if I were to speculate on the cause of my obsessive behavior as an adolescent, I think maybe I was trying to find some order in what I perceived as an increasingly untidy world. And the world only gets more chaotic when you have marriage and mortgages and mouths to feed, so naturally it follows that I have become an even bigger freak. I suppose I am trying, in my idiosyncratic way, to distill the universe into manageable chunks. By collecting information and organizing it, whether recording rainfall or runs batted in, you don't make life any more predictable. But at least you have a handle on the disarray. After all, weather is only truly bad if it catches you unprepared.

"I don't predict anything," says Ray. "A meteorologist predicts it. A climatologist records it."

But that doesn't mean Ray hasn't been in the predicting business. He spent much of his life as a farmer — growing corn, wheat, sugar beets, alfalfa, tomatoes. Farming is man's attempt to predict nature's whims. Although there is a routine to life on a farm — in everything from the chores to the seasons — it is a famously unpredictable way of making a living. Just ask Ray about the time two feet of rain fell in May, June, and July of 1943, causing him to lose half his sugar beet crop. Or about the drought in the early '50s. Or that early freeze in the fall of '74. Still, Ray seems to be fueled by the irregularity of the weather.

"In the month of February, for example," he says, a hint of giddiness in his voice, "we've had as high as seventy-three and as low as twenty-three below zero. That's a ninety-six-degree difference. . . . "

Ray Burkholder in his backyard

So I think he and I have another thing in common, in that there is a curious dichotomy to my relationship with randomness. Although I tend to sweat the small stuff, trying to make order from chaos, I think I prefer the unpredictability of the big picture. I am proud of the fact that Amy and I have crafted a lifestyle built around flexibility, that we don't have much of a set daily routine, that we can go off and do something together in the middle of the day and the middle of the week, that we can pick up and travel with our kids every summer. My profession isn't at the whim of the weather, but it has much the same haphazard quality. I draw energy from the notion that every time the phone rings or the e-mail clicks it might be an editor or publisher with some exciting news that takes me in a new direction.

Most of all, I like the fact that I can inform my wife that not only would I like to embark on a soul-searching journey to Ithaca, I also would like to write about the experience without the pressure of a publisher looking over my shoulder — in other words: Can I take several months off to walk a tightrope without a net? And she can turn to me and say, "I think that sounds like a great idea." And I love her for it. I can only hope, once the journey is over, that the feeling is mutual.

Of course, the other side of the coin is that we don't always know when our next paycheck is coming or even where it is coming from. And don't even get me started on the cost of health insurance. But I must admit, there is a sick part of me that takes pleasure in teetering on the edge of financial calamity without quite falling over it.

I suppose I tend to think of us as having steered closer to Charybdis than to Scylla. Odysseus opts for the latter, feeding the monster. On the other hand, I see a certain courage in navigating the maelstrom. During this cross-country trek, I have embraced the unknown. I don't want to have my life completely mapped out before me. I don't necessarily want to know where my path leads. I have come to understand that life without unpredictability is essentially lifeless. I want to let the wind take me where it might. *Que sera sera.*

Meanwhile, ol' Ray is still talking. "In May this year we had 1.22 inches of rain. Last year, we had 8.90. So it was over seven times as much last year as this year . . ."

He can go on like that forever, and he just might. "How long do you plan on doing this?" I ask, as he walks me to his front door.

He shrugs. "As long as I'm able."

"So about forty years or so?" I give him a wink.

He laughs, knowing full well the death-and-taxes axiom. "More or less."

XIX
omphalos

a pledge and ruin is near

The Seven Sages, a sort of Dream Team of ancient philosophers and legislators, were said to have left a trio of pithy maxims engraved upon a column at the site of the famous Oracle at Delphi. The seer who served as the oracle spoke in cryptic riddles, which were interpreted by the priests of the temple and then often misinterpreted by those who received them. The oracle was enormously influential, determining everything from city construction to strategies of war, so all the Greek states would send riches to satisfy the seer. While the treasures have long vanished (the shrine was destroyed at the end of the fourth century), it is said that the greatest fortune remains — in the form of the words of the Seven Sages.

"A pledge and ruin is near" is a suggestion to refrain from over-commitment and to act with caution, which does seem antithetical to the role of the hero with its traditional undertones of unwavering devotion to a cause or perhaps flirtation with disaster. Carefulness and courage would seem to be unrelated attributes. This I ponder as I watch men steer modern-day chariots around a muddy oval at break-neck speeds.

It is Burns Electric Night at the Attica Raceway, a weekly summer rumpus in an Ohio hamlet named (perhaps by some transplanted residents) after Attica, New York (home of the infamous state prison), which was itself named after the Greek peninsula jutting into the Aegean Sea. This is Friday-night dirt track racing, and even here — in the minor leagues of a blue-collar pastime in a sparsely populated region — there is money to be made. Tonight's event is sponsored by a local electronics store (a few weeks earlier, it was Martin Koop Attorney at Law Night). Concessionaires in trailers behind the grandstand are selling the four racetrack food groups — hot dogs, popcorn, funnel cakes, and ice cream. A garage gift shop peddles T-shirt iron-on slogans making pleas for faith (IN DODGE WE TRUST) and tolerance (GOD MADE ADAM AND EVE, NOT ADAM AND STEVE).

I find a seat in the corner of the wooden grandstand. Squinting through the dust, I can see moths and clouds of gnats waltzing beneath the trackside lights above a fence adorned with the names of local construction and farm drainage companies. As two dozen sprint cars spin and slide around the track, they kick up gusts of wind that send flecks of filth into the crowd like a nuclear winter. They say true dirt racing fans go home wearing part of the track. I have dirt in my eyes, splinters in my ass, and a ringing in my ears. The clamor comes from all sides — from the growl of the cars, from the rumble of trackside freight trains passing in both directions, from the yaps and howls of assorted angry dogs imprisoned in Pontiac Grand Ams in the parking lot, from the garbled exhortations of a public address announcer, and from the full-throated rapture of a few thousand locals, many of them cleverly adorned in protective goggles.

So this is where I have come to in my journey — sitting amid a rain of dirt and watching men drive machines in circles. Eventually, the engines go quiet and the gusts go soft and a young driver climbs out of the victorious No. 4 car. As he waves to the grime-soaked masses, a blonde a few feet away from me is exhorted by her soused friends to jump over the chain-link fence separating the riffraff from the dirt. She flips them the bird, climbs slowly down to the track, swivels her hips the length of the front stretch, and hugs tonight's hero.

nothing in excess

My journey to Attica had been a serene excursion, the early-evening tableau offering long shadows creeping down silos and cherry-red barns, which looked almost regal amid the approaching sunset, as if drawing life from the dying light. But now it is morning, and the light of day is a letdown as I head eastward another fifteen miles along Highway 224 — a gouged and roadkill-strewn stretch of road — to a crossroads known as Delphi.

The prophetess at ancient Delphi was usually an older woman who foretold men's futures by climbing atop a tripod over a fissure in the earth and receiving the divine breath of Apollo. All I can find in Ohio's version is an overweight woman holding a toddler and strad-dling an ATV. I arrive hoping for some sort of sign, a glimpse of my future. Instead, I find a muted oracle — a plain DELPHI sign next to a blank marquee and an arrow pointing to an empty parking lot. As I stand there, wallowing in pessimistic metaphors, a goateed guy on a Harley rumbles to a stop. His name is Joe. He owns the garage next to the empty lot. "Why don't you go to Greenwich. It's five miles up the road," he says. "That's a real town." So a few minutes later I find my sign: GREENWICH ROTARY TRUCK AND TRACTOR PULL — JUNE 4, 1 P.M. It is almost noon on June 4.

Like the pilgrims who used to seek the Oracle from all over Greece and Italy and Asia Minor and Egypt, folks are converging on this stretch of sludge in north-central Ohio, five miles east of Delphi. They arrive here from Jeffersonville and Fairfield and Richland and Bowling Green — grandfathers and grandsons in matching camou-flage caps, straw-haired women in tight tank tops, beefy men hiding their gravity-defying guts beneath T-shirts that say things like "My drinkin' team has a truck pullin' problem."

The trucks and tractors have names like Farm Boys Toys and Mighty Mac, and the mission is to use one to pull the other as far as you can before you get stuck in the muck. Which is about as simple as it gets. But amid the whiff of Sloppy Joes and the whine of country music and the whirr of souped-up machines, I find myself pondering the dichotomy of the tractor pull. Horsepower and traction. Energy and control. It's all about balance really, a mud-soaked equilibrium.

A tractor pull competition

Which brings me back to the Oracle at Delphi. It was said to be located at the geographic center of the inhabited world — marked by a dome-shaped rock, the *omphalos*, as the navel of the earth. According to myth, Zeus charged two eagles with finding this magical midpoint. He released one to the east and one to the west, and they met at Delphi, where the Greeks built a temple to Apollo. This striving for centeredness was evident in the second of the Seven Sages' maxims: "Nothing in excess." It is a recurring notion in Greek philosophy.

Socrates taught that a man "must know how to choose the mean and avoid the extremes on either side." Aristotle referred to the "golden mean" of life, a balance between the excesses of youth and age — between extravagance and frugality, optimism and pessimism, passion and temperance. One should be courageously temperate, he said, and temperately courageous. Of course, Aristotle also believed that thirty-seven-year-old men should marry eighteen-year-old women, as he did. So apparently the ancient Greeks had an understanding of the midlife crisis, even when the average life span was about thirty-five years. And here I am, headlong into my late thirties, trying to approximate Aristotle's balance, if not his libido.

On the one hand, mine is a youthful quest — a mission to savor experience and explore the unfamiliar. On the other hand, I feel like an impostor — not only out of place (I wonder if the assembled race and pull fans can sense my unease, whispering to each other about that sushi-eating, Gap-wearing, left-leaning interloper) but also out of time. Am I too old for exploration? Too old to be hitting the road in a search for some tenuous link between myth and reality? Jack Kerouac once commented that the East represented his past and the West his future. Am I heading east just to stave off time?

My friends from my college days perform intricate surgeries and negotiate multimillion-dollar deals and own more than one necktie. They have reached the cusp of middle age with a certain level of adult responsibility. And what am I doing? I am nearly two thousand miles from home, watching trucks spin their wheels and feeling as if I have been doing the same. I find myself struggling with the psychic equivalent of a tractor pull. I used to be fueled by energy. Now I yearn for traction.

Aristotle would tell me that if I seek self-worth, I have to stop thinking that aiming for the center is the same as aiming low. He believed the mean to be the very opposite of that. Rather, he favored teaching moral reasoning so that adults would instinctually locate the mean. Actually, I think I have done the opposite. Having been born into a pretty standard Midwest suburban existence, I drifted toward the fringes, at least professionally and geographically. But I have been temperately courageous at best.

Most important, Aristotle would tell me to stop viewing the pursuit of the center in absolute terms and instead aim for, as he put it, "the mean considered relatively to ourselves." In other words, stop measuring myself against my peers and come to grips instead with my own golden mean, which is a good bit of advice for someone headed toward a college reunion.

Here is what Joseph Campbell wrote about that: "To a man not led astray by sentiments from the surfaces of what he sees, but courageously responding to the dynamics of his own nature — to a man who, as Nietzsche phrases it, is 'a wheel rolling of itself'—difficulties melt and the unpredictable highway opens as he goes."

So I vow to do that with greater frequency, as I continue along Highway 224 — to find the center of my universe by looking inward. And maybe I will find I have struck a respectable balance. After all, Campbell also stated this: "The hero as the incarnation of God is himself the navel of the world."

know thyself

The third of the Seven Sages' maxims is easier said than done. The Zen-like notion that who you are informs what you do (rather than what you do defining who you are) would suggest that I am a writer because I am an observer. Of course, I also chose the profession because I like to sleep late, shave once a week, and wear ratty clothes. But mostly it is because I am a spectator and extrapolator, someone who tries to draw profound meaning from a constant carnival of minutiae. It is a curse, really.

I sit at baseball games and find myself people-watching until startled by a foul ball that lands in my nachos. I go to bachelor parties and find myself pondering not the stripper's backside but rather her backstory. I attend social gatherings and tend to watch from the corners, from where I make broad generalizations about humankind by observing the way people dress or congregate or hold their liquor. I know I possess decent social skills. Indeed, occasionally I can come across as charming. But beneath that confident exterior is a man who is desperately ensnared in an almost pathological cycle of analysis — self and otherwise. A cocktail party becomes an inner Albert Brooks monologue.

Frankly, it has made me cynical. I detect a certain trend or behavior that bothers me, then I dissect it, explore its source, assess the societal imperfections represented by it . . . and suddenly I find myself making some broad indictment against a component of modern culture. It drives my wife crazy. Heaven forbid somebody drops a cigarette butt on the sidewalk. She has to hear me rail against the diffusion of responsibility in modern industrial societies. Or if the television happens to catch a breathless account of Tom Cruise's wedding, she has to roll her eyes while I embark on a sixty-second invective about the culture of celebrity worship. So that may be why I became a writer. It was an outlet for me, like boxing is to Mike Tyson and bullying is to Bobby Knight.

Of course, Knight once famously contended that we all learn to write in second grade and most of us move on to greater things (somebody should have pointed out that we learn our X's and O's in kindergarten). In fact, I could afford to start my own publishing house if I had a dollar for every time someone has told me, "You know, I was thinking of writing a book . . ." When that happens, I am always tempted to refer to an anecdote I once encountered from an author who heard that same line from a neurosurgeon at a cocktail party. She turned to him and said, "You know, that's weird. Because I was thinking of trying brain surgery."

Then again, while not everyone is a wordsmith (this is made clear as I pass a hotel that offers — and this is a permanent sign — rooms at RESONABLE RATES), I am well aware that writing is not brain surgery. And what I have long tried to figure out is where it falls on the scale of worthwhile professions.

I muse about this because I have arrived once again, quite literally, at a crossroads. This one, twenty-three miles east of Delphi, is called Homerville. A block away from the amazingly tiny Homerville Post Office sits the yellow-brick Homerville Community Center, which was once known as Homer School. CONGRATULATIONS

GRADUATES, it says on the marquee. This being early June, I have been seeing variations on that theme repeatedly over the past couple of weeks — above gas stations, movie theaters, even Dunkin' Donuts. Middle America is sending its children into the real world, hoping, one must assume, that they will achieve something admirable, something that contributes to what George W. Bush called the "embetterment" of mankind.

I am staring at the sign when a fellow wearing a camouflage cap and a torn muscle shirt rides up on his ATV. He looks to be in his early twenties. His name, it turns out, is also Brad, and he tells me that thirty-seven people live in the village of Homerville, which is in the township of Homer.

"So what do you do around here?" I ask.

He points to a dairy farm just down the road. "I milk cows."

I detect a self-effacing tone in his voice, as if he is saying, "Sorry, that's all I do." But in the context of my state of mind at the moment, he may as well have told me that he invents vaccines or builds skyscrapers. Here is tangibility personified. *He milks cows! He turns nature into nurture! He is a vital cog in the circle of life!*

And what do I do? I turn phrases. I craft transitions. I milk metaphors. I don't save lives like Sheriff Dean Roland in Siren. I don't risk my life like Sergeant Scott Frey in Sparta. I haven't dedicated my life to civil service like Commissioner Bill Hansell in Athena. I simply chronicle life. And when I think of it that way, my role seems embarrassingly passive and reactionary. I don't even milk cows; I just write about the guy who does. How essential am I?

This being Homer Township, perhaps I should look for the answer in the wandering minstrel himself. But beyond the existence of the *Iliad* and the *Odyssey*, there is no proof that the alleged author of those epics actually walked the earth. There may have been a fellow named Homer who lived around the eighth century B.C. and committed to memory tales of heroism from centuries past. Or it may have simply been an appellation given to an amalgamation of rhapsodes who crafted and refined the stories of Achilles and Odysseus over the centuries. So the singular literary icon may have been as much a product of wish fulfillment as the stories attributed to him.

However, there is no denying the Homeric legacy. By the fifth century B.C., the *Iliad* and the *Odyssey* were inextricably interwoven in nearly every facet of Greek culture. They were the Old and New Testament of a polytheistic society and a staple of academic curricula. They informed social custom. Homer himself became the focus of a hero cult. At least half a dozen cities in Asia Minor claimed him as a native son. He was celebrated — in shrines, paintings, even religious sacrifices — as more than a poet, as something of a divinely inspired progenitor of literature.

Homer makes no attempt at modesty. Through the words of Odysseus, he comments that singers have honor and respect "in every nation upon the earth." He tenderly praises Demodocus, minstrel of Scheria, "whom the Muse loved dearly, and she gave him both good and evil; of his sight she reft him, but granted him sweet song." So Demodocus was blind, as Homer was said to be. This tradition of sightless singers may stem from two long-held beliefs: that the absence of sight strengthens the acute memory needed to recall an oral epic and that ancient poets were seers who could glimpse the future but who were unable to perceive the present. Or it could be that the blindness suggests a different symbolism, the idea that a knack for storytelling can be accompanied by a lack of more basic capacities. This is what worries me.

There are times when I feel as if I am experiencing life only so that I can present it to others — much like the way you see some people walking around with a video camera sutured to their eye at a tourist attraction. There have been several occasions when I have implored my wife to stop trying to pose the family for a vacation picture, to just enjoy the moment instead of trying to capture it for posterity. Yet, hypocritically, I tend to view life's little moments through a writer's lens, as if everything that happens to me is fodder for an essay or a screenplay or a children's story.

I tend to prefer nonfiction, both as a reader and writer, trying to make sense of reality rather than putting forth an imagined version. But there are times when I wonder if all I do is report the experiences of others. Garrison Keillor once stated that writers are "vacuum cleaners who suck up other people's lives and weave them into stories like a sparrow builds a nest from scraps." Perhaps he is right. Maybe my career, which is second only to my family as a manifestation of who I am, is merely a shadow of others' achievements. Whatever skills I possess as a writer, where would I be without the experiences of the heroic people — activists, conservationists, philanthropists, survivors, pioneers — whose deeds I have recounted over the course of my career?

Then again, Brad from Homerville couldn't do much without the cows.

Long after Homer, Walt Whitman chimed in on the role of the writer in the world. He claimed that a heroic people cannot exist without heroic literature to provide a blueprint for an era-appropriate moral conscience. Whitman believed the ancients needed Homeric legends and the Europeans needed Arthurian tales and, presumably, America needed progressive dreamers like himself. He wrote that great literature "penetrates all, gives hue to all, shapes aggregates and individuals." Fine, I'll give him that. Great literature can, indeed, change the world. Once in a while a Homer or Shakespeare comes around — or even a Steinbeck or a Sinclair. But what about the rest of us hacks?

However, when I ask what I am contributing to society on a daily basis, maybe I am asking the wrong question. What do we know about Homer? Nothing, really. We have no information about his birth, his life, his death. All we have is his legacy. And maybe that is what I will have too.

Ask a writer for whom he is writing, and if he points to himself don't believe him. To a certain extent, we all do. If I am not satisfied by my work — not only by the output, but by the cathartic act itself — then at the very least I am disappointed. But if I am the only one who matters, then I may as well write in invisible ink. On the other hand, I don't entirely write for the reader either — mainly because doing that is like trying to stereotype a snowflake. You can't possibly please everybody. Do I write for the rewards? Sure. It is a job that (sometimes) pays the bills. But again, that isn't my primary goal either. If it were, I would be far less selective in my subject matter, and I would be able to afford two cars.

So what's left? There are times when I feel as if I write for posterity.

I know it sounds incredibly pompous, particularly for someone whose books have been known to go out of print with as much speed as the winged feet of Hermes. But if I could publish my magazine articles on nondegradable paper, if my books could be handmade and bound in leather — hell, if I could carve an essay into the North Face of Grand Teton — I most certainly would. Mine is a quest for knowledge and a mission to distill it. My goal is to leave something tangible, something lasting. And maybe it begins with simply considering the parameters of courage.

So I vow to remember, as well, that without scribes, there is a lack of models to which the masses can aspire — no Superman, no Hercules, no Lancelot, no Atticus Finch, no Frank Merriwell. And if you can't create a champion out of whole cloth, you can do worse than trumpet the true-to-life protagonists in our midst. We can't all be heroes, but we can leave a greater understanding of the heroic ideal. And at the very least, I can boast the courage of my convictions.

"The true artist has the planet for his pedestal," Emerson declared. "The adventurer, after years of strife, has nothing broader than his own shoes." As I leave the township of Homer, I take solace in that.

XX

new castle

Late in my maternal grandmother's life, when she was confined to a wheelchair and her mind was grasping at coherence, she never lost her generosity of spirit and her sense of humor. Every time I visited her, I could expect an exuberant greeting, usually some sort of singsongy piece of flattery. "Well, if it isn't Mr. America!" I knew it was because she probably didn't remember my name (and I knew, too, that her eyesight had long been failing her), but I reveled in the welcome. We would chat as best we could, considering that her short-term memory challenges created an endless loop of conversation.

"So what are you doin' to make money?" she would ask.

"I'm a writer, Grandma."

"A what?"

"A writer."

"A writer! Can you make enough to eat?"

"We'll see . . . ," I would answer, playing along.

"You married yet?"

"Not yet. Pretty soon, Grandma." Indeed, I was about to propose to Amy.

"Well, what the hell are ya waitin' for?" And then she would ask again, "So what are you doin' to make money?"

"I'm a writer, Grandma."

"A writer!"

Anyway, it was the act of conversing that was important, rather than the practical benefits of it. We were sharing time together, nothing less, nothing more. As the months passed, I could see her eyes growing more vacant with each visit. The conversation grew loopier. She wasn't so much interested in my answers to her questions as she was in offering up the questions themselves. A third and fourth time she would ask, "So what are you doin' to make money?" So I would start to get creative.

"I'm a rocket scientist, Grandma."

"Oh, that's nice . . ."

I would try to probe her memories, but eventually they were largely relegated to vague generalities and shrugs. She could talk a bit about her youth in Pennsylvania or iconic figures from her era, but I sensed no real emotional connection in her recollections — until I would ask her about Grandpa Bunny. At the mention of his name, Grandma Ida's eyes, all too often glazed over by then, would brighten noticeably. Suddenly, she was all there again — alive in the moment.

"Oh, he was somethin' else," she would say. From there, she would wander into an anecdote, usually the same story, about how his pals on his football team greeted Bun (that's what everyone called him) outside the temple doors following Yom Kippur services one evening, looking all glum on the Jewish Day of Atonement and telling him they would have won the game if he had only played. She would punctuate the tale with laughter. And then always, with absolute predictability, she would lean forward — as if imparting information of great consequence — and end the reverie with the same line: "And you know, he was damn good lookin', too!"

It always made me smile. Still does.

I never knew Bernard Rosenblum. He died fifteen months before I was born. From what I can gather, he was quite the character. He was a football star, a soldier, and a loyal son who toughed it out in the family business. He was an accomplished painter and a musician who liked Dixieland jazz. He was a beer drinker, known for uncapping beer bottles with his teeth. He had a reputation as a bit of a playboy, but he also sang with the temple choir. It can be wonderful to get to know your maternal grandfather through gushing platitudes and earthy anecdotes. Isn't that how myths are born? My imagination conjures up a larger-than-life figure: heroic, talented, charming, and irreverent.

"He would be proud of you, as you should be of him," my great-uncle Marc, my grandfather's brother, wrote to me a few years back, just before he passed away. Uncle Marc outlived his brothers and sisters by nearly three decades and was the only one of my grandfather's eight siblings whom I ever met. He was a writer, brilliant and esoteric and opinionated, and he tended to think of himself as the intellectual outsider of the clan, a poet amid the prosaic. He was the family's genealogist and keeper of historical anecdotes, and he would send me occasional letters offering memories of my grandfather, who was eleven years older than he. But always he would throw in a line of regret. "As I write this," he admitted once, "I realize how little I knew him and how miserably I failed to show appreciation of his generosity and his unadvertised talents and virtues."

It has been nearly four decades since Bunny passed away. Now that I see the significant roles that grandparents play in my sons' lives, I find myself wanting to know more about not only who my grandfather was, but where he came from. After all, to learn more about him is to discover the genesis of myself.

Several centuries ago, my maternal ancestors lived in the Lithuanian capital of Vilna, once known as the "Jerusalem of Lithuania" for its role as a center of Judaic culture and a preeminent site for rabbinical studies (later, the Nazis turned it into an overcrowded ghetto where as many as 100,000 Jews were killed). Sometime in the eighteenth century, a group of immigrants from Vilna settled in the village of Vilke, along the Nieman River. Known as Vilenchik, they made their living by bartering, because Jews were not admitted to the craftsmen's guilds. One of the most important members of the community was a fellow named Osher. The manager of a nobleman's estate, he lived in a fine house in Vilke and gave his family an official surname — Rosenblum.

One of Osher's sons, Chaim David, settled down on a little farm a few miles from Vilke and operated a flour mill. Unlike his father, he was a poor man, barely able to feed his brood. In an attempt to find greater opportunity (and to escape the general anti-Semitism afflicting nineteenth-century Russia), his children were among thousands of Jews who decided to emigrate to America.

Chaim David's third son, Isaac Samuel Rosenblum, followed his two older brothers west just after his sixteenth birthday. According to a letter he wrote to his own children toward the end of his life, Sammy (as he would later be known) arrived in New York in September 1883 with little understanding of English and twenty dollars' worth of rubles in his pocket. He immediately began looking for work and was offered a four-dollars-a-week job. But when he discovered that his room and board would also cost him four dollars weekly, he asked his employer for a five-dollar salary, so that he might send the extra dollar home to his parents. "That's a greenhorn for you," the man said scornfully. "You give him a job and before he starts working he already wants a raise." So Sammy stomped away in disgust and instead took a train to the western Pennsylvania borough of Sharon, which was then a bustling industrial center hard against the Ohio state line.

Sammy joined his brothers, Nathan and Harry, who were sleeping in an attic in a small home in the factory district and paying twenty cents per meal. These immigrants made their living much as the Vilenchiks had done in Vilke. Sammy was given a half-bushel basket containing various articles — pins, buttons, socks, handkerchiefs. His brothers taught him the names of the objects, the selling prices of the goods, and how to count from one to one hundred. They taught him how to approach a lady and ask, "Do you want to buy anything?" and how to ask once more if the first reply was negative. Within months, he was strapping eighty pounds over his shoulders, slogging along the dirt roads of western Pennsylvania day after day, literally peddling the wares on his back.

So here was the iconic immigrant patriarch, a man whose descendants would number sixteen grandchildren and some three dozen great-grandchildren spread from coast to coast. They became school-teachers and pediatricians and advertising executives and attorneys. Considering this is a family with solid working-class roots, a surprising number of my cousins have made their mark in the arts. Among them are several painters, at least three professional musicians (including a San Francisco Symphony violinist and a Broadway musical director), a host of National Public Radio's *All Things Considered*, and more than a half-dozen authors. And all because a sixteen-year-old had the courage to set off for a mysterious land across an ocean and start at the bottom rung of the American Dream.

I asked my Greek chorus about this sort of hero: the Underappreciated Personification of Resolve. The single mother who works three jobs and raises five kids. The factory worker who trudges to work daily and saves his nickels so that maybe his children can go to college. The home health care worker who patiently caters to the most intimate needs of an elderly client in her last, dying days. If, as has been postulated before, heroism happens when courage meets circumstance, what if the circumstances are mundane? "If someone chooses to be a carpenter, for instance, rather than a doctor or firefighter or soldier," I asked my chorus, "what can they do to be heroic?"

The answer: "Maybe we shouldn't define them by profession. Often heroism is a lot less conspicuous. . . . Maybe one quality has to do with stamina and effort and resolve." Perhaps elements like tenacity and humility combine to form a heroic compound. What's that line from Gilbert and Sullivan? "If everybody is somebody, then nobody is anybody." Perhaps. But maybe nobody would be anybody without the somebodies who came before them. And I am willing to bet that most every American's family history can be traced back to epic immigrant tales of valor and fortitude.

"I had my troubles, but also my pleasure. Just be carefull [*sic*] and keep on." That was how Sammy Rosenblum concluded the letter he wrote to his children not long before he died, as if summing up his life and his lessons.

• • •

My great-grandfather married a woman named Rachel, whose family also came from Vilna in Lithuania and emigrated to the United States via Dublin. Her father was a Jewish scholar named Litvinovski until an immigration inspector suggested, "Why don't you use a good Irish name like Harris?" So Litvinovski from Lithuania became — and this is the part I like best — Harris from Troy (albeit Troy, New York).

By the turn of the century Sammy and Rachel lived in the city of New Castle, Pennsylvania, another industrial center about a dozen miles southeast of Sharon. The city's origins are far from gallant: in 1798 a civil engineer named John Stewart traveled to western Pennsylvania to resurvey lands granted by the government to revolutionary war veterans. In the process, he discovered that the original survey forgot to stake out fifty acres at the confluence of Neshannock Creek and the Shenango River. So he grabbed it for himself. A century later, with the arrivals of canals and railroads and mills and immigrant labor, it had become the tin plate capital of the world. New Castle may sound like a town named after grand aspirations, but it is and always has been a bastion of the proletariat. Sammy and Rachel started a bare-bones furniture store there — just dining tables and chairs to start with — and raised a family that eventually would grow to five girls and four boys. Bernard — Bunny, my mother's father — was the middle child.

Sammy still struggled to make ends meet. In the letters he wrote to his children later in life, his grasp of English still somewhat tenuous after six decades in America, he recalls a time when the mills were shut down for several weeks. When they reopened, the mill workers were to receive three weeks' pay on a particular Saturday, meaning business would be booming. But that Saturday also happened to be Yom Kippur, the holiest day on the Jewish calendar. Sammy was faced with a dilemma — in his eyes, he had to choose between feeding his family and feeding his soul. So he tried to do both. Believing he couldn't afford to lose the few hundred dollars in sales, he came up with a plan. He sold the store outright to a Mrs. Fulton, his chief assistant, for five dollars, intending to buy it back immediately after the holiday. It might have worked, but Rachel got wind of the scheme. She retrieved the key to the store from Mrs. Fulton at sundown, just before the family was to sit down for its final supper before fasting, and laid it on the table next to her husband. "Your store will be closed tomorrow," she told him. End of story.

Now that I think of it, I find it curious that some of my ancestors' most prominent tales seem to revolve around making moral choices on the Day of Atonement. Most interesting, we seem to find comedy in it.

Meanwhile, I head to New Castle, which is an hour's jaunt east along that same Highway 224. As I get closer, I fiddle with my radio dial, trying to locate AM 680, a CBS affiliate broadcasting out of the nearby city of Butler, where the Rosenblum family moved in later years and where Isaac Samuel Rosenblum's eldest son, David, started the news talk radio station and called it WISR. I can think of no better memorial to the man than an AM station — a simple source making waves that travel great distances.

Butler is where my Grandpa Bunny ran a furniture store, gaining a reputation as someone who may have been a bit too willing to do favors for friends and a bit too reluctant to collect unpaid bills. It is where my mother was born and raised (in a house that happened to have bunnies on the window shutters) and where Bun and Ida are buried. But on this particular journey, it is New Castle that draws my attention. This is where my ancestors gained some traction, the place that transformed an immigrant peddler into a patriarch. And it is a city where his middle child, my grandfather, set off on a life course that barely missed intersecting with mine. So today I visit New Castle for the first time, searching for a connection.

Although the city is in the midst of a revitalization, my initial reaction upon seeing it is that it feels old-fashioned, almost as if I have driven into the past, *Back to the Future* style. Along Washington Street, the main thoroughfare through town, I pass businesses with antiquated names that seem to match their faded storefronts — Hall of Hobbies, Malloy's Cameracade, Fountain Restaurant. I spy what looks like a redbrick warehouse overlooking the creek that meanders through town. The fading words "Dry Goods" are still noticeable on its facade. A Civil War monument rises from the center of a traffic circle. It is fronted by a cannon, which is aimed, I am discomfited to notice, directly at my Winnebago.

I have parked the Aspect across from a three-story brick Italianate building. This was the site of the Warner brothers' first permanent nickelodeon — the Cascade, which opened nearly a century ago. Today, Warner Brothers has financed construction of the Cascade Center here, an enterprise that includes a re-creation of the brothers' first theater. I peek into a large ground-floor window to see an unfinished room already furnished with eighteen seats and a massive antique movie projector. According to the family stories, my grandfather used to run the Warner brothers' projector as a child. I squint in an attempt to picture an eleven-year-old boy gaping in wonder at the magic of an early silent film. But like an ancient piece of celluloid, the image flickers for me and then goes dark.

So I head for the public library instead, sifting through the archives and thumbing my way through old high school yearbooks until I come across a photo of my grandfather, a leather-uniformed adolescent in prideful pose — Captain Bun of the dominant 1916 football squad. My research tells me that a number of notable New Castle natives were his schoolmates. One girl became a philanthropist and married Spencer Tracy. Another led the field trials for Jonas Salk's polio vaccine. But back then the part of local hero was played by Captain Bun.

The gushing accounts of the New Castle football team speak of "a steady procession up and down the field by our husky warriors." Many of the accolades are reserved for the captain. Bun scoring three touchdowns against New Wilmington High and recording the team's only points in a win over Rochester. Bun "smashing the opposing line to pieces with his plunging." Bun's return to the field after a knee injury, which "renewed the life of the team." And what is this I see? "In our next game with Beaver, crippled by the absence of Captain

Rosenblum, we were held to a scoreless tie." That would have been September, possibly around Yom Kippur. Perhaps my grandmother's oft-told tale was accurate after all.

Staring at the photograph of him in his football leathers — a Jew among broad-shouldered Gentiles, with his thick, wavy hair and his large, expressive eyes — I try to imagine myself in his place. But again I can't. I am too far removed — in time, in distance, in appearance, in generational assimilation. Not to mention athleticism.

So I decide to search for his childhood home. I locate a 1915 city directory, and once again irony creeps into my journey. The address listed for the Rosenblum family is 108 Quest Street. How satisfyingly appropriate. I have never in my life heard of a street named Quest; unfortunately, neither have the residents of New Castle. I approach a man in an establishment called House of Brews. He has lived there his entire life, but he knows of no Quest Street. A woman at a parking meter simply shrugs and shakes her head. I walk into a store called American News Stand, where a handful of old Italian men hem and haw for a while. One fellow, chewing a hand-rolled cigar, takes control.

"Quest? Isn't that in the Croton area?"

"Is it?"

"You have to get to Croton Road." He starts giving tortuous and mischievous directions, things like "There's a yellow building painted white. Don't turn there." I leave with only a vague notion of which direction I should point myself, but I slide behind the wheel and try anyway, climbing the hills on the outskirts of town, picking my way among the maze of streets in the Croton neighborhood. Nothing. The folks there can't recollect a Quest Street either. My quest for Quest appears to be at a dead end.

Frustrated, I pull to a stop in the lot of what looks like an abandoned gas station and turn off the engine. I think back to my visit to Dayton, Washington, and my attempt to find the house of my murderous great-great-uncle Henry Roth. The address no longer existed, but at least the street was still there. Here, in New Castle, it feels as if a whole page has been torn out of my family's history. I thought perhaps the setting that shaped my grandfather would help me perceive him in greater definition. But I am left with only recreated theaters and sepia photographs and vanished roads.

All of my life I have learned about him through the recollections of others — his little brother who outlived him by more than thirty years; his best gal who clung to the memory of him like a life preserver in her final days; his daughter, who still lights a candle every May to honor her dad, who died when she was only twenty-three. I always wished I could hear about him in his own voice. I would hear the pitch and timbre, what kind of laugh he had, the peculiarities of his northern Appalachian accent. Thanks to a package sent to me by my mother before I embarked on my expedition, I can.

I climb into the back of the Aspect and pull out a file containing a mishmash of genealogical references, collected over the years but never organized, an assortment of names and dates and a family tree so scrawled and indecipherable that it looks more like family kudzu. Carefully, I remove a folder inside the file, to find a series of letters saved over the decades, dated from June 1918 through February 1919. Most of them begin "Dear Folks," and end with "Corporal Bernard Rosenblum, Company 7, 332nd Infantry, American Expeditionary Forces." I spend the next few hours immersed in the Great War with the grandfather I never knew.

I cannot picture myself in Europe's trenches during World War I, no more than I can imagine being at the gates of Troy, wearing a golden corselet over my chest and a plumed helmet atop my head. But I can identify, at least on some level, with the fear of the unknown and the angst of separation from family. I suspect this is why a soldier's letters home can be so moving. They are an attempt to maintain a grasp on humanity in the midst of dehumanizing warfare. Amid the savagery, there can be a powerful poetry.

Wartime correspondence can be purposefully unrevealing — self-edited of information and emotion in an effort to protect both the soldiers and the readers. But even the most mundane missives are windows into a young man's soul during what is surely the seminal experience of his life. It is possible that my grandfather had never before left the confines of western Pennsylvania, except perhaps for a handful of regional football games. Suddenly, at age twenty-two, he was shipped halfway around the world, marched through towns with names — Valleggio, Sommacompagna, Villafranca di Verona — that he probably couldn't pronounce, and deposited into the middle of an epic battle dubbed the War to End All Wars. It must have been terrifying and electrifying.

You don't hear much about the 332nd Infantry during World War I. Entire books have been written about the battles in Europe without mention of the regiment, which was the only American unit to serve on the Italian front. Under the command of Colonel William Wallace, the 332nd was formed in August 1917 at Camp Sherman in Chillicothe, Ohio. The soldiers, mostly from Ohio and Pennsylvania, came from a variety of socioeconomic and ethnic groups, and my grandfather says as much, in his own inimitable way: "Each corporal has a squad of seven men and himself. Eight in all. I've got a bunch of good fellows and every one is older than I am. Me, the youngest and the corporal. I inquired around and discovered I had a full blooded German, a Russian Pollock (Polish), a real Irish man and me a Jew."

After several months of intensive drills and training, in May 1918 the soldiers of the 332nd left for the eastern seaboard via the B&O Railroad. Twelve days later, they boarded the Cunard liner HMS *Aquitania* for the voyage to Europe (Bun's take: "I got slightly seasick the first day out, but after that it was just like riding one of New Castle's street cars"). A train to Southhampton. A transport across the English Channel, during which they passed the wreckage of ships sunk by German submarines. And into France, where, says Bun, "The cutest little French girl is teaching me to speak the language." He talks of playing his mandolin for the women in the village, and then, almost offhandedly, he adds, "I'll be playing for the Senoritas soon."

Unlike the vast majority of American forces, the 332nd didn't stay in France. Instead, the regiment arrived in Milan in midsummer and was greeted by throngs of Italians shouting "Viva l'America" and showering the soldiers with flowers. But in Italy the soldiers also suffered infestations of mice and fleas, bouts with dysentery, and the threat of an influenza epidemic that so ravaged the northern part of the country that bodies were piling up faster than they could be buried. ("Spanish Flu, as they call it here," writes Bun. "It's very bad and I do wish you folks would be careful you wouldn't get it.")

My grandfather doesn't reveal his exact location or mission. Instead, he talks in peripheral details and sweeping generalities — how the houses in Italy are "infested with the prettiest little black swallows with white bodies underneath" or how the Kaiser is "trying to drive a nail thru the world with a sponge, but he can't do it no matter how hard he soaks it." As I wade through my grandfather's handwriting, I learn little about the war. But I feel as if I am gaining great insight into the warrior.

Bernard (Bunny) Rosenblum, during World War I

I see evidence of his earthy charm when he uses phrases like "straight dope" and "don't worry yourselves bowlegged." When he asks about the state of the family business ("I guess we'll have a pretty good store soon"), I sense his regret at leaving his parents and siblings to fend for themselves. When he writes that one of the worst things his father can do is "mention gefilte fish and pie to a fellow and then say don't get homesick," I understand that, while his quirky gastronomical preferences may have been passed down to me, it isn't the food that he misses. I imagine a young man itching to reveal his myriad experiences to his loved ones, but forced to offer only cryptic comments ("I could tell you more, but not now. Lots of things that nobody in America knows") and youthful bluster ("The Kaiser's nose is red. His eyes are blue. His chin recedes. His army, too").

He must have been an overwhelmed twenty-two-year-old, but he adopts a tone of nonchalance interspersed with occasional false bravado, and I know that it must be for the benefit of his worried readers, if not a means of diminishing his own fears. Once in a while, I can glimpse an attempt to encapsulate the enormity of it all, as when he uses three simple words to describe his epiphanies while at the front: "Funny, funny world."

For the most part, he seems a young man who knows he is mortal but prefers to think he isn't. So when he sends his regards to a neighbor, Mrs. Wallace, and her dog—"Tell her I can teach Zeus to lay for me"—I resist the temptation to treat it as a metaphor.

The 332nd lost only a handful of soldiers. In early September, a mortar exploded during drills, killing seven and wounding several dozen. That proved to be more casualties than the regiment suffered in combat. To some extent, the regiment's role in Italy was meant to be symbolic. It was there to serve as proof of American-Italian cooperation, and this may be my favorite thing about the 332nd. Although they trained and fought and died for the cause — and although they did suitably heroic things like crossing rivers, traversing the Alps, knock-

ing out machine gun nests, and capturing supply depots — it might
be argued that this particular regiment represented an army of ideas.

Let me explain: my grandfather's letters speak occasionally of
marching through the countryside. Never of fighting. Always marching. Although he makes it sound dreary and insignificant, this seems
to have been the regiment's primary responsibility. The 332nd staged
a series of long marches in which each battalion would take a separate
road out of the city of Treviso. Hauling different equipment and
adorned in an ever-changing assortment of headgear, each battalion
would circulate in sight of the Italians (our side) and the Austrians
(their side), boosting morale for the former and (hopefully) confusing the latter before returning as inconspicuously as possible after
nightfall.

"War sure is a joke on this front," Bun writes at one point. He was
surely trying to assuage his parents' worries. But in some respects, the
American presence in Italy was all a big strategic gag. And the deception worked. Austrian generals later admitted that they thought there
were at least six American divisions and possibly as many as 300,000
soldiers in Italy. Austrian morale plummeted, and it may have short-
ened the war on the Italian front, saving thousands of lives.

For someone like me — my place on the combat courage spectrum likely falling somewhere between pacifist and petrified — these
are my kinds of soldiers. In fact, these are Odysseus-like warriors.
Homer said repeatedly that resourcefulness was Odysseus's strong suit.
He was the "man of many wiles"—heroic in thought as well as deed.
Achilles had his spear. Ajax has his pike. Odysseus's most potent
weapon was ingenuity.

Was Bun a hero? Well, 350,000 New Yorkers cheered the regiment's parade down Fifth Avenue in the spring of 1919. Which certainly beats Odysseus's return — to encounter a bunch of suitors trying
to bed his wife. Homer may have constructed an epic poem about the
Trojan War, but Bun Rosenblum did the same following the Great
War, a handful of rhymes summarizing his year in the service: "Soon
our day came to go across . . . To show old Heinie who is boss . . . We

went thru England, France, Italy . . . And saw some country I longed to see." Nice, perhaps, but I get the feeling my puckish grandfather would rather have written a scandalous limerick about Nantucket.

My great-grandparents, I assume, were proud of their son. But mostly I suspect they were relieved. In fact, I can hear their concern through Bun's responses in his letters. At one point, he tries to soothe his worried mother's mind, telling her, "The fact your dream of me coming home was not true at the time does not say it won't be true."

It turns out she worried about the wrong son in the wrong war. Early in his letters, my grandfather offers words of sympathy for his seven-year-old brother Hank: "I hated school when I was a kid, too." Twenty-four years later, Hank served as an M.D. on a Coast Guard weather observation ship, the USS *Muskeget*, which cruised the Atlantic during World War II. But a communication on September 9, 1942, was the ship's last. The *Muskeget* had been patrolling waters teeming with enemy submarines, and it was later suspected (though never confirmed) that a German U-boat fired two torpedoes into her side. A couple of weeks later, Sammy Rosenblum received a telegram informing him that his youngest son, who had a two-year-old son of his own at home and a baby girl on the way, was "missing in the performance of his duty." The two-year-old went on to become a doctor, just like his dad.

There are shades of Odysseus here — the man lost at sea, thousands of miles from his wife and son. But in this story, all 121 men aboard the *Muskeget* disappeared without a trace. Haskell "Hank" Rosenblum attended the same university as I, the one on the hill in Ithaca. And he remains there, his name engraved on a World War II memorial above a quotation by Abraham Lincoln: "So costly a sacrifice upon the altar of freedom."

Should it be a badge of pride to me that some members of my ancestral family were American heroes in a most traditional manner? My great-grandfather turned a sack full of knickknacks and a strong back into the foundation of a widespread and broadly successful family. My grandfather played a role in outwitting the Austrian army. My great-uncle gave his life as one of the good guys in the Good War. They represent a sort of holy trinity of American attributes — perseverance, inventiveness, and sacrifice.

However, valor is not inherited. Prejudging others based on ancestry is the root of bigotry, just as self-satisfaction based on the feats of one's forebearers is false conceit. It might have been customary in Homer's day, when men would introduce themselves as "Mentes, son of Anchialus" and "Ilus, son of Mermerus." I have never once had anyone refer to me as Brad, son of Myron. But nonetheless, I take great pleasure in these stories of ancestral courage. At least, when I look back on the lives of the people who gave me the opportunity to aspire, I have something heroic to aim for.

XXI
apollo and cassandra

Apollo was the sun god, the archer god, the god of youth and truth and poetry and painting and prophecy — multitalented and unmatched in beauty and virility. Basically, he was the Elvis of Olympus. Indeed, he was also the god of music, so I pay careful attention to the sound track offered by various local radio stations, as I head for the Pennsylvania hamlet bearing his name.

Robert Palmer croons ("She's so fine . . . there's no tellin' where the money went . . .") as I pass through the Fort Pitt Tunnel, emerging to encounter a striking view of blue-collar Pittsburgh — skyscrapers rising like concrete Titans and PNC Park gleaming like a twenty-first-century Parthenon. East on Interstate 376, I follow the north bank of the Monongahela River for a while, along with the Young Rascals ("Groo-oo-vin' . . . on a Sunday afternoon . . ."). Highway 22 and Faith No More continue the theme ("Ooh, that's why I'm easy . . . easy like Sunday morning . . ."). Finally, as Highway 66 takes me north and into a hamlet situated on a hill above the Kiskiminetas River, U2 seems to have a grasp on my state of mind ("I still . . . haven't found . . . what I'm looking for . . .").

Here is what I know about this place: it is a palindrome. Apollo, PA spelled backwards is . . . Apollo, PA. My great-grandfather, who supposedly so despised the name Otto that he ditched it entirely, would have avoided this town like the Black Death (Apollo was the god of plagues, too). Although the town is named Apollo and it is in a county called Armstrong, neither has any association with Neil

Armstrong and Apollo 11. Still, the town hosts a Moon Landing Festival every July.

It is a patriotic place with stars and stripes flying every twenty feet throughout the business district. But the Kiski Valley area has sacrificed more than its share of soldiers in the sands of Iraq: Stevon Booker, a thirty-five-year-old posthumous Purple Heart winner, killed by enemy fire in Baghdad during the first weeks of the war. Lonny Wells, a twenty-nine-year-old father of an infant daughter, fatally shot in the leg in Fallujah, an incident captured in a *New York Times* photograph. Billy Sturges, a twenty-four-year-old father of two and husband to an army medic in Iraq, mortally wounded when a car bomb exploded next to his Humvee near Khalidiyah. Joshua Henry, a twenty-one-year-old former local football star, killed by small arms fire in Tikrit.

And nineteen-year-old Brad Coleman, who had joined the military hoping to be trained in office management and finances and had been in the army all of eight months.

His father had served in the navy. His grandfather had served during the Korean War. His great-grandfather had seen action in the Philippines during World War II. His great-great-grandfather had fought in Europe during World War I. "Brad is the only one of us who hasn't come home," his father told a reporter. He died while he was sleeping, when mortar rounds hit his living quarters in Mosul.

Apollo is exactly the kind of place that bears the brunt of distant dysfunctional politics, but it certainly produces heroes, and not all of them are fighting men. Apollo is the birthplace of Nellie Bly, the crusading nineteenth-century journalist, feminist, humanitarian, and adventurer. Her childhood home, a nondescript two-story house on Terrace Avenue with peeling siding, seems unworthy of a woman who had herself committed to a public mental asylum to expose horrific conditions there and who outdid Phileas Fogg by completing a trip around the world — by train, boat and horse — in seventy-two days. She was born Elizabeth Cochran, but took her new name from a Stephen Foster song, and then she became the subject of songs herself.

So again, there is music on my mind. I stop by the Apollo Post Office, closed on this Sunday, and note fliers in the window for an all-day music festival and a Gospel Glory Gathering. I make my way to the Roaring Run Trail along the east bank of the Kiskiminetas River. Here, the sun is just beginning to dip below a forested mound on the other side, leaving a ridge of trees reflected in the water, which is flowing at about the pace of a brisk walk. And I hear an orchestral ensemble of birds — the metronomic "witchety-witchety-witchety" of a yellowthroat, the flutelike "ee-oh-lay ee-oh-lay" of a wood thrush, the tympanic "dink-a-tee, dink-a-tee" of a towhee.

This is one of those times when I feel pangs of spiritual belief, a wish to believe in the theory of intelligent design. I must admit, there have been many such moments on this journey — while staring at the splendor of Mount Rainier, for instance, or the limestone formations carved by the Missouri River, or the pointed pines rimming Lake Itasca. Immersed as I have been in the polytheistic practices of the ancient Greeks, I have been further emboldened as a nonbeliever. The more I contemplate the blurred lines between history and science and spirituality and literature, the less I can stomach the presumptuousness and dogma of organized worship. The fact that the *Odyssey* is studied in English class while the Bible is studied in church seems to me to be an accident of the course of history, rather than a discovery of universal truth. But still, there are those times when my faith in faithlessness falters a bit.

I rumble up the hill, toward the edge of town, until I see a handful of people strolling into a redbrick building — the Apollo Assembly of God. LETS GET ONE THING STRAIGHT! shouts the front-yard marquee. DEVIL BAD, GOD GOOD. There is music coming from within, and I hear a calling, albeit one stemming mostly from the curiosity of a soul-seeker and a journalist.

At the entrance to the church, I pick up a pamphlet, as if I were shopping for real estate. It explains that the church interprets the Bible literally and that its primary message is salvation. Because of Jesus Christ's sacrifice, each person can be "cleansed from wrong and

saved from the real and impending hell awaiting the nonbeliever."
I sneak in and grab a seat in the back, a lapsed Jew's attempt at
inconspicuousness.

The two dozen worshippers, most of them in their seventies, are
scattered among the green suede pews. A bespectacled woman is playing the organ, and the congregation is singing "Give Them All to
Jesus." The lyrics are displayed in large print on an overhead projector. "Shattered dreams . . . wounded hearts . . . broken toys . . . Give
them all, give them all, give them all to Jesus. . . . And he will turn your
sorrow into joy. . . . "

"Music can minister to you or to anyone at times when you are
down, defeated, when you're feeling low," Pastor Zetch tells me afterward. "Music has a tendency to lift you up, and I believe you can go
all the way back into scripture, like when David would play his harp
for Saul when he would get into one of his moods. And Saul would
come out of his depression." Or you can go all the way back to Homer
and notice that Apollo was both the god of music and the god of
healing.

Pastor Zetch is a large man with a handshake so firm that it is actually alarming. He stands in front of the congregation, sweat already
leaving a trail from his shock of white hair down his jowly face.
"God's speaking to us, and he's trying to tell us something," he says,

directing us to the first book of Kings, chapter 18, in which Elijah convinces the prophets of Baal that the Lord is God: And Elijah said unto them, Take the prophets of Baal; let not one of them escape. And they took them, and Elijah brought them to the brook Kishon, and slew them there.

"The toughest place to stand up for God is in the devil's territory!" the pastor explains, and as he gains momentum his preaching is punctuated by unexpected giggles, exasperated pauses, and exhortations for amens — a sort of subdued frenzy.

I am supposed to be focused on the book in front of me, but the passage reminds me of one of the final scenes of Homer's epic, when Odysseus reveals to the suitors who have taken over his house that the king has returned, apparently with the blessing of the gods. Having just proven his worth with his bow, he strips off his beggar's rags and shouts, "And now for another mark, which no man has ever hit: I will see if Apollo will hear my prayer and let me strike it." With that, he sends an arrow into a suitor's neck.

"Dogs!" he cries. "You thought I would never come back from Troy, so you have been carving up my substance, forcing the women to lie with you, courting my wife before my death, not fearing the gods who rule the broad heavens. . . . And now the cords of death are made fast about you all!"

Odysseus, with the help of his son and his faithful swineherd and cowherd, proceeds to slay the scores of suitors, almost as if it were a religious sacrifice. He spares only two men — a herald and a minstrel. Only then does he reveal himself to his wife and make love to her for the first time in nineteen years.

Most people believe this is where the story ends, but there is a final scene in which the friends and relatives of the slain suitors angrily confront Odysseus. A battle to the death begins, but Athena, who has guided our hero throughout, has seen enough. "Stay your hands from battle, men of Ithaka," she commands. "Be reconciled and let bloodshed cease." The men drop their weapons, but Odysseus, still enraged, swoops on them "like an eagle from high heaven."

However, Zeus stops him by casting a blazing thunderbolt at the feet of Athena. The gods have deemed it time to end the bloodshed. Peace and mercy dominate the final lines. Tell that to the 450 prophets of Baal.

Paradoxically, perhaps, I find this final scene to be unsettling. If Odysseus's adventure is to be read as a template for all of our life journeys, heroic or otherwise, then this suggests that the conflict never ends except arbitrarily by some sort of fiat — even after we reach our ultimate goal or return triumphant or finally regain that true love that carried us in spirit through dark times. Even if the gods are on our side.

"It's not supposed to get easier!" shouts Pastor Zetch, as if reading my mind. "The more we do for God, the more we're going to encounter! Just what you wanted to hear!" He laughs, almost maniacally, and wanders halfway down the aisle, his hands positioned like claws. "But not only will you encounter more opposition, you will receive more power from God!"

He pauses, lowers his voice, and reminds the congregation that the way of the Lord is and always has been a mystery. "If you can evaluate who did it, then God didn't do it," he says, his voice now nearly a whisper. "Because we'll never figure God out."

Amen to that.

When he felt disrespected, Apollo's reprisals could be merciless. He used his lyre to beat the flute-playing Marsyas in a musical contest, then added injury to insult by hanging the impudent musician from a pine tree and flaying him alive. When King Midas, an observer of the contest, contended Marsyas made the better music, Apollo called him an ass and then gave him the long ears of a donkey. When the Sibyl of Cumae, a priestess of Apollo, agreed to a night of hanky-panky in return for immortality, she realized too late, after failing to keep her end of the bargain, that she hadn't read the fine print. She lived for a thousand years, but youth and beauty weren't included.

After a few centuries, she was nothing more than a tiny and wrinkled little creature encased in a jar hanging from a tree and repeating endlessly, "I wish to die."

So Apollo could be a bit of a prick.

This leg of my voyage takes me eastward as always, through the deep dips and steep rises of central Pennsylvania — from Apollo to Cassandra, which is a tragic tale all its own. Cassandra is described in the *Iliad* as the most beautiful of King Priam's daughters, a princess of Troy. Unfortunately for her, Apollo thought so, too. His lust suitably aroused, he promised to teach her the art of foreseeing the future in return for sexual favors. Cassandra agreed to his terms, but then shunned him after accepting the gift of prophecy. So Apollo added a twist to her gift: She will tell the truth, but no one will believe her.

Countless times before and during the Trojan War, Cassandra predicts Troy's fall, to no avail. Her father keeps her away from the Trojan warriors, afraid that her rants about impending disaster will harm morale. (Imagine that: the leader of a great kingdom silencing any detractors, surrounding himself with only yes-men and unremitting optimists while pursuing a doomed course of action. What a frightening thought.) In ancient paintings and tales, Cassandra is usually portrayed as a raving lunatic, her hair flying wildly, her face contorted in frustration. Shakespeare contributed to the consensus, depicting her as a madwoman in *Troilus and Cressida*, and her name has come to mean a person who utters unheeded prophecies. But the fall of Troy is only the beginning of her travails. She is raped by Ajax and then stolen into sex slavery by Agamemnon before being murdered by his vengeful wife. All in all, not a fate befitting a princess.

At first glance, the Pennsylvania hamlet bearing her name seems unworthy as well. About midway between Johnstown and Altoona, I descend into a lush valley and then take an oddly angled offshoot of a road through a one-lane tunnel under a series of railroad tracks. The entrance to town makes it feel like a place apart. It is also a bit horrifying, as the first sight in town is an abandoned bloodred building that was once a proud three-story hotel, but now looks as if it will collapse at the tiniest puff of wind — the kind of place unfit for even the first of the Three Little Pigs.

The rest of Cassandra is, if not beautiful like its namesake, at least sporadically charming in the checkerboard fashion of many small towns trying to recover their youth one lot at a time. For every heap of rubble or rusted facade or park overgrown with weeds there is an upright house with a neat stack of firewood and a well-manicured lawn. Overlooking the hamlet is a Catholic church atop a knoll, just above the volunteer fire department, which is across the road from a tiny post office serving 136 residents. Nearby, a family is having a mid-afternoon barbecue and listening to the radio. Ted Nugent's "Cat Scratch Fever" echoes through the hills.

In the middle of everything is the Cassandra Railroad Overlook Motel & Gift Shop, adorned with various railroad-crossing signs, and alongside it a child-sized, brightly painted wooden train — red caboose included.

Cassandra's origins are tied to the railroad. In the mid-nineteenth century, a group of mostly Welsh and Irish immigrant laborers pushed across the Alleghenies and laid the old Portage Railroad. They established a small settlement along the roadbed, built a store and a hotel, and called it Derby. A town was laid out on thirteen acres owned by a fellow named Mathiot Reade. As coal mines in the area prospered, Derby grew to nearly one hundred homes. A new Pennsylvania Railroad Line was completed, and by the turn of the century the community was thriving. In 1908, the town was incorporated as a borough, and it was renamed Cassandra, after Reade's daughter.

Cassandra's future may be tied to the railroad, too, as it has become a popular destination for a curious subculture of aficionados known as railfans. These folks like to watch trains, and they come from far and wide to do so. The motel and gift shop are closed for the season, but the overlook is only five hundred feet up a hill, just past a sign that says, WELCOME RAILFANS. The sky is foreboding and the air thick as I cross the railroad tracks along a pedestrian bridge lined with purple and white wildflowers. Sure enough, there are two middle-aged men sitting on a bench, cameras in hand, waiting for the trains to come.

They tell me they came in from Washington, D.C., for the annual convention of the Railroad Station Historical Society. This year it's in Altoona. Gordie has ruddy cheeks beneath brown-tinted sunglasses. He is an astronomer at the Goddard Space Flight Center. Mike wears a hangdog expression beneath a comb-over. He works for the Census Bureau. He doesn't say a word the whole time.

Gordie holds up his Nikon. "I've been shooting slides for thirty-five years. I've got about fifty thousand of them. We're both into what's called Railroadiana. There are big train shows every year — huge buildings filled with timetables, books, calendars. I have every monthly *Trains* magazine from its first in November 1930 to the current one. People have different subhobbies. Some people are into dining car china. We're both into railroad stations. In the heyday of the railroads, from about 1910 to 1930, they built really elaborate stations. But not everyone who likes to watch trains is into the stations."

He says this like a proud multidimensional devotee of a single-minded obsession. But I have to admire his enthusiasm. Here I am searching for answers about a life well lived, and should it not include a certain passion for life's little treasures? My sons collect seashells and stuffed animals and pennies and action figures and beaded neck-laces and painted pebbles disguised as nuggets of gold from Lep-rechaun Day at the preschool. As a father, I revel in their zeal, and I realize that I used to have a zest for this, too. I collected old coins — Indian Head pennies, Mercury dimes, Buffalo nickels. My brother and I amassed boxes of baseball cards, thousands of them, some dat-ing as far back as 1959. I owned every J. R. R. Tolkien book and thumbed *The Complete Guide to Middle Earth* into tatters. But somewhere along the slog toward adulthood, I lost the passion.

I would blame it on maturity, but then I look around. I have a friend who treks to world-class golf courses around the country, and another who surfs and kayaks any chance he gets, and another who plays the bagpipes. His wife raises rabbits in their backyard and has collected enough bunny memorabilia — coasters, dishes, salt-and-pepper shakers, door knockers — to stock a gift shop. Eccentric, yes. But more than that, it is an extension of her character. My sister has season tickets to the Chicago Cubs (bringing shame to the family). For many years, my father had box seats at the horse races. My wife and her girlfriends schedule marathon scrapbooking sessions in which they record the highlights of their children's lives, adorning the moments with patterned paper and pithy phrases.

What do I do? Play golf twice a year? Whip a computer program at Scrabble? I need a hobby, a real passion apart from my profession. It may be why I've lost a sense of self.

"When I got into the hobby about thirty-five years ago, there were about one hundred Class I railroads in the country," Gordie is saying. "Now we're down to six. All of them merged together. This used to be the main line of the Pennsylvania Railroad, then it became Penn Central, then Conrail, and now Norfolk Southern."

"Sounds like the nostalgic aspect of this appeals to you."

He nods. "I work for NASA. We have an instrument orbiting Saturn right now. So when I get back to work, I'll be looking at information that's sent back from there. I go out to Hawaii a couple times a year and use telescopes on big mountaintops. So I have a forward-looking job and a backward-looking hobby. It's kind of a nice balance."

Do I lack a sort of equilibrium of attentions in my life? Unlike my new railfan friend, my passion is also my job. This is a source of satisfaction for me in that I generally enjoy my working hours. But might it also be stifling me a bit? Am I collecting only words and phrases and observations and opinions? I can make a point, but that doesn't make me well rounded.

"In this part of the country, the trains are fighting their way up the mountains. They put on quite a show," Gordie is saying. "Monday is pretty dead, but in general you have anywhere from forty to eighty trains a day."

There is thunder in the distance, and I begin to suspect that railfans are much like storm chasers. They travel from site to site, guided by their expertise, straining for what sounds like a roaring locomotive and thrilling at the variety of each discovery.

Gordie shrugs at my analogy. "There will be another train in an hour. There's no real point in chasing."

He is carrying a railroad radio, a VHF scanner. "The trains talk to the dispatchers, and they're required to call signals. That's the best hint. The signals are identified by the number of miles from Philadelphia . . . "

Just as he says this, his radio blares, "Milepost 253.1, track three."

Railfans Gordie and Mike in Cassandra, Pennsylvania

"The tracks are numbered," Gordie explains. "Far track is three. Middle is two. Near track is one. From the milepost, we know that the train is in the town of Cresson, just a few minutes away. So we know in the next five minutes, there'll be a train coming on the far track."

Gordie and Mike get organized, standing up and readying their cameras, and I realize this isn't like storm chasing at all. It relies not on randomness, but on predictability — or at least an attempt at prediction. It reminds me of old Ray Burkholder in Pandora, recording the weather, looking for patterns in whatever arrives. Were it not for the VHF scanner, this railroad overlook would serve as one of my metaphors. To the east, the track curves. Trains coming around the bend would be unexpected, unforeseen. To the west is a three-mile straightaway. You can see what's coming.

I am about to tell them how appropriate all of this is — predicting the near future here in a place called Cassandra — when a train comes around the bend and Gordie and Mike start snapping photographs, calmly but with a hint of excitement. Afterward, like a trackside Sherlock Holmes, Gordie explains to me the nuts and bolts of what we just saw — a double-stacked train, probably ocean containers from California or the Pacific Northwest that have traveled across the country, maybe empties going back west. These are intermodal trains, he explains, transporting products from truck to train or train to ship. There were three locomotives, he says. The black one was Norfolk Southern; the two oranges ones were Burlington Santa Fe, one of the two big western railroads.

"What happened to the caboose?" I wonder. This is all I noticed.

"Yeah, that's another part of cost-cutting. Up to the mid eighties, they were a permanent fixture on every freight train. Now they've been replaced by what's known as a FRED — Flashing Rear End Device. It's like a sentence that doesn't end with a period."

We sit some more, feeling an occasional raindrop as the air grows muggier by the minute. Then Gordie turns to me with a slight grin on his face. "There's supposed to be a rare circus train coming through town at about a quarter to four. Ringling Brothers. Circus performers ride on it, too, with elephants and lions. I'm actually excited to —"

He never finishes the sentence because a terrifying bolt of lightning explodes above Cassandra, followed by a bone-shaking cannon blast of thunder. The trickle of rain becomes a torrent, and we rush across the footbridge and duck for cover in our respective vehicles. Moments later, a siren rings out from the Cassandra fire station. With the devastation of Siren, Wisconsin, still on my mind, I am a bit skittish, to say the least.

Gordie fiddles with his radio, switching channels, holding it to his ear. Then he climbs out of his car and holds the radio up for me to hear. Someone is talking about a tornado, how it is expected to make its way through various towns at five-minute intervals, how it would arrive in Cassandra at 3:45, just like the circus train.

The two railfans huddle for a moment and decide to race back to their hotel in Cresson. I jog down to the fire station and wait out the rain — and the possible twister — with a trio of volunteer firemen alongside a gleaming yellow pumper. CASSANDRA is emblazoned beneath the windshield. The men don't seem particularly concerned.

"Yeah, we get a couple of these every year," one of them says. "Nothing really happens. They don't tend to touch down here in the mountains."

By 4:00 p.m., the warning has been canceled and the lesson has been learned: Life is a locomotive without a dispatcher to warn you what's coming. Still, it would have been nice to have seen the circus.

XXII
hell and back

After spending the night in State College, almost exactly at the midpoint of the state, I steer onto Highway 45, which cuts through the Appalachians and through various central Pennsylvania burgs — Aaronsburg, Mifflinburg, Lewisburg. All manner of business establishments line the highway, and I notice a sort of intimacy to the names on the marquees. In Aaronsburg, Gary's Kountry Kitchen. In Harleton, Harry's Repair and Harvey's Gas. In Mifflinburg, Fisher's Meat Market and Zimmerman's Bike Shop and Dave's Automotive. Who can blame them for putting a part of themselves on the signage of their pride and joy? It is the same reason I don't use a pen name.

Just west of Lewisburg, traffic stops suddenly for several minutes, and I can see red siren lights in the distance. It is one of those accident scenes that you come upon late, and then you try to piece together what happened. I reach the intersection just as the clues are dispersing — an ambulance going in one direction and a flatbed tow truck going the other way. In the bed of the truck lies a horribly mangled motorcycle.

A sign on Highway 15 south, along the Susquehanna River, says, AGGRESSIVE DRIVER HIGH CRASH AREA NEXT 5 MILES — a somewhat grammatically vague, but nevertheless understandable warning. Too late, I fear, for the motorcyclist. There are also signs for Moyer's Marine Sales and Kulp's Transmissions and Ollie's Bargain Outlet. Crossing the Susquehanna, as wide a river traverse as I have yet experienced, Highway 61 takes me through Sunbury (Schindler's Studio,

Spangenberger's Family Drive-in, Kenny's Vacuum Sales and Service)
and Shamokin (Maurer's Ice Cream Shoppe) and Kulpmont (Pete's
Restaurant and Pizzeria).

Immediately after the hamlet of Strong is the village of Atlas.
Which is appropriate, of course, because after Atlas led the Titans
against Zeus in the Titanomachy, the great battle for supreme power,
Zeus singled him out for punishment by making him hold the heav-
ens apart from the earth. He has been referred to as the God of Heavy
Burdens, and I find this village to be nearly as uninviting as his task.

A half mile away, across a viaduct, the town of Mount Carmel
looks, from certain angles, like a magnificent city of spires with its op-
ulent churches, wide streets, clean parks, tidy houses, banks, delis, craft
stores. A proud-looking Anthracite Fire Company sits at the crest of
a hill. An enormous high school boasts a football team that has won
more games than any other school in pigskin-crazy Pennsylvania.

Atlas, on the other hand, is like the twin who didn't get enough
nutrients in the womb. It is the other side of the tracks. The 1,100-
some people are packed together here in narrow houses, side by side,
that look like trilevel tenements. "Mining houses," they call them here.
There are boarded-up windows, rusting canopies, crumbling concrete,
graffiti, countless BEWARE OF DOG signs and basketball nets hanging by
a single string.

The folks here are clearly trying. They hang flags and wind
chimes from their porches. They sweep their front stoops and put out
welcome mats. They stick eight-foot jungle gyms into nine-foot alleys.
On one side of town, a rather feeble community park with a flag at
half-mast is dedicated to "all Atlas men and women who served their
country" and "in tribute to all firemen of Atlas Fire Company." But
on the other side of town, the Savitski Brothers Coal Company — or
what is left of it — is dominated by a collapsing building and a bro-
ken-down school bus hidden in the weeds. I see streets named Willow,
Oak, Laurel, Juniper . . . but I don't see many trees.

At the corner of Saylor and Hemlock Street (Socrates be
warned), I run into a fellow named E.B., a township police officer

sitting in his squad car. Holding tightly to a pack of Skoal, he tells me that the attitude in Atlas is pleasant enough. "The people are helpful — family people," he says. "But you can't find jobs around here. When I started twenty-five years ago, Savitski Brothers was booming."

It is that same old tale that I've seen in numerous towns across Appalachia — a coal region depleted. In 1790, a Quaker named Isaac Tomlinson found some black stones lying in the bed of a stream of water crossing his farm. Within a century, there were fifteen coal mines within a five-mile radius, and the population had soared to more than 15,000. But now, two centuries later, there are half as many people, and the region is still asking itself whether there is life after the death of coal.

The birth of coal is pretty remarkable. Essentially, plants capture energy from the sun for photosynthesis, then die and find themselves buried under layers of vegetation, which become so heavy that they squeeze out the water and other compounds that would aid in decay. So the compressed vegetation forms coal. The longer and deeper the coal is buried, the higher its quality. Peat is the first stage of coal formation, lignite the second, bituminous coal the third. Anthracite is the highest grade, and it was anthracite coal that Isaac Tomlinson first discovered in this area. Because it burns very hot, people have long described it with a rather poetic phrase: they call it "buried sunshine."

I am sitting in the first-floor den of one of the row houses, close enough to the highway that I can hear the trucks roaring by. Behind me in a glass-enclosed cabinet is a collection of *Little Rascals* dolls — Alfalfa, Buckwheat, and the gang. Sprawled on a chair in front of me, wearing a dirty white T-shirt, is fifty-seven-year-old Nick Vincenzes, the de facto mayor of Atlas. He is a big fellow with large square glasses and a beach-ball belly. What is left of his hair is matted in sweat. Nick has lived in Atlas since 1958. His wife, Linda, was born here. Her father was born in this very house.

"It's a nice place to live. It really is," Linda says, almost apologetically. "I think we have a decent school district compared to a lot of places you read about. And the neighbors are good. My neighbor next door, I grew up with her."

"We thought about movin' to da city years ago, but we didn't want anything dat fast-paced," Nick explains in a pronounced deez-dem-and-dose dialect.

"You mean, like, Philadelphia?"

He shakes his head. "Reading."

Nick and Linda have three grown sons. "One lives across da street," says Nick, "anudder lives two doors down, and da third lives with us."

"So the one two doors down is the one who moved away," I joke, weakly.

Nick erupts in guffaws, and I soon realize this is typical of him. He appears to be one of those men without much of a barrier between his thoughts and emotions and his words and actions. He does not seem to own a PC gene, occasionally allowing phrases like "Jewish lightning" and "colored folks moving in" and "drinking Irishmen" to escape his lips, matter-of-factly. And when he gets especially excited, he punctuates his conversation with exasperated sighs.

"Dis place has been Atlas fer at least sixty years or more, but it used ta be called Exchange." He winks. "I hear dats cuz da husbands and wives always used ta be swapping."

Nick sits up in his chair. "Do ya know about Centralia?" he asks.

I nod. Just a few miles away are the remnants of a town that has been condemned. Because it has been burning. Underground. For more than four decades.

"I was thinking of checking it out," I tell him. "Is it dangerous?"

He waves off the thought. "Oh, don't worry 'bout going up ta Centralia. Anywheres ya walk in dis whole region, you can fall into a sinkhole."

Nick drives a truck, delivering home fuel oil throughout the area. But around Atlas he is best known for driving the pumper as a longtime member of the all-volunteer Atlas Fire Company. It is a bit of a family business. One of his sons is the fire chief, the other two are captains.

"We might get fifty, sixty calls a year — car accidents, smoke incidents, brush fires . . . We had a big fire right up da street here. Lady torched three homes. I was scared. We're trained, and we try ta do everything calm and tink straight, ya know?"

"Ever do anything you consider heroic?"

He shrugs and gives one of his sighs. "We just like doin' this. Firefighters need this rush or somethin', ya know? I dunno what it is. Ya gotta help somebody."

"That's one thing about the Atlas firefighters," says Linda, a look of pride in her eyes. "They don't do it for the glory or recognition. They just get up and go."

"I used ta work a night shift job, and I was able ta be aroun' during da daytime," says Nick. "So if a call went out, at least I was here

Nick Vincenzes at "da Hosey"

ta make sure da truck got ta da fire. I did all my fire training and every-thing, but my main ting was I made sure da truck got there. I was da pump operator. Even today, when I go ta da station, if dey see me comin' and someone's in dat engine seat, dey gotta get out."

Nick decided I should see the station, which is located in a con-crete block of a building, pink on the top half, maroon on the bot-tom, almost like a chunk of Neapolitan ice cream. Behind it, a peach-colored slab serves as the police department, although it looks more like a Mexican cantina.

"Everyone calls da fire company da Hosey. They say, 'We're goin' down to da Hosey,' " Nick explains as he leads me to a second-floor room where a handful of people are chatting, surrounded by pool and pinball tables, video poker machines, and NASCAR posters. This is the Bar, Atlas's version of a members-only club. You have to fill out a form and be accepted by a committee. "There are about four hun-dred members, about eighty lifetime members, only about twenty-five firefighters," Nick explains. "I tell ya what, years ago it was two, three deep at da bar. But now with all da liquor laws, it's dyin' out. Some of your hardcores are still hangin' out, though."

He points me to the basement, the fire station's rental hall, where locals celebrate birthdays, small weddings, and fund-raisers, with the money going to the fire company. Then he leads me into the garage, past lockers brimming with boots, gloves, helmets, coats, and bunker pants. The walls are lined with trophies, dozens of them — trophies for having the cleanest trucks and the best skill test scores and the top finish in a pumping contest and the finest overall appearances in a parade.

"Dis is only half of 'em," Nick boasts, and then he turns to his treasure, gently patting the bumper of a gleaming yellow fire engine. "Dis here's da baby. It's an old Hahn 1250 Pumper. Can fit five men. It's my favorite. Dis brought us outta da Stone Age. We had a trustee who went down to Harrisburg and begged 'em. We got one of 'em one percent or two percent loans, ya know? Actually, we just purchased a new one last year, but dis baby gave us a lotta service."

I hear the pride in his voice. I think of the committee judging worthiness for entry into the Bar upstairs. I glance at the assortment of trophies around me — miniature pumpers on pedestals and tiny firefighters gripping hoses. And it strikes me that, one way or another, we all find our place of belonging. We all find a way to obtain life's little satisfactions and the occasional shot in the arm of self-esteem. Sometimes it means digging deep, but we can all find some buried sunshine.

A sign: WARNING—DANGER . . . UNDERGROUND MINE FIRE . . . WALKING OR DRIVING IN THIS AREA COULD RESULT IN SERIOUS INJURY OR DEATH . . . DANGEROUS GASES ARE PRESENT . . . GROUND IS PRONE TO SUD-DEN COLLAPSE.

Naturally, I walk right in, Nick's words of comfort ringing in my ears: *Anywheres ya walk in dis whole region, you can fall into a sinkhole.* Why I find that reassuring, I don't know.

As I stand in front of the largest building in town, a municipal building housing the local branch of the county fire department, an older gent with his granddaughter in the car stops along Highway 61 and asks me if I need any help.

"Nope, just wandering around."

"Don't wander around here," he says. "I've seen holes open up. And the other day, some government people took the top off an or-ange vent there, and man, you could run a steam engine off of that."

I give a wave of thanks to the man and watch him drive away. But if the sign isn't going to deter me, and if the bleached trees and smok-ing hillsides and noxious fumes don't stop me from exploring, then an unsolicited warning isn't going to do it either.

This surreal landscape, only a few miles east of Atlas and Mount Carmel, is the once-thriving hamlet of Centralia — Pennsylvania's version of hell on earth. One local legend suggests that a priest, who had been badly beaten by a band of rebel Irish miners here more than a century ago, climbed into his pulpit and cursed the town: that it should burn in hell forever. And it just may.

It is certainly not the nation's only mine fire; there are some four dozen in Pennsylvania alone. Nor is it the state's longest-burning underground fire; one up near Wilkes-Barre has been blazing since 1915. It isn't even the only town named Centralia to experience an underground disaster; in 1947 a coal mine explosion in Centralia, Illinois, claimed 111 lives. But this may be the most famous of the bunch.

Centralia was once a booming community, riding the discovery of an anthracite vein into something resembling prosperity. By the mid-twentieth century, there were nearly two thousand residents and a thriving business district — banks, churches, saloons, a high school. Then, in 1962, the residents had the grand idea of burning trash in an old open pit mine. Gas venting from beneath the surface ignited and carried the fire to a coal vein that runs beneath most of the town. Nobody took any action for a few months because nobody knew about it — until some local churchgoers near the landfill began to complain about foul-smelling odors. Authorities arrived to test carbon monoxide levels and they determined that, yes, the mine was on fire — and little could be done about it. The fire department tried pouring in thousands of gallons of water, to no avail. Anthracite coal is almost impossible to extinguish. After a few more halfhearted attempts to douse the flames, the fire began spreading along the subterranean seams. It has been burning ever since — upward of five hundred acres underground so far. Some say it may burn a thousand years.

For about a decade and a half, the state and federal government spent more than three million dollars in an attempt to control the fire. All sorts of solutions were proposed — flooding the mine, stripping it to expose the fire, deflecting the course of the blaze with explosives, even digging a massive trench around the town. Most ideas were unaffordable or unworkable, so a study was commissioned. The U.S. Office of Surface Mining (OSM) estimated that it would cost $663 million to extinguish the blaze.

Meanwhile, Centralia began a slow death from deep within. Smoke began to rise from the earth. The pavement grew hot. The toxic fumes grew more potent. Eventually, the fumes and the possibility of widespread subsidence — that is, the ground opening up to consume people, trees, cars, houses — became life-threatening. In 1981, a preteen boy was playing in his grandmother's backyard when the ground suddenly began to swallow him up. He clung to tree roots above an eighty-foot-deep sinkhole until someone heard his screams for help and saved him.

Now Congress stepped in, setting aside $42 million to turn Centralia into a ghost town. Between 1985 and 1991, more than five hundred homes were purchased and razed and more than one thousand residents evacuated. But a handful of folks wouldn't leave. *It's our hometown,* they said, but there was another All-American motive at work — greed. With anywhere from twenty to forty billion tons of coal beneath the rotting earth, the diehards believed that the government wanted them out so that it could buy up the rest of the land and strip-mine the valuable anthracite. Otherwise, the coal belonged to the borough of Centralia.

In 1992 the OSM authorized condemnation procedures for the state to acquire the remaining fifty-three properties. The residents responded with legal objections, which inched through the court system — all the way to the state supreme court — and were ultimately unsuccessful. In 1996 the state Department of Environmental Protection sent thirty-two certified letters to the Centralia residents who were still there, notifying them that health and safety issues made it imperative to relocate. "By remaining," the letters warned, "you are assuming the risk that subsidence, gas, or other events may result in injury to you or your family." At the time of my visit, a dozen people still live here.

Under sunny skies, the Centralia of today doesn't look so hellish, really, as much as it reminds me of a Monopoly board. Or perhaps a Monopoly board left too close to the fireplace. The few remaining houses, once part of a neighborhood collection, rise up sporadically, separated by several acres, looking rather naked and emaciated without their counterparts alongside them. So there is one house on Boardwalk, another on St. Charles Place, a third on Marvin Gardens, a couple on Pennsylvania Avenue. No hotels, though there used to be one here, back in the day.

One of the few houses remaining in Centralia, Pennsylvania

In some parts of town, if you squint a bit and narrow your focus, you wouldn't know the place is on fire. Flowers are planted, lawns tended, wreaths hang on doors. A few cars are parked curbside. A handful of mailboxes are still serviceable. Irony of ironies, there are even a few fire hydrants. A green bench next to a tiny grassy park seems to invite people to sit for a while, take a deep breath, inhale the poisonous fumes. A monument in the park is dedicated "to all those who served their country in all wars" and topped by a large bell (constructed, I notice, in New York — in the city of Troy). Alongside the monument sits a time capsule planted in 1966, four years after the fire started and one hundred years after the town's founding. It is to be opened in 2016.

But Centralia doesn't look as if it will last that long. It is one enormous pressure cooker, as there is so much steam from the burning coal that a handful of vents have been placed in the ground to relieve the pressure. I walk through a grid of empty streets and truly dead ends, past driveways leading to nowhere, toward a hilltop cemetery that appears to be where the fire is closest to the surface. Here, the local joke goes, you can be buried and cremated for free. Thin clouds of steam and smoke billow from the craggy hillside, which looks as if it has collapsed upon itself. Sinkholes are filled with spare tires and broken glass. Trees lie dead and dying — once leafy maples bleached into zombie forms. It is as if Hades is bubbling over. As I lift the neckline of my shirt to shield my nose and mouth from the pungent smell of sulfur, a father, mother, and daughter stroll by.

"Daddy," says the girl, "is it bad for me to breathe in what I'm smelling?"

He puts his hand on her shoulder. "No, honey. We just won't stay here very long."

There is a haunting quality to Centralia, as if the steam rising from the hillsides represents the spirits of the dead. Mind you, I don't believe in ghosts. In fact, I am a skeptic about most everything. I don't believe in Bigfoot or the Loch Ness Monster or werewolves or UFOs or horoscopes or compassionate conservatives (well, maybe a few of them are roaming around). I do believe that the moon landing was very real and Lee Oswald was a very lucky shot. I was never a fan of President Dubya, but I believe all 9/11 conspiracies are hogwash. I think psychics are full of crap, and those creepy charlatans who tell people they can communicate with their dead grandmother on *Larry King Live* are devoid of conscience. And I think anyone who claims to see the Virgin Mary in a slice of burned toast is either too hard up for miracles or not hungry enough. I am agnostic on some days, atheist on most, superstitious only very rarely. So I believe when you are deceased and departed, that's it. You are dead and gone. Of course, you will notice that my visit to spooky Centralia occurs during daylight hours. I am skeptical, but not stupid.

The ancients believed that the return of the dead was an unwanted deviation from the soul's proper path to the underworld. And there is an element of this path that seems relevant to my journey. Ironically, the same god charged with protecting lost travelers — Hermes — also led deceased mortals to Hades and the banks of the river

Styx. It wasn't a place for evil men; it was more like a bus station —
a rather dismal setting where the will of the gods determined the
pleasantness of your stay. But even Hades had its ticket to paradise —
Elysian Fields, a dwelling place for mortals made immortal by the
favor of the gods. It was said to be a happy land located in the very
western part of the world, where it was always sunny and warm and
fanned by life-giving breezes. The denizens of Elysium were free to return to their native lands if they wished, but few chose to give up the
pleasures of residence. It all sounds a lot like Newport Beach, but
what I like about the notion of Elysium is this: it was the hero's
reward.

Whether we actually believe it or not, most of us are comforted
by the notion that a life well lived leads to a magnificent afterlife.
However, I never could accept the notion that, say, Mother Theresa
and the lead singer of Twisted Sister are headed to the same place.
But a Heroes' Heaven strikes me as a fine idea, sort of like that inner
room at a nightclub reserved for only the hippest of the hip. I can
picture Hercules playing Texas hold 'em with members of the New
York City fire department. Perseus and Gandhi would be comparing
tunics. Maybe my Grandpa Bunny would be there, too, teaching Theseus how to tell a dirty joke.

And here is my favorite thing about Elysian Fields: some poets
were sent there, as well. So maybe if I tell enough stories about heroes,
I can sneak in the back door.

Still, this stop in Centralia is appropriate — in the sense that, if
I want to approximate a heroic adventure, I should make a trek to hell
and back. This figurative notion has its origins in ancient mythology,
where the journey was literal. More than a few Greek adventurers had
to experience a trip to the underworld to earn their stripes. Along
with conquering the realm of the living, they had to survive the kingdom of the dead. It became a literary motif.

Odysseus appears to be the first such adventurer. Toward the end
of his long journey, our hero is told by the sorceress Circe that before
he can reach Ithaka he must let the north winds blow him to the house

of Hades. He must descend into the underworld and consult with the dead prophet Tiresias, who will presumably tell him all he needs to know about the remainder of his voyage home. Once there, he encounters a who's who of dead icons. There is Sisyphus, sentenced to the task of forever pushing a huge boulder up a hill, and Tantalus, punished by starving while having food and water just out of reach. Odysseus encounters his comrade Elpenor, who died in an accident at Circe's house, and his mother Anticleia, who took her own life while mourning her missing son, and the ghosts of Agamemnon and Ajax and Hercules. But it is his brief encounter with the phantom of Achilles that most intrigues.

"You, Achilles, are most blessed of all men who ever were or will be," says Odysseus. "When you lived, we honored you like the gods, and now you are a potentate in this world of the dead. Then do not deplore your death, Achilles."

But Achilles won't have it. "Don't bepraise death to me, Odysseus," he answers. "I would rather be a plowman to a yeoman farmer on a smallholding than lord paramount in the kingdom of the dead."

The statement has also been translated as "I would rather be the serf of a poor man than king of the dead." And it is the speaker himself who makes the speech so remarkable. Achilles was doomed to a short life. We can no more imagine him as an elderly man than we can picture James Dean plugging Viagra. But his existence was long on exaltation, and he craved the glory that he felt he was due. He is the personification of Jack Kerouac's preference for "the mad ones . . . the ones who never yawn or say a commonplace thing, but burn, burn, burn, like fabulous yellow roman candles exploding like spiders across the stars."

Yet upon reflection in the realm of the dead, the ultimate warrior seems to be rejecting the warrior life, as if to say that he would have chosen the candle burning longest over the one burning brightest. It makes one wonder about the diehards in Centralia who are opting for risk-and-reward, chasing some future notion of financial glory — a vein of anthracite all their own — while inhaling deep draughts of toxic fumes.

Later Greek myths actually give their heroes the chance to choose all over again. Here I return to Plato's *Republic*. In the last of the ten books of his masterwork, Plato introduces an analogy known as the "Myth of Er." It tells the story of a warrior named Er, who dies in battle but is brought back to life ten days later. In between, he travels to the underworld and witnesses the judgment of the dead, a scene in which Plato introduces the notion that one is either rewarded or punished in the afterlife, depending on one's moral behavior. At the time, it was a bit of a radical concept. In the philosopher's vision, lots are drawn, and every soul has the opportunity — before drinking from the River of Forgetfulness — to select his next life, be it human or animal, in the order of the number he received. It is like a cosmic delicatessen that serves corned beef and rebirth.

"The life which he chooses shall be his destiny. Virtue is free, and as a man honors or dishonors her he will have more or less of her; the responsibility is with the chooser," Plato writes. "He should consider the bearing of all these things which have been mentioned severally and collectively upon virtue; he should know what the effect of beauty is when combined with poverty or wealth in a particular soul, and what are the good and evil consequences of noble and humble birth, of private and public station, of strength and weakness, of cleverness and dullness. . . . Let him know how to choose the mean and avoid the extremes on either side, as far as possible, not only in this life but in all that which is to come. For this is the way of happiness."

The choice of a new life seems to be predicated on previous experiences. Orpheus, who was inconsolable at the loss of his wife, opts to become a swan, which usually mates for life. Agamemnon, still smarting from alleged injustices, chooses to be an eagle, so as to remove himself from humanity. Ajax, still craving his due reverence as a warrior, selects the life of a lion. Then comes Odysseus, choosing last.

"Now the recollection of former toils had disenchanted him of ambition, and he went about for a considerable time in search of the life of a private man who had no cares," Plato explains. "He had some difficulty in finding this, which was lying about and had been neglected by everybody else; and when he saw it, he said that he would have done the same had his lot been first instead of last, and that he was delighted to have it."

I wonder, if given the option, what I would select. Like Orpheus, would I reflect on failures and losses, striving to correct or recover them in the next life? Like Ajax, would I lament unaccomplished goals and unrealized respect, opting for a life that might allow me to be a paragon of reverence and achievement? Like Agamemnon, would I look back through a cynical prism and then distance myself from the perpetrators of perceived slights? Or, like Odysseus, would I recall that for all the battles we fight and quests we undertake, it may just come down to living a life for yourself, not for posterity?

Odysseus, adventurer and king, yearns for the life of an ordinary citizen. Achilles, the greatest of warriors, would give back all his glory for another breath of life. The ancient myths of the underworld seem to be the very origin of the Trite Epiphany — that all the renown and riches and trophies and triumphs are meaningless if you don't have your family and you don't have your health.

XXIII

labyrinth

Finally, after nearly a month of heading east, I change direction. Northward now, toward Ithaca.

Highway 42 takes me through Columbia County and into Sullivan County, where it hands me off to Route 220. There is a Rock Run Church here and a marquee: HEAVEN. DON'T MISS IT FOR THE WORLD. Not three hundred feet later, a sign: WORLDS END STATE PARK — IO MILES. I notice it is Worlds End, not World's End — no apostrophe, as if it is not a place but rather a declaration of inevitability. Moving from irony to paradox, this stretch of Pennsylvania's Appalachians, a gorgeous drive through farmland and foliage, is known as the Endless Mountains.

Up I climb now, steeply. Not circuitously up. No switchbacks or wide loops. Just straight up, endlessly it seems, toward the crest of the Endless Mountains and the county seat of Laporte. I have a mission here, somewhat reminiscent of Theseus in his ancient quest to kill the man-eating Minotaur: I am looking for a labyrinth.

Actually, the Minotaur's labyrinth was more of a maze. There is a significant difference. A maze is a challenge, a puzzle to be solved, replete with blind alleys and dead ends. It is multicursal, offering many choices — a left-brained task requiring an active and analytical mind focused on details. A labyrinth is unicursal. It has one path, well defined, leading to the center and back out again. There are no intersections, no tricks. It is a right-brained experience, passive, intuitive. One makes choices in a maze, but one is led by a labyrinth. As such, it has for centuries been a sort of strolling meditation, the only choice being whether or not to walk a spiritual path.

Since 1992, when an Episcopal priest in San Francisco began touting the mind-clearing benefits of labyrinth walks, thousands have been created in a variety of places and for diverse purposes. Some call it a path of prayer; others a mirror of the soul. Still others use terms like *harmonic convergence* and *alternance of energy* and *imprinting a royal groove*, which all sounds like the sort of New Age twaddle at which I typically roll my eyes. But in truth, the spiritual attraction of the labyrinth is ancient. A labyrinth-inscribed tablet found in the Greek city of Pylos is more than 3,200 years old. A design on a wine jar from Tragliatella, dating to Homer's era, depicts soldiers on horseback running from a labyrinth. Inscribed in its outermost circuit is the word *Truia* — or Troy.

These patterns, often based on spirals occurring in nature, have been part of any number of spiritual traditions around the world — in Egypt and India, Peru and Sumatra, Iceland and Arizona. They have been carved on rock faces, etched into sand, painted on pottery, woven into baskets, engraved on silverwork, embossed on coins, inlaid into tile floors of great cathedrals, and — as is the case with my destination today — cut into grassy fields. As such, they are not unlike the Homeric legends in that they are archetypes — universal patterns that emerged out of the collective human psyche and were passed down through the millennia so that we may still experience them directly. Like Odysseus's voyage, the labyrinth can be seen as a metaphor for a heroic journey — toward the center of one's identity and back again, hopefully with a greater understanding of self.

I pull into a driveway just north of the state police barracks, where I am greeted by a woman with brown hair cropped short on the sides but tied tightly into a long thin tail. Immediately, I notice that she has an aura of serenity about her — soft-spoken, poised, self-assured. It is a comfortable vibe. I had discovered the existence of her labyrinth by coming across an online press release, which referred to her by what is now her legal name — Mollie Sheldon Eliot. So I called her Mollie when I phoned her and asked if I could explore the mystical shape that she has mowed into her property, and I greet her as Mollie now, too. But it turns out to be far more complicated than that.

She leads me to her backyard, where there is, indeed, a labyrinth — about sixty feet in diameter — sheared amid the weeds and wildflowers. A Native American lodge pole rises from its center. "If you were native, and you were walking through our backyard, you would look at the lodge pole and say, 'Wow, I can tell a lot about these people,'" Mollie explains, as we sit on folding chairs in an open-air barnlike structure with children's drawings of spirals pinned to its walls. "You would know that we're affiliated with the Eastern Delaware Nations. Our clans are on the pole. You would also know that we practice a respect for the four directions and that we use tobacco as a sacred herb."

Born and raised in New Jersey but with ancestral ties to Sullivan County, Mollie is Native American mixed with French, English, Scottish, and German. The "we" of which she speaks seems to refer to an extended family, currently staying at her house, that includes her sons Zac and Lee (Mollie has four children in all, from two former marriages) and Lee's friend from college, who is boarding there for the summer. The group also includes Mollie's life partner, Lisa, and Lisa's daughter, Jennifer.

The relationship with Lisa, whom she met a decade ago, is more person-based than gender-based, she explains. "People say they have midlife crises. Well, I learned a lot about myself at midpoint. I had been looking for someone to complete me, and it just seemed to fit. It was comfortable. And it blossomed from there. My kids felt like they had another parent they could count on."

Interesting, I am thinking. But at this point, I have no idea just how interesting. Lisa and Mollie were married a year before my arrival. The chief of the Eastern Delaware Nations performed the ceremony, right in the center of the labyrinth.

"The labyrinth has become the focal point of our family life.

And for a lot of the people who come here, it's a healing place," she says, peering toward it. "We thought when we were building it, we were doing it for us and our family. But a friend of ours said, 'You know, it's going to call people to it.' We thought that was funny — you know, *Field of Dreams* or what? But it does. We put out a couple of press releases, and people come. They show up." She turns to me. "You showed up."

Even in an informal conversation, Mollie's words seem well chosen, the rhythm of her phrasing well balanced. In another age, she might have been a bard. In this age, she is a freelance journalist, photographer, and advertising and PR consultant, as well as the owner of a small company that produces publications and designs Web sites. She calls it Quest Publishing.

"Life is a quest, you know?" she says.

I smile, perhaps a bit wryly. "I certainly do."

"My belief is that everybody has a story to tell, and everybody's story is important. It's those stories that make us human, make us connect," she says, echoing the very philosophy that informs my travels. "When I was working as a reporter at a daily paper, I would always get the job to interview a person who was turning one hundred years old. Everybody hated that job. I loved it. I would sit at their feet and just soak it up. I'd say, 'Tell me your story . . . ' "

"Okay." I lean back in my chair and fold my arms. "Tell me yours."

She pauses for a moment, then chuckles. "It's almost funny to me because, looking back, when I started out I would never have said that I was looking for a heroic life. But I've lived one, and I like that I've lived one."

She clears her throat and then hits me with this piece of information: "Part of the reason I'm with Lisa is . . . I'm a multiple personality."

As I have indicated before, I am a skeptic of the highest order. So normally, if someone were to insist that their body was a vessel for a

series of disparate characters, I would raise an eyebrow and mentally
raise a few red flags. But something about Mollie's demeanor — her
matter-of-factness, her quiet confidence — has me immediately convinced of her authenticity.

"I've learned about the disorder — if you want to call it that, but
I don't," she continues. "In general, it takes a lot of abuse to make a
multiple — on pretty massive levels for a long time. You become dissociative. It was gruesome, and I really don't want to dwell on it. It was
more than one person, and it was fairly consistent until I was in school.
So it was when I was very young.

"When we were growing up, we thought everybody had an inner
family like we did. At that time, there were four of us. We knew each
other very well. We talked to each other inside. And some therapists
will tell you that's the difference between a multiple personality and
a schizophrenic. A multiple hears voices within and knows on some
level that they are Self. A schizophrenic hears voices outside and is
directed by those voices. And yet we are still atypical. Most multiples
have missing time in their lives. They have people they don't recognize
and clues they can't follow, and they usually become suicidal because
things become so chaotic. We're atypical in that we have this inner
family, and we've worried about each other from the time we were
tiny. We remember playing together and going to school together. And
some of us were like, 'I hate math. I'll do history, you do math.' It's a
great strategy for life," she laughs, "but the way you get multiple isn't
very cool."

"I notice you use the pronoun 'we' quite a bit. . . . "

"We're pretty co-conscious, but we're not integrated into one person," she explains. "That's usually the goal of therapy. But we were
steadfastly against that because three of us were professional writers,
and one of us was very little at that point. She's grown up quite a bit,
but—"

"You aren't all the same age?"

She shakes her head. "We started out with four of us who were
together all the time, and then we began to suspect — and that was

part of the midlife crisis — that there were other personalities hanging around. We sensed that there were more, and we've had a series of
alters — that's the word psychologists use — show up. We kind of
view it as coming in from the cold. They can choose to remain au-
tonomous and live their life, or they can integrate with one of us.
And both things have occurred."

A few years back, she wrote an autobiography about her experiences living with multiple personality disorder, or as it is technically
known these days, dissociative identity disorder. She called the book
Portrait of Q, which is what she calls the system that constitutes herself.
The Trekkie in me understood the reference immediately. Q was a recurring character on *Star Trek*, who possessed both an individual and
communal perspective as part of the Q Continuum, an omnipotent
collective of beings who seemed to guide the fortunes of mankind.
The man who played Q, actor John de Lancie (whom I actually met
once while standing in line at O'Hare Airport), portrayed him as mer-
curial, boastful, condescending, often comical, sometimes threatening, occasionally compassionate — many of humanity's extremes
combined into one all-powerful character who acted with much the
same superciliousness as the ancient Olympians.

Mollie Sheldon Eliot is her legal name. She officially adopted it
after divorcing her second husband. But it turns out that Mollie, Sheldon, and Eliot are actually three of the four original personalities in
her Q collective.

Mollie is the bearer of her given name. Her appearance and age
match the chronological age of the body. She is generally cautious,
nurturing, an excellent cook. Eliot is male, tall and rangy and Native
American in appearance. He is quite nearsighted and tends to be a
health food addict. Sheldon, also male, is blond with Native American features. Until about a decade ago, he was a lifelong teenager who
liked to skip school and steal candy. Now, Q informs me, he is in his
early thirties. He is charming and streetwise and a protector to the
others, generally being the one who converses with strangers. It is
actually Sheldon, not Mollie, with whom I have been speaking.

"If you become really comfortable with me, would, say, Mollie or Eliot appear?"

"They're lurking now," Q replies. "Everyone's really interested in the fact that we're talking to you."

The last of the four original personalities is known simply as Baby, a blue-eyed, curly-haired blonde who stayed three years old for about four decades. Developmentally, she is now in her early teens. In recent years, however, as Q began to come to grips with her abusive past and her current relationships through therapy and introspection, the other alters who had been hidden emerged.

"I remember, when I graduated high school, I went into business. All my friends were going off to college, and they said, 'What are you doing?' And I said, 'I'm still trying to find out who I am.' And that was pretty literal." Q smiles. "It started out with me taking a different tack from my peer group, but it's really become a quest to find Self and to be Self and to be true to that."

The Q collective — the system constituting who she is — includes a burly fellow named Orion, a wise Native American elder who goes by Dakota, and personalities named Shadow and Watcher and Keeper. There is Gwen, a young adult who views herself as the babysitter of the youngest personalities and who likes to take over when the body goes shopping. There is a little boy named Chad, who used to crawl under clothing racks in stores when he was scared, forcing Q to pretend she had dropped something. Susie is fluent in French; Dani is a shy, mute child; Vinnie is her confident twin.

"They all held bits of our childhood trauma apart from the four of us who kept us safe and interacted with the outside," she explains, and she offers an example: "Very soon after I met Lisa, I was driven to distraction by a baby crying — not out there, but in here." She points to herself. "Finally, one of the very small children came forward and said, 'I know where the baby is.' Internally, we visualize as much of a world as there is out there. So what I visualized was picking up the baby, and the baby stopped crying. That baby — a little girl named Lily — is now developmentally twelve or thirteen." Q shrugs. "She may be the original child who was hidden from the abuse, who we protected. We don't know."

Q describes her inner world as similar to virtual reality, only more complex. Sometimes the various personalities communicate audibly; other times it is through what she calls "mindtouch," although it is apparently impolite to mindtouch someone who is asleep or engrossed in a task. Naturally, this system — usually co-conscious but not integrated — can turn simple tasks into complexities. When Q goes to powwows of the Eastern Delaware Nation, for instance, she isn't quite sure whether she should dance with the men or the women. And consider the common frustration of forgetting where your car is parked at the mall. Q has to first figure out who drove.

Mollie Sheldon Eliot and her labyrinth

"It just takes another minute to make that leap," she explains.

Apparently, this may also include a leap into past lives. One member of Q's collective, an eccentric chap named Ian, loves to drink

Guinness, speaks in an Irish brogue, and claims to have been born in
Ireland in the Middle Ages. Sheldon tends to pick on Ian, pointing
out to him that they didn't talk like that back then. They spoke
Celtic. And nobody much believed Ian's contentions about being born
a thousand years ago. But then one time Q and Lisa were playing
Scrabble (Q can team-play, and nobody knows it), and Ian put down
an unusual word that Lisa challenged. After a trip to the dictionary,
it was discovered to be an archaic Celtic term.

And then there is the way Ian rides horses. Each personality has
its own riding method. Sheldon does it western-style. Eliot holds both
reins in an English fashion. But Ian sits forward in the saddle and
bends the horse around the opposite way, a style so foreign that Q did
some research and discovered it was something called sidepass, which
was especially popular in the Middle Ages.

"That's when we started to believe him," says Q. "I can intellec-
tually understand that we are all fragments of the same self. And I'm
comfortable with the idea that some of that self may have lived in
other lifetimes."

For much of her life, Q's primary focus was protecting her
inner family from discovery. Nobody caught the clues when she was
young — how her school performance would fluctuate between A's
and D's, how she would play with dolls one day and brawl with boys
the next, how there were times — when Sheldon was in control —
when she was suddenly left-handed. It wasn't until her early twenties
that the memories of her childhood trauma began to emerge, and she
managed to stave them off until she reached her forties, when they
came in torrents. She entered a deep depression and came close to
suicide, finally deciding that keeping her big secret was dragging her
into an abyss.

"One personality married the boys' dads, and the rest of us were
one hundred percent trying to have a normal life, and sort of staying
behind that, always hiding," she explains. "After that fell apart, we just
had a rough year, a very rough year. And the outcome of that was we
decided not to hide anymore."

When Q and Lisa decided they wanted to vow their fidelity to each other, Lisa was adamant that all of the co-conscious personalities in Q had to agree to the union. You think there is pressure in asking a future father-in-law for his daughter's hand in marriage? Try asking several wildly different parts of a whole. But they all agreed.

"Meeting Lisa was kind of critical because what we said was, 'Let Eliot have a turn.' Mollie was adamant that she'd had two failed relationships. And Eliot had this growing relationship with Lisa, and we were all friends with her. We figured maybe he would do it better. I — Sheldon — was infatuated with her, but she said, 'Sorry, Shel, I don't get involved with sixteen-year-olds.' "

"But during times of intimacy, can it get . . . awkward?" I feel awkward asking it.

"Lisa and the continuum kind of addressed that early on because the possibility of further victimization was there, even if it was inadvertent. So we had to sort of set some ground rules. The biggest rule is if somebody says you need to stop, then we stop."

For someone who has undergone so much turmoil, not only in her childhood but throughout her life, this person sitting alongside me seems to be in a good place. In fact, I find myself admiring her introspective abilities. She calls people like herself "multiples," while folks like me are "singletons." But I hear that, and I can't help but think of "simpletons." Compared to Q, I feel somewhat inadequate in my difficulties coming to terms with a single personality, a solitary journey. Could it be that what makes us special is not necessarily the whole, but actually the sum of the parts?

When Q disclosed her multiplicity to her friends and her family, she was surprised — in a sort of tragicomic way — by the *lack* of surprise that registered on her sons' faces. With acceptance came confidence, and her decision to go on with her life led her to pursue meaningful goals. She began offering her story to victim service agencies and organizations interested in the effects of sexual assault and domestic violence. This is what Q means when she says she has lived a heroic life.

"Just by saying who I am," she explains, "and not hiding any-more."

"Hi, I'm Eliot," says Q, offering a hand.

Briefly taken aback, I recover quickly. "Nice to meet you."

Our conversation has veered into the metaphysical — spiritual journeys, life connections, fate, purpose — and apparently intellectual Eliot has decided to make an appearance. "I believe that I'm here for a purpose, and we connected for a purpose, and I don't have to know what that purpose is."

The labyrinth, Q later explains, is something Eliot has been aware of since about the age of three. "He would go into the bathroom, lock the door, lock the window, and then suddenly we would be under a spruce tree. And he had his sacred things there — little bits of glass and feathers and things. And he would take us on an inward journey that always involved a spiral path. We would sit under that spruce tree where nobody could get us, nobody could find us, nobody even knew we were there."

As many of us do, Q still sought a place of tranquility well into adulthood. "It used to be that when I came to a crossroads in my life, I had a tendency to get on a horse and go up to a mountaintop. I'd just drop the bit out of the horse's mouth and let it wander, and I'd stay there until I understood what I needed to do," she says. "Now I don't have to go to the mountaintop. It's right here. And that was the lesson, too, because it was right here all the time."

She walks into the house, leaving me staring at the labyrinth, and then returns moments later with a parting gift for me — a white-phase feather from a wild turkey. "It's significant," she explains, "because we believe the more the animals turn white, the more we have to pay attention to our spiritual realm."

With that, she returns to the house, leaving me to perform my labyrinth walk in solitude. It is a longer journey than it appears — a quarter-mile to the center, and a quarter-mile back — and at first, despite being very much alone but for the sound of the crickets in the trees flanking the labyrinth, I feel a bit self-conscious. There are said to be three stages of the experience — releasing, receiving, and returning. The act of releasing is supposed to allow us to shed the distracting details of life, essentially quieting the mind so we can open the soul.

This effort is assisted by the fact that, unlike in a maze, no thought is required. I just focus on the narrow pathway, putting one foot in front of the other. And there is a certain catharsis in such a simple task. This cross-country trek of mine has been predicated on trying to place myself — to locate where I am in my life, where I fall on some sort of heroic scale, in an effort to jump a few steps forward and perhaps get a glimpse of where I might be headed. But a labyrinth asks that you simply focus on the path right in front of you. When you don't have options to divert your focus, and when you aren't consumed by roads not taken or the vagaries of an uncertain future, you feel a sort of timelessness and, yes, a certain release.

"It's a metaphor for life," Q told me. "You go into it, and you can't get lost. How can you get lost in your own life? You might lose your path, in a sense, and not know the way, but you can't lose yourself."

The goal, quite literally, is centeredness, and in that, a labyrinth can be quite the tease. Several times it looks as if I am approaching the center, so close that I want to simply hurdle the tall grass to get there, only to be unexpectedly guided back to an outer path again. Q had told me that some people actually start running when they come to this realization, which also, of course, is symbolic of life. "There are times," she said, "when everything is perfect. It's one of those golden moments. And the next thing you know . . ."

So I keep walking, taking the long way because I know the path will take me there eventually. And then it does. I stand in the center, feeling surprisingly safe and serene, and only now do I take a good look around and see exactly where the labyrinth has led me. "Where we had thought to travel outward, we will come to the center of our own existence," Joseph Campbell declared. "And when we had thought to be alone, we will be with all the world."

Q had said that the labyrinth journey can be a crucible of exchange, a means of revelation. Or it can simply be an exercise in nothingness, a time to clear your head and revel in purposelessness. Sometimes you receive an epiphany; sometimes you notice only the wildflowers. It has become a bit of a ritual for her to reach the center and make an invitation to any parts of her who have not come forward. "If there's anybody still outside our circle," she says in what must be an inner dialogue, "come on in."

Peering at the feather that I still hold in my hand, I consider the various parts that make up the whole of my recent journey. Gift giving was a significant part of ancient Greek culture. With travelers so dependent on the hospitality of strangers, gifts were a means of telling wanderers that they were welcome in that house, which is why Odysseus, despite losing everything en route, still doesn't come home empty-handed. Of course, in those days the gifts were resplendent robes and tunics and magnificent goblets. But I have managed to collect a few gifts of my own, some of them just as valuable.

Bill Hansell presented me with a book in Athena. Mary Haughian gave me some old newspaper clippings near Calypso. Linda Vincenzes sent me off from Atlas with a bag of *pizzelles* — traditional Italian waffle cookies. And somewhere in the Aspect I still have a printed track meet program from Marathon. I received an intellectual feast in Olympia, a wanderer's tale in Iliad, a soldier's story in Sparta, a simple dialogue in Plato, a chariot race in Attica, a guided tour in Siren, a sermon in the temple of Apollo. Standing here in the center of the labyrinth — and toward the end of the road — I try to find a pattern in the bits and pieces of my journey, try to arrange the gifts I have received into One Great Insight. But it eludes me.

"The adventure of the hero," Campbell summarized, "represents the moment in life when he achieved illumination." His steps of the hero's journey correspond roughly to the traditional stages of a labyrinth walk — the Call to Adventure, then Initiation and Transformation, then the Return with a gift, a boon of knowledge. So now I make the return, realizing only that the end of this path also happens to be the beginning.

On the way back, the path looks new. The sun, grown low, throws longer shadows. The grass and weeds are bent at fresh angles. The clumps of wildflowers, seen from another perspective, form unexpected designs. A quarter-mile later, I find myself back at the small barn alongside the labyrinth, where there is a guest book in which people have scribbled their thoughts after each soul-cleansing stroll. I hold the pen in my hand for a while, thinking — musing, I suppose.

"A journey to punctuate my journey," I write. "Maybe that's our life purpose — a journey to the center in the Endless Mountains."

XXIV

ithaca

The road to Worlds End takes me toward the sun, which is just about to disappear behind the hills. A few miles in, I come to a shack of sorts on the side of the road, alongside some abandoned semi trailers and piles of neatly sawed logs. The orange sign atop the building is the only commercial signage at all along this stretch of country road, and it seems to indicate that a specific brand of chain saws is sold here — or at least used to be. The sign says OLYMPYK. I am no longer surprised.

By the time I set up camp at the state park and eat a quick meal, night has fallen, and a squadron of fireflies has appeared. It is a cloudless night, and there is only a single stoplight in all of Sullivan County. When I look up, I find an explosion of constellations, the heavens sprinkled with the light and dust of the cosmos.

Directly overhead is Boötes, which some say is the most ancient constellation in the firmament, a collection of stars first referenced by Homer himself. Its story concerns a typical Zeus-and-Hera spat. Zeus beds a woman named Callisto, who gives birth to a son, Arcas. Jealous Hera turns Callisto into a bear, who is almost killed by her unknowing son while he is hunting. To protect them both, Zeus places them in the sky in the form of Boötes, the Hunter, and Ursa Major, the Great Bear — one eternally circling the other around the North Pole. The brightest star in Boötes — indeed, the most brilliant star in the Northern Hemisphere during late spring and summer — is Arcturus, whose name means "guardian of the bear." Homer refers to it in the context of guide and protector. Upon leaving Calypso's island, Odysseus uses Boötes as a means of navigation, as he commences the final leg of his journey toward Ithaka.

In the morning, I begin mine. From here, which happens to be called Forks Township, the way is straightforward — due north over the state line and into rural New York, where the names of the communities — Spencer, Van Etten, Newfield — take me back a decade and a half to my days as a cub reporter at the *Ithaca Journal*. One of my responsibilities was to take phone calls from weary high school coaches late on Friday nights, as I earnestly scribbled all the relevant information they offered in an effort to compile a box score and a paragraph about that all-important basketball matchup between the Spencer–Van Etten Panthers and the Newfield Central Trojans.

I find myself grinning at the memory. I would scramble for a couple of hours, gathering data from a dozen regional contests, barely managing to complete my task before our 12:30 a.m. deadline. Afterward, Amy would meet me at the newsroom, having just served last call at a pub a few blocks away. Still dressed in her work clothes — a skirt-suspenders-and-bowtie ensemble — she would look pretty darn adorable, even with the inevitable beer stains. We would walk home, hand in hand, to our studio apartment above a jewelry store, and we would fall into bed, exhausted and in love.

We seem so far away from that now — miles and years distant. But as I pass the WELCOME TO ITHACA sign and catch a glimpse of the university rising from the hill like a castle in the kingdom, I realize that I don't miss what we had then but what we have now. "There is hardship enough here to make one go home disgusted," Odysseus comments, early in the *Iliad*. "If a man has to stay one month from his wife, he is impatient."

I understand perfectly. In the two decades since the gods brought us together as a couple of teenagers living only for the present, Amy and I have crafted the future to our liking, and it is a collaborative masterpiece. "For nothing is greater or better than this, when man and wife dwell in a home in one accord," says Odysseus toward the end of his great voyage. No longer surrounded by the sounds of a newsroom and a college tavern, our epic tale is now set amid the constant pitter-patter of little feet and boyish giggles and tattletale whines and cartoon theme songs. And we still fall into bed at the end of the day, exhausted and in love.

I drive through town and up the hill to the campus, parking the Aspect in the lot adjacent to my old fraternity house. Across the street, a woman is perched near the top of a tree, protesting the proposed creation of a parking lot. A bumper sticker shouts from a car on the street: MY KARMA RAN OVER MY DOGMA. Ah, it's good to be back.

Inside the fraternity house, several residents are milling around, playing foosball and billiards, watching TV. The place is a bit quieter and much less filthy than I recall. They must have cleaned it up for us crotchety alumni, mistakenly thinking that we prefer it that way. It doesn't seem to smell like stale beer and feet anymore.

"Hi. I'm a . . . I used to live here."

They nod and offer handshakes and return to the foosball and billiards and TV. So I walk around the house briefly, peeking into my old bedrooms — the tiny one with a yin-and-yang symbol still painted on the wall, the room with the built-in waterbed that made me sea-sick, the space downstairs next to the kitchen and the endless supply of Cap'n Crunch. Returning to the Great Hall, as we used to call it, I stop and stare at myself. Smiling back from a photo composite on a wall is the eighteen-year-old me, boasting a head full of hair and am-bition. When Odysseus finally arrives in Ithaka, he is unrecognizable even to his own family. Athena has disguised him for his protection, giving him the appearance of an old, bald beggar. I wonder if that is what these undergraduates make of me.

Even when he reveals himself, when Athena removes the cloak of age and poverty, his son, who hasn't seen him in a generation, is so awestruck by the transformation that he doesn't recognize the man. Telemachus averts his eyes, suspecting it might be some sort of deity. "I tell you, I am no god; why do you rank me with the immor-tals?" says Odysseus, and then he adds, Vader-like, "No, I am your father."

Odysseus left Ithaka a king and returned a vagabond, so his per-ception of his homeland was colored by his perceived station in life and, subsequently, his treatment by the Ithakans. In addition, Athena disguised Ithaka, covering it with a mist so that Odysseus knew it not at first. But as I climb steep Libe Slope toward the center of campus, I remember my Ithaca well — sore muscle memory.

At the top of the hill is the Arts Quad, normally an open ex-panse of greenery, crisscrossed by walkways, where students toss balls back and forth with lacrosse sticks or rest their heads against their backpacks and catch a few moments with the elusive Ithaca sun. Today, however, three massive tents have been erected for the hordes of achievers who have returned to bask in the glow of the institution that served as their springboard. The southernmost tent, aimed at the younger returning classes, will have the biggest crowd and the loud-est music. The northernmost will feature a comparatively quiet brass band playing oldies. It will be populated by blue-haired women wear-ing matching red blazers and bent old men in straw hats and buttons that say "Class of '45." The middle tent is meant for the middle-aged, the alumni with one foot in each phase of life. It strikes me, rather powerfully, that this is where I now belong.

I stroll farther up the hill to Uris Hall, an ugly box of a building where I took most of my psychology classes. Next to it, constructed out of automobile bumpers, is a silver sculpture entitled *Herakles in Ithaca*. Presented to the university a quarter-century ago by one of its deans just before he succumbed to cancer, it was meant to represent the strength needed to live an inspired life (never mind that Herakles — or Hercules — likely never set foot in ancient Ithaka, except within the plot of a 1962 time-travel film called *The Three Stooges Meet Hercules*). Interesting, though, that Homer's fully rounded portrait of Odysseus, a man both intrepid and imperfect but who actually ruled Ithaka, was passed over in favor of the archetypal brawny hero — even on a college campus.

Herakles statue at Cornell University

Making my way back to the Quad, I duck into Goldwin Smith Hall, a broad, columned edifice where I used to attend writing seminars. Just to my right as I enter is a tiny sandwich shop, its entrance lined with statues of ancient Greek athletes holding javelins and throwing discuses. This café of long standing is known as the Temple of Zeus. I sit here for a while, reflecting on my Greek chorus and one philosopher's notion that perhaps a hero is simply somebody who has achieved his purpose, whatever that might be.

Reaching into my backpack, I retrieve a poem I have carried with me for three thousand miles — an ode called "Ithaka," written by Constantine Cavafy, one of Greece's most distinguished poets. It is recorded that Cavafy's last act before his death in 1933 was to draw a circle on a blank sheet of paper and then place a dot in the middle of the circle — a cryptic final motion, yes, but one that might be interpreted as a sort of labyrinth-like epiphany that centeredness is the purpose of any journey.

Much of Cavafy's poetry was inspired by the Hellenistic era. "Ithaka," written in 1911, is a celebration of the journey to that ancient isle. The poet wishes that the voyage be long and full of great joys and pleasures and new encounters, and he insists that the perils of the quest — the Laestrygonians, the Cyclops, Poseidon's wrath — can be overcome with lofty thinking and a pure soul. He closes with the following:

> Always keep Ithaka in your mind.
> Arriving there is your destination.
> But don't hurry the journey at all.
> Better if it lasts many years,
> and you moor on the island when you are old,
> rich with all you have gained along the way,
> not expecting Ithaka to make you rich.
>
> Ithaka gave you the beautiful journey.
> Without her you would not have set out on your way.

She has no more to give you.

And if you find her poor, Ithaka did not betray you.
With all your wisdom, all your experience,
you understand by now what Ithakas mean.

Placing the poem in my pocket, I amble back into the sun and sit on the steps of the building, beneath the great marble columns. A few hundred feet away, the university clock tower rises 173 feet into the sky like a spear point, and I close my eyes as the chimes begin to ring out, echoing through my memories.

Suddenly, even more familiar sounds — a couple of young voices, high-pitched and earnest. And then a woman's exhortations, unmistakable. Opening my eyes, I can see them at the other end of the Quad, and I get to enjoy a few seconds of focused infatuation before they notice me. When they finally do, I watch them gasp and wave maniacally.

"Daddy! There's Daddy!"

The two boys start to run toward me, their hair a bit longer than when I last saw them, their strides more confident. Amy walks slowly behind, undoubtedly tired from the airline flight and the long climb up the slope, but she is beaming. As the boys reach me and envelop me in a hug, she approaches, and our eyes meet. We don't have to say a word.

Here is what Joseph Campbell had to say about the woman as symbol of the heroic monomyth: "She is the 'other portion' of the hero himself — for 'each is both': if his stature is that of world monarch she is the world, and if he is a warrior she is fame. She is the image of his destiny."

My four-year-old son climbs into my lap and places his hands on either side of my face, as if double-checking my identity. "Did you drive all the way here, Daddy?"

"Yep. Across the whole country."

"Wow," the two boys say in unison, easily impressed.

As all three of them squeeze me harder, a singular perspective from my Greek chorus echoes with the chimes: "If one person in your life recognizes you as a hero, then you're a hero."

It may not last forever, but it's a beginning.

acknowledgments

Any book is a journey, sometimes an epic one. At times, the road to publication for this one felt like Odysseus's version — a passionate and personal voyage that was a bit meandering, fraught with obstacles and dilemmas, and at the mercy of the vagaries of fate. But just as the king of Ithaka had the benefit of Athena to guide him, so did I have friends and colleagues to help steer the ship.

First, I would like to thank the dozens of people whom I encountered during my cross-country excursion. This isn't a work of fiction. Every single event, every quotation, every location is real and true to life. So without the folks whom I met along the way, the journey had nowhere to go. In my book, you're all of heroic stock. Thank you for taking the time to tell your stories. You are what I treasure most about writing books like this: random encounters that offer lasting revelations. No matter where I went — an army base near Sparta, a squad car in Siren, a living room in Athena, a coffee shop in Troy — I was made to feel welcome. Along the sparsely traveled road I had taken, that made all the difference.

That road would have been far less comfortable had I not had the luxury of traveling in style in a Winnebago Aspect. In fact, it might not have been possible at all. I am grateful to the fine folks at Winnebago Industries, especially Sheila Davis and Kelli Harms, for being so helpful and so generous through the years. There are no better examples of American perseverance than the people who have dedicated themselves to that iconic brand in Forest City, Iowa.

I would like to acknowledge the good people at Arcade Publishing, who sent this book toward home before reluctantly closing their doors following the death of founder and publisher Dick Seaver. Cal Barksdale was a pleasure to work with, offering the perfect editor's dichotomy—an eye for the smallest details and a sense of the big picture. Michaela Hamilton, Karen Auerbach, Arthur Maisel, Susan Barnett, and especially Amy Pyle at Citadel were brave enough to help me finish the journey, and their faith in the project turned frustration into optimism.

My literary agent, Laura Rennert, and I found each other, somewhat randomly, in northern California a few years ago. I appreciate her enthusiasm, her broad expertise, and her commitment to me and my career—she's one of the best in the biz. However, it wasn't until after we solidified the deal that we discovered a remarkable coincidence: a quarter-century earlier, her late brother Ian (then from Oklahoma) and I (then from Chicago) had been friends and cabin mates at a summer camp in northern Wisconsin. I like to think of it as evidence of some sort of literary karma, particularly because this book—my first with Laura—includes a chapter about a return to that very same camp. I dedicate that chapter to Ian's memory.

Before we settled on a publisher, I sent the manuscript to a handful of friends and family who served as my version of a respected editorial board. Ruthie Adler wields the pen of an English teacher and the insight of someone who has known me since forever. Aimee Jackson has an editor's mind and a friend's heart. Jeff Lewis is smarter than he looks, and he looks pretty smart. Greg Marshall is a mensch (look it up, Greg). Helen Palmer, my eleventh-grade expository composition teacher who set me on a path to becoming a writer, has become a valued friend and supporter. And Carol Hillsberg, well, if all mothers-in-law were like her, there wouldn't be any mother-in-law jokes. I can never fully express my gratitude for her unwavering encouragement through the years. The same goes for my dad-in-law, Richard. I think I'll keep them.

This book is dedicated to my own parents, Bud and Hazel Herzog. One never fully appreciates those who raised you and provided for you until one takes on that same challenge a generation later. I owe them everything. A mere book dedication doesn't suffice. So in addition, I'll call them more often. My own sons, Luke and Jesse, had to sacrifice a bit for me, as well. Trying to complete a book at home while a couple of energetic boys bounce around is a bit like attempting to perform brain surgery while riding a snowmobile. But they did their best to let Daddy write when the muse called.

Finally, of course, there is that muse. Her name is Amy. She is my wife. If I write a thousand books in my lifetime, hers will be the face that launched a thousand ships.

No longer the property of the
Boston Public Library.
Sale of this material benefits the Library.

WITHDRAWN

**No longer the property of the
Boston Public Library.
Sale of this material benefits the Library.**